ASPEN PUBLISHERS

MW01688265

E-Z RULES®

FOR THE FEDERAL RULES OF CIVIL PROCEDURE

With Selected Statutes

2008-2009 Edition

Jack S. Ezon, Esq.
Jeffrey S. Dweck, Esq.

Wolters Kluwer
Law & Business

AUSTIN BOSTON CHICAGO NEW YORK THE NETHERLANDS

Aspen Publishers
Attn: Permissions Department
76 Ninth Avenue, 7th Floor
New York, NY 10011-5201

To contact Customer Care, e-mail customer.care@aspenpublishers.com, call 1-800-234-1660, fax 1-800-901-9075, or mail correspondence to:

Aspen Publishers
Attn: Order Department
PO Box 990
Frederick, MD 21705

Printed in the United States of America.

1 2 3 4 5 6 7 8 9 0

ISBN 978-0-7355-7222-5

Library of Congress Cataloging-in-Publication Data

Ezon, Jack S.
E-z rules for the federal rules of civil procedure : with selected statutes/Jack S. Ezon and Jeffrey S. Dweck.—2008-2009 ed.
p. cm.
Includes index.
ISBN 978-0-7355-7222-5
1. Court rules—United States. 2. Civil procedure—United States. I. Dweck, Jeffrey S. II. Title.

KF8841.E96 2008
347.73′5—dc22 2008033681

Cover illustration: Paul Schulenburg/Images.com

NOTE: E-Z Rules is not a substitute for the actual text of the official Federal Rules of Civil Procedure, and should not be quoted or cited to. E-Z Rules is meant to be used as a quick reference and guide to understanding the Federal Rules, and cannot completely replace them. In addition, the "Overview" for each section of the Federal Rules is not meant to be a comprehensive teaching tool, as it does not consider case law. It is merely meant to provide the general scheme and remind the reader of certain key points of the Federal Rules of Civil Procedure.

About Wolters Kluwer Law & Business

Wolters Kluwer Law & Business is a leading provider of research information and workflow solutions in key specialty areas. The strengths of the individual brands of Aspen Publishers, CCH, Kluwer Law International and Loislaw are aligned within Wolters Kluwer Law & Business to provide comprehensive, in-depth solutions and expert-authored content for the legal, professional and education markets.

CCH was founded in 1913 and has served more than four generations of business professionals and their clients. The CCH products in the Wolters Kluwer Law & Business group are highly regarded electronic and print resources for legal, securities, antitrust and trade regulation, government contracting, banking, pension, payroll, employment and labor, and healthcare reimbursement and compliance professionals.

Aspen Publishers is a leading information provider for attorneys, business professionals and law students. Written by preeminent authorities, Aspen products offer analytical and practical information in a range of specialty practice areas from securities law and intellectual property to mergers and acquisitions and pension/benefits. Aspen's trusted legal education resources provide professors and students with high-quality, up-to-date and effective resources for successful instruction and study in all areas of the law.

Kluwer Law International supplies the global business community with comprehensive English-language international legal information. Legal practitioners, corporate counsel and business executives around the world rely on the Kluwer Law International journals, loose-leafs, books and electronic products for authoritative information in many areas of international legal practice.

Loislaw is a premier provider of digitized legal content to small law firm practitioners of various specializations. Loislaw provides attorneys with the ability to quickly and efficiently find the necessary legal information they need, when and where they need it, by facilitating access to primary law as well as state-specific law, records, forms and treatises.

Wolters Kluwer Law & Business, a unit of Wolters Kluwer, is headquartered in New York and Riverwoods, Illinois. Wolters Kluwer is a leading multinational publisher and information services company.

IMPORTANT NOTE

All rules follow the format of the Federal Rules of Civil Procedure. Where the actual subsection letter or number of the rule is used, it is enclosed between parentheses "( )." All other numbers and letters are produced by E-Z Rules and, therefore, should not be cited to when discussing a rule. These numbers and letters, and other E-Z Rules "bullets" have been added in addition to the official subsections found in the actual code in order to make the substance more comprehensive.

For example, in Rule 4 there are 13 sections, referred to in E-Z Rules as (a)-(n). These are actual sections used in the Federal Rules of Civil Procedure and may be called, for example, "subsection (a)." Under Rule 4(b), however, there are items labeled "1.", "2.", and so forth. Since these are not enclosed in parentheses, they are not the letters or numbers used by the Federal Rules.

USING E-Z RULES FOR THE FEDERAL RULES OF CIVIL PROCEDURE

Why E-Z Rules?

Welcome to ***E-Z Rules***, a new way of presenting rules and laws, designed to put the "ease" into *legalese*!

E-Z Rules translates the confusing statutory language of the Federal Rules into plain and simple English. ***E-Z Rules*** are designed to give you quick access to the important information you often need, without the unnecessary strain of dissecting long, monotonous, statutory texts. And remember, ***E-Z Rules*** does this *without excluding any key points of the actual rule or statute*!

How Is It Organized?

E-Z Rules is easy to use. It has been carefully tailored to meet the needs of both the law student and today's active law firm.

E-Z Rules for the Federal Rules of Civil Procedure begins with the *Roadmap to the Federal Rules of Civil Procedure* to the key topics of the litigation process, service, jurisdiction, removal to federal court, pendant jurisdiction, venue, pleadings, pretrial conference, discovery, summary judgment, third parties, jury, judgment, and appeals. With its Overview, Relevant Rules, and actual Federal Rules of Civil Procedure in ***E-Z Rules*** format, the *Roadmap* will help you quickly grasp the concepts of the featured key topics.

Following the *Roadmap* are the actual Federal Rules of Civil Procedure (with selected statutes) — again, in ***E-Z Rules*** format.

What Is the E-Z Rules Format?

- ***E-Z Rules*** is laid out so that the entire substance of a rule or statute can be grasped at a single glance.
- Rules are boldly titled for quick spotting.
- Key words and phrases are emphasized with either **bold**, *italic*, or <u>underline</u>. This not only helps in making the rules easier to understand, but has been proven to help the user focus on pivotal words or phrases that may otherwise go unnoticed. In addition, certain words have been abbreviated in order to facilitate quick referencing and easier reading. A list of abbreviations appears on page ix.
- All rules follow the format of the Federal Rules of Civil Procedure. Where the actual subsection letter or number of the rule is used, it is enclosed between parentheses "( )." All other numbers and letters are produced by ***E-Z Rules*** and, therefore, should not be cited to when discussing a rule.

When the actual subsection letter or number of the rule is used, it is enclosed between parentheses. These are actual sections used in the Federal Rules and may be called, for example, "subsection (a)."

All other numbers and letters, not enclosed in parentheses, are produced by *E-Z Rules*. They are not the letters or numbers used by the Federal Rules, and therefore, should not be cited to when discussing a rule.

Rule 9. Pleading Special Matters

(a) **Capacity**
- (1) Other than to show jurisdiction, there is no need to allege:
  - (A) capacity to sue
  - (B) authority to sue as a representative
  - (C) an organized association's legal existence
- (2) If a party wants to raise a capacity issue, it must do so in a *specific negative* allegation (which must be stated with particularity, (i.e. with a specific factual foundation)).

(b) **Fraud, mistake, condition of mind –**
1. Accusations of fraud, mistake – must be stated with *particularity* (i.e. with a specific factual foundation).
2. Accusations of malice, intent, knowledge, and conditions of mind – may be alleged *generally*.

(c) **Conditions Precedent:**
1. A Denial that a Condition Precedent has not been fulfilled must be stated with *particularity*.
2. An allegation that a Condition Precedent was performed may be alleged *generally*.

(d) **Official document or act** – It is sufficient to simply say that it was done in compliance with the law.

(e) **Judgment** – Domestic or foreign court judgments are sufficient to aver a judgment or decision. There is no need to describe the jurisdiction of the court.

(f) **Time and place** – Allegations of time and place are material.

(g) **Special damages** – must be specifically stated.

(h) **Admiralty and maritime claims**
- (1) How Designated.

For Example, in Rule 9 there are eight sections, referred to in ***E-Z Rules*** as (a)-(h). These are actual sections used in the Federal Rules of Civil Procedure and may be called, for example, "subsection (a)." Under Rule 9(b), however, there are items labeled "1." and "2.". Since these are not enclosed in parentheses, they are not the letters or numbers used by the Federal Rules of Civil Procedure.

> *Note:* ***E-Z Rules*** is not a substitute for the actual text of the Federal Rules of Civil Procedure and should not be quoted or cited to. ***E-Z Rules*** is meant to be used as a quick reference and guide to understanding the Federal Rules and cannot completely replace it. In addition, the Overview for each section of the *Roadmap to the Federal Rules of Civil Procedure* is not meant to be a comprehensive teaching tool. It is merely meant to remind you of certain key points.

ABBREVIATIONS USED IN E-Z RULES FOR THE FEDERAL RULES OF CIVIL PROCEDURE

π	Plaintiff
FRCP	Federal Rule of Civil Procedure
FRE	Federal Rules of Evidence
PJ	Personal Jurisdiction
SMJ	Subject Matter Jurisdiction
SJ	Summary Judgment
TRO	Temporary Restraining Order

SUMMARY OF CONTENTS

Part One

E-Z RULES™

ROADMAP TO THE FEDERAL RULES OF CIVIL PROCEDURE

The E-Z Rules Roadmap to the Federal Rules of Civil Procedure is designed to put everything you need for a given topic at your fingertips. It is organized by key topic (the litigation process, service, jurisdiction, removal to federal court, pendant jurisdiction, venue, pleadings, pretrial conference, discovery, summary judgment, third parties, jury, judgment, and appeals) and provides complete coverage in a format designed to guide you easily through the material.

Each topic begins with an Overview. In the Overview, terms are defined and salient points are highlighted. Following the Overview are (1) a list of the rules applicable to the topic and (2) the actual rule in E-Z style, that is, in language that makes the rule easy to understand.

The Roadmap will help you analyze problems. By using it as a checklist, you can break down a problem and "attack" it in a comprehensive and organized fashion in accordance with the Rules.

Studying the Roadmap will help you grasp the concepts behind the Federal Rules of Civil Procedure and gain an overall picture of the relevant law.

Let the Roadmap guide you to a solution!

CONTENTS TO ROADMAP TO CIVIL PROCEDURE

I. THE LITIGATION PROCESS

A GENERAL OVERVIEW

1. **LITIGATION DECISION**—Before beginning, it is imperative that one determine:
   - Is there a cause of action?
   - Is there a legally cognizable claim?
   - Did the Plaintiff or victim suffer at the hands of the Defendant?
   - *Standing to sue*—Does the party have a legal interest in the suit?
   - What are the chances of succeeding, based on facts and precedent?
   - *Burden of proof*—Is there enough evidence available to prove the case?
2. **FORUM DECISION**
   A. **Subject matter jurisdiction** (e.g. exclusive, concurrent, limited, general, diversity, etc.)
   - State court (the FRCP do not apply)—Does the issue have state court jurisdiction (must look to state laws)?
   - Federal court (these FRCP apply)—A suit will have Federal SMJ if it is *either*:
     - A **Federal question**, or
     - A case with **Complete diversity**
       - There must be diversity of citizenship between all Plaintiffs and Defendants (Note: 2 Plaintiffs or 2 Defendants may reside in the same state), and
       - The claim must be $\geq$ $75,000

   B. **Personal jurisdiction** over Defendant—The court must have personal jurisdiction over the Defendant (see state laws and "Jurisdiction" rules below).
3. **PLEADINGS**
   - **Summons and Complaint**:
     Complaint must contain the following:
     - ALLEGATIONS—π's claims and arguments
     - RELIEF—π's relief requests

     Summons:
     - The Summons must demand an Answer
     - The Summons must also state that if the Summons is ignored, a default judgment may be entered in favor of π.
   - **Filing:** Federal Rules require the π to file the Complaint *before* serving.
   - **Service** of Summons and Complaint (see Rule 4)
   - **The Answer**—Defendants have **20** or **30** days to Answer
     - Types of allegations allowed in Answer
       - Deny
       - Deny knowledge or information sufficient to form a belief as to the truth of the allegation ("DKI")
       - Admit

- Disputing facts—partial admittance
- *Affirmative defense*—admitting to the allegations, yet including a "but" clause (usually claiming contributory fault)
- Counterclaim—Defendant presents claims against π or third parties
- Implead—bring in a third party
- Motion to dismiss (e.g. *lack of claim, jurisdiction*).

4. **PRE-TRIAL CONFERENCE, MOTIONS AND JUDGMENTS:**
   - **Motions** (see Rule 12):
     - Examples:
       - Motion to dismiss
       - Motion for summary judgment
     - Motion papers
       - **Notice of motion**
       - **Affidavit** of facts
       - **Brief/memorandum of law**—stating legal arguments
   - **Pre-Trial judgments**:
     - Examples:
       - Summary judgment
       - Motion to dismiss granted
       - Writ of sequestration
     - Appealing pre-trial judgments:
       - Final judgment rule (Federal): can appeal decisions *only after final judgment*
       - Interlocutory appeal—(used in many state courts): allows appeal of motions immediately after they are granted or denied.
   - **Pre-trial conference** (see Rule 16)
5. **DISCOVERY**
   - Parties must exchange information with other parties.
   - Allowable forms:
     - Depositions—oral or written
     - Interrogations—written
     - Documentation requests
   - Rule 26 (1993) requires parties to make certain disclosures, while the former rule required the party seeking the information to specifically request it.
6. **JURY SELECTION—*"Voir Dire"***
   - **"Venire"**—potential jurors
   - Once a group of potential jurors is chosen, the parties may select or eliminate jurors with or without cause:
     - Each side has limited **peremptory challenges** to eliminate jurors *without reason*
     - Challenges for cause—eliminating jurors *with reason* or based on law.
7. **TRIAL**
   - **Plaintiff's case**
     - Direct examination—π may question its witnesses.
     - Cross examination—Defendant may question π's witnesses.

- Re-Cross Examination is optional.
- **Objections** may be made at any time if Counsel objects to any evidence. Counsel **must** *specifically object* on the record for purposes of appeal.

- **Defendant's case**
  - Motion for directed verdict (Judgment "As a Matter of Law")
    - This motion may be made by the Defendant on grounds that the π's case was too weak to continue proceeding.
    - Even if the motion is denied the court may still *reserve judgment* to override the jury after trial.
    - Defendant's examination of its witnesses (to which π may cross examine)
  - Both Parties may request a **Directed Verdict** before the jury makes a decision.
  - **Charging the jury**—closing comments made by the parties and the judge to instruct the jury.

8. **VERDICT**
   - **General**—"Yes," "No," "Guilty," "Not Guilty" answer requested
   - **Special**—the jury must answer specific questions posed by judge (i.e., telling the judge what they think the facts are)
   - **JNOV**—("Judgment Notwithstanding the Verdict") the judge overrides the jury's decision
   - **Remittitur**—the judge may reduce damages in exchange for a party's promise not to appeal
9. **MOTION FOR A NEW TRIAL**—may be granted based on:
   - A judgment error
   - or New evidence
   - or Jury or attorney misconduct
   - or Unfair award to plaintiff
10. **APPEAL**
    - Appellant brings the appeal against the Appellee
    - Each side submits a brief describing why they should prevail, based on:
      - Judgmental errors (e.g., the wrong law or statute was followed)
      - Jury problems
      - Insufficient evidence
    - The Appeals Court may **affirm, reverse**, or **remand** a case back to the trial court
    - If a "Writ of Certiorari" is granted, a Party may appeal a case from the *Appellate Court* to the *Supreme Court.*
    - Interlocutory appeal may be granted based on a Motion for Lack of Jurisdiction.
11. **"RES JUDICATA"**—once appealed to the highest allowable court, a case will be *closed* for good.
12. **PRECEDENT**—*"Stare Decisis"*
    - **Lower courts** must follow precedents of higher courts
    - **Higher courts:**
      - May REVERSE decisions/precedents of lower courts
      - May OVERRULE *itself* in a later, *factually similar* case.

II. SERVICE

OVERVIEW

- Service is the means by which the Plaintiff notifies the Defendant of its impending action. Minimum constitutional requirements have been established to assure that the Defendant is properly notified before a judgment may be taken against her.
- **Constitutional minimum**
  - Requirements for a court to have the power to adjudicate a case:
    - "*Nexus*" — a relationship must be established between the Defendant and the Forum State (i.e. the state in which the suit is being brought must have "Jurisdiction" over the Defendant (no need to have jurisdiction over the plaintiff).
    - Valid service
  - **Due Process minimum requirements for service**
    - "*Reasonably Calculated Notice*" (actual notice is not the standard)
    - Specific circumstances are not factors
    - *Interested parties* must be afforded an opportunity to present objections
  - Even if it is clear that a Defendant has no chance of winning, service must be made (perhaps to afford the Defendant a chance to negotiate a settlement). The State cannot waive service.
- Fraudulent service:
  - People cannot be brought into a jurisdiction by fraud.
  - Service only induced by fraud (to a Defendant already in the Jurisdiction) is acceptable.
- Immunity from service:
  - People making "*special appearances*" or "*voluntary appearances*" to dispute claims/jurisdiction in an unrelated case are immune from service, *unless*
    - A new case directly results out of the case inducing the appearance
    - or The case involving the appearance involves the same subject matter
    - or The case is a criminal case
- Immunity rules:
  - The court must examine the pleadings or the surface of the lawsuit to establish connections between the two cases.
  - The Defendant has the burden of showing that there is no connection between the two cases.

Relevant Rule: 4

Rule 4. Summons

(a) Summons form (contents and amendments):

(1) Contents: The Summons must have the following:

(A) The court and the parties' names
(B) It must be directed to the defendant
(C) The name and address of plaintiff's attorney (or the plaintiff if he is unrepresented)
(D) Specify the time for the Defendant to appear to defend himself (before a default occurs).
(E) Notify the Defendant that the consequence for failing to appear would be default judgment in favor of π.
(F) Be signed by the clerk
(G) Bear the court's seal

(2) Amendments: The court may allow a summons to be amended.

(b) Issuing the summons:

1. After the π files the complaint, he may present the summons to the clerk for a signature and seal.
2. If the summons is in proper form, the clerk must sign, seal, and issue it to the π for service on the Defendant.
3. The clerk will issue as many summonses as there are Ds.
4. π or π's attorney is responsible for delivering the Summons and Complaint to Defendant.

(c) Service:

(1) Plaintiff's obligations:

1. A Summons shall be served together with a copy of the complaint.
2. π is responsible for service (see Rule 4(m) for time limits).
3. π must furnish the process server with the necessary copies of the summons and complaint.

(2) Qualifications to serve:

- Anyone *at least* 18 years old

and • a Non-Party to the suit

(3) U.S. Marshal to serve:

- *may* request a U.S. Marshal or a specially appointed agent to serve.
- π *must* request a U.S. Marshal or a specially appointed agent to serve if the π is proceeding in *forma pauperis* (pursuant to 28 USC § 1915) or as a seaman.

(d) Waiver of Service:

(1) Sending a Waiver of Service Notice:

i. To avoid costs, the π may notify the Defendant of the action with a *"Waiver of Service Notice"* and request that the Defendant waive service of the summons.

ii. Any Defendant who has received a proper Waiver of Service Notice has a duty to avoid unnecessary costs of serving the summons.

iii. If the Defendant refuses to waive good cause, the Defendant must pay the costs of service.

iv. Requirements for Waiver of Service Notice:

(A) **In writing**:

(i) Individuals: Notice must be addressed directly to the Defendant.

(ii) Corporations/associations: Notice must be addressed to either an officer, managing/general agent, or agent appointed by law.

(B) Name the **court** in which the complaint has been filed.

(C) **Copy of Complaint:** The notice must:

1. include a copy of the **Complaint**

and 2. 2 Extra copies of Notice and Request

and 3. Prepaid means of return (e.g., Self-Addressed Stamped Envelope)

(D) **Consequences** — π must specify the consequences of compliance and of failure to comply with request (see official form 1A for text)

(E) **Date** — The date when the waiver request was sent must be specified.

(F) **Time limit**

1. π must inform the Defendant of the time limit by which the Defendant must notify π of his intention to waive service.

2. The time limit must be at least 30 days from the *date sent* for return (60 days if sent to a foreign country).

(G) **First class mail** — π must send the notice by first class mail or other reliable means.

(2) Costs to Defendant for denying waiver: The Defendant will be responsible for the following costs if he does not consent to the waiver of notice:

(A) Cost subsequently incurred in order to effectuate service and (B) Reasonable costs of any motion needed to collect service costs, including attorney's fees.

(3) Time for answer with waiver: Defendant may wait 60 days after the request is sent to furnish an Answer (90 days if sent to a foreign country). Note: Although the Defendant may send an *answer* after 60 days, the response to the notice of waiver **must** still be sent within 30 days.

(4) Commencement of action with waiver: The action proceeds as normal (except for the time for filing an Answer) and is considered to have started once π has filed the waiver notice with the clerk. No proof of service is needed.

(5) A Defendant who waives service does not waive any objection to *venue* or *jurisdiction* of the court.

(e) Service on individuals: If the Defendant does not waive service, π may serve according to:

(1) The state law for service—π may rely on the state law of *either*:

a. The state where the District Court (in which the action is being brought) is located

or b. The state where service is being made

or (2) The federal law for service—π may choose any of the following methods to serve under Federal law:

(A) Personal service—π must personally serve the individual (actual hand delivery).

or **(B) Abode service**—to a resident in Defendant's *usual* place of abode (no business service).

or **(C) Substitute service**—to an authorized agent.

(f) Service upon individuals in a foreign country—Unless waived, service may be made outside of the U.S.:

(1) By any internationally agreed method if it is *reasonably calculated to give notice* (e.g., Hague Convention).

or (2) If no internationally agreed method of service, then:

(A) Service laws of the foreign country

or (B) As directed by a foreign authority (in response to a letter rogatory/request)

or (C) By (unless prohibited by the foreign country):

(i) **Personal service**—delivery to the individual of the summons and complaint

or (ii) **Mail**—registered mail to be dispatched by the court clerk in Defendant's country.

or (3) As directed by forum court (i.e., in the U.S.) as long as it is not prohibited by an international agreement.

(g) Service upon infants/incompetents — According to state law (if outside of U.S., refer to 4(f)).

(h) Service on corporations/associations:

i. Applicability: This subsection applies
  a. Unless another federal law provides otherwise.
  and b. If the Defendant is *either:*
    1. A domestic or foreign corporation
    or 2. A partnership
    or 3. An unincorporated association subject to suit under a common name
  and c. A Waiver of Service has not been obtained and filed.

ii. Service under this subsection shall be effective when:
  (1) State law is followed
    (A) Rule 4(e)(1) for an individual
    (B) Delivering a copy to an *authorized* **General Agent**, **Officer**, or **Manager** (and mailing a copy to the Defendant if the statute so requires).
  or (2) If the Defendant is a foreign corporation, and Rule 4(f) is followed

(i) Serving the United States, its agencies, corporations, or employees

(1) Effective service
  (A) Delivering to:
    (i) The U.S. Attorney for the forum district or the U.S. Attorney's assistant or clerk
    or (ii) Registered or certified mailing to civil process clerk
  and (B) Sending a registered or certified mailing to the U.S. Attorney General
  and (C) Delivering a copy to an officer or agency, if a U.S. agency or officer is involved

(2) Suits against the officer or agency in their official capacity*:*
  1. Serving the United States pursuant to Rule 4(i)(1)
  and 2. Sending a copy of the Summons and Complaint by registered or certified mail to the officer, employee, agency, or corporation.

(3) Suits against the officer or agency in their individual capacity:
  1. Method of service:
    a. Serving the United States pursuant to Rule 4(i)(1)
    and b. Serving the officer or employee pursuant to Rule 4(e), (f), or (g).
  2. "Individual capacity"
    a. This subparagraph applies to officers and employees sued for acts or omissions while performing their duties on behalf of the United States.

and b. This section applies even if the officer or employee is also sued in his official capacity.

(4) *Reasonable time* is allowed to cure a failure to serve the following parties pursuant to Rule 4(i):*

(A) Anyone sued pursuant to Rule 4(i)(2)(A), so long as the Plaintiff properly served either:

1. The United States Attorney

or 2. The Attorney General of the United States

(B) The United States, where it is sued pursuant to Rule 4(i)(2)(B), so long as the Plaintiff properly served an officer or employee of the United States that is being sued in his individual capacity.

(j) Service upon foreign, state, or local governments:

(1) Foreign state, political subdivision, etc.: Service is made pursuant to 28 USC § 1608.

(2) U.S./state/municipal corporation or organization *either*:

(A) Serve the CEO

or (B) According to state law service

(k) Territorial limits of effective service

(1) Service of a summons or filing of a 4(e) waiver is sufficient to establish **Personal jurisdiction** if:

(A) The forum district's state laws allow it

or (B) The Defendant is a Joined Party (per Rules 14 and 19) and is served within 100 miles from where the summons was issued

or (C) It is authorized by a federal statute

(2) Defendant not subject to jurisdiction of any state court: A waiver of service notice or service of a summons is effective to establish personal jurisdiction in a federal case if:

(A) The Defendant is not subject to the jurisdiction of any state court

and (B) The exercise of jurisdiction over the Defendant is consistent with the Constitution and laws of the U.S.

---

* **Summary: "Reasonable Time" to Cure a Failure to Serve**

Failed to Serve	Rule Governing Service	Properly Served
Officer, Employee, Agency, or Corporation	4(i)(2)(A)	U.S. Attorney or Attorney General
United States	4(i)(2)(B)	An Officer or Employee sued in his individual capacity

(e.g., State Minimum Contact is greater than the Constitutional Minimum Contact)

(l) Proof of service (if service is not waived):

(1) If service is not made by a U.S. Marshal, an affidavit of service is required as proof of service.
(2) Foreign countries: Proof of service may be attained:
  (A) According to treaty agreements (if served pursuant to 4(f)(1))
  or (B) With a registered mail receipt—if mailed (pursuant to 4(f)(2), (3))
(3) Validity, amendments
  a. Failure to prove service does not affect validity of service.
  b. A Court may allow proof of service to be amended.

(m) Time limit for service

1. Service must be made within 120 days after filing the complaint.
2. If service is not made in time the case will either be:
   a. Automatically dismissed (without prejudice)
   or b. Service will be demanded within a specified time
3. If π shows *good cause*, the court may extend the time to serve (or the service period).
4. This subsection does not apply to service to foreign persons (Rule 4(f)) or foreign corporations (see Rule 4(j)(1)).

(n) Seizure of property:

(1) Federal law
  a. A court may have jurisdiction over property if a federal statute so provides.
  b. Notice to claimants of the property to be seized shall be sent, *either*:
    1. As provided by the statute
    2. By service of a summons under this rule
(2) State law
  a. If personal jurisdiction (in the district where the action is brought) over Defendant cannot be obtained with *reasonable effort* the court may assert "in rem" jurisdiction by seizing the Defendant's assets that are located in the forum district.
  b. The court must seize property according to the state law (in which the forum district court is located).

III. JURISDICTION

A. PERSONAL JURISDICTION

OVERVIEW

A court cannot hear a case unless it has "personal" or "territorial" jurisdiction over the parties to a suit. A court may have personal jurisdiction over a Defendant only if it can establish a valid connection between the Defendant and state (Nexus). Questions on personal jurisdiction mainly arise with regard to a court's power to bind Defendants not physically present in the forum state.

1. **In-state personal jurisdiction:**
   - Courts have jurisdiction over anything within their borders:
     - People—"*Personal Jurisdiction*" over state citizens or transient "visitors"
     - Property—"*In Rem*" Jurisdiction over owners or those using or possessing property in a state
   - **Transient jurisdiction**—A state even has jurisdiction over people visiting a state without any other contacts.
   - Corporate presence—Jurisdiction may be established by:
     - Citizenship: A Company is a Citizen of a state in which:
       - It is incorporated
       - It locates its principal place of business

     or
       - Any state in which the Corporation maintains enough activity to establish a Minimum Contact (as discussed below for out of state)
2. **Out-of-state personal jurisdiction:** To establish out-of-state personal jurisdiction two questions must be addressed:
   - Is there a statute or rule that gives the court jurisdiction over the parties?
   - Is the exercise of personal jurisdiction pursuant to the rule or statute constitutional?

   a. **State long-arm statutes:**
   - Courts may extend their jurisdiction beyond their boundaries with long-arm statutes, so long as there are some ties or "contacts" with the forum state.
   - For Corporations, many states *Imply Consent* to Nexus, appointing the *State Secretary* as *Service Agent* when such "minimum contact" is established (E.g., business, driving through state).
     - Corporate presence
       - Courts always have jurisdiction over Corporations that are "citizens" of the forum state (i.e., the state where the court is located).
       - A Corporation is deemed to be a citizen of the state:
         - In which it is Incorporated

         and
         - In which it has its Principal place of business—where most activities occur, where its headquarters are, or where it has the greatest number of employees

b. **Minimum contacts test**:

The "*Constitutional Minimum*" must be satisfied whenever a Long-Arm Statute is used to establish personal jurisdiction:

1. The Defendant has "*minimum contacts*" with the forum state

and 2. The claim arises from those contacts (with certain exceptions in special cases)

and 3. Maintaining the claim does not offend "*traditional notions of fair play and substantial justice.*"

- *Constitutional Requirement for Service of Notice:* Constitutional Due Process also requires that the Defendant receive notice and a chance to be heard, which is usually satisfied by complying with Service of Process requirements.
- Parties who conduct activities in a state accept the risk that those activities will give rise to suits, and understand that they may have to return to the state where the activity was "conducted" to defend themselves.
  - Requirements to establish a constitutional minimum contact:
    A Court must establish *Both*:
    - That the jurisdiction is *fair and reasonable*

    and • *Purposeful Availment*
  - **Fair and reasonable standard**
    - The court weighs the Defendant's contact with the state and the inconvenience for Defendant to defend himself in that state.
    - Factors weighed in determining the **Fair and Reasonable Test**
      - Interest of the Forum State
      - π's Interest in obtaining Relief
      - Most efficient resolution
      - The shared interests of several states
      - Burden on the Defendant vs. the benefits the Defendant obtained from the Forum State
- **"Purposeful availment"** is the "*Quality and nature*" of Defendant's contact with the state.
  - The π must show Defendant's *Purposeful availment of the privilege to conduct activities in the forum state*
- **Requirements for "Purposeful availment":**

  1. *Conducting activities within state*

     a. The Defendant must have *understood* that its activities will "impact" the state

     and b. The Defendant must have anticipated that its *activities* may lead to controversies or lawsuits

     and c. The State has a right/interest to enforce orderly conduct

     and d. Either

        1. The Defendant takes advantage of the "benefits & protection" of state

        or 2. The Defendant must have made contact by *his own* activity

        or 3. The Defendant solicits business

or 4. The Defendant signs a waiver clause to be subject to suit in that state

or 2. <u>Goods placed in stream of commerce</u>—
- Goods must be placed in the stream of commerce in that state.
- Foreseeability that a product may end up in a certain state is <u>not enough</u> to establish minimum contact—the π must show that the Defendant Company's *intentional conduct* should have caused it to anticipate a lawsuit.

or **3. <u>Harmful activities</u>**
- *<u>Actual harm</u>*—if actual harm results in the forum state (e.g., car accident), jurisdiction is established.
- *<u>Intentionally</u>* committing activities that the Defendant *knows* will have a harmful effect on the state will also establish jurisdiction.

- **<u>Scope of accountability</u>**
  - *<u>Specific jurisdiction</u>* (relationship needed) if a person:
    - Commits a Single Act (e.g., car accident)
    - Transacts Occasional Business
  - *<u>General jurisdiction</u>* (no relation needed)—may be established if a person/company
    - Has <u>continuous & systematic</u> contacts
    - or Is "<u>Doing *substantial* business</u>"—usually extensive facilities, contact, market directions
    - or Conducts harmful/pervasive activities

- **Note:** Most state long-arm statutes limit foreign jurisdiction beyond the Constitutional Minimum (i.e., they make it harder to establish jurisdiction)

B. IN REM JURISDICTION

OVERVIEW

- Jurisdiction over property:
  - Real Property
  - Personal Property (Chattels)
  - Intangible Property
- Attachment:
  - When a Defendant is not subject to personal Jurisdiction, the Court can *sequester* property
  - The Court's power over the Defendant is limited to the value of the property
  - The Defendant is *obligated* to enter the Court's jurisdiction to defend the property (if he wants it back)
  - General requirements for attachment:
    1. Notice of Attachment to Defendant

    and 2. Attachment must be by *Judicial Order*

    and 3. π must post a bond

    and 4. Opportunity for Defendant to have an *Immediate Hearing*

    and 5. Required facts/proof by plaintiff (not just conclusory evidence)
  - The Burden of proof is on the *Plaintiff* to prove that the facts warrant attachment.
- Quasi-in-rem jurisdiction — Jurisdiction obtained by attaching Defendant's property in the State (Note: Damages are limited to the value of the in-state property). Quasi-in-Rem Jurisdiction is subject to:
  - **Fair and reasonable test/purposeful availment** — Expectation of being sued when the property was acquired
  - **State interest** — Property must be "*related*" to the action for the state to have an interest *unless* (no relationship needed if):
    - In-State service is made (i.e., Transient jurisdiction is established)
    - The company engages in continuous and systematic activity/doing business (i.e., General Jurisdiction)

C. SUBJECT MATTER JURISDICTION

OVERVIEW

Aside from personal jurisdiction, the second requirement for a Federal Court to hear a case is that the court have the power to hear the kind of claim being brought (i.e., Subject-matter jurisdiction). There are two major categories of Subject-Matter jurisdiction:

1. *Federal question*: The action involves a Federal Question

or 2. *Diversity of citizenship*: There is both:
   - Complete diversity between the Parties

   and • The amount in controversy is > $75,000

- **Complete diversity**:
  - Complete diversity is needed between ALL Defendants AND ALL Plaintiffs (Note: Plaintiffs may live in the same state as other Plaintiffs and Defendants may live in the same state as other Defendants)
  - Corporate diversity (§ 1332): As stated above, a Corporation is deemed to be a citizen of:
    - The State of its incorporation

    and • The State in which it maintains its principal place of business
  - Third party interpleader (see below):
    - Any third party must be subject to personal jurisdiction
    - A third party may dissolve SMJ if it destroys the diversity requirement (e.g., if the third party lives in the same state as the π)

Relevant Rules: 28 U.S.C. § 1331, § 1332

§ 1331. Federal Questions

All civil actions *"arising under"* the U.S. Constitution, U.S. laws, or U.S. treaties have original federal jurisdiction.

§ 1332. Diversity of Citizenship

(a) District courts have original jurisdiction if the matter in controversy is *greater than $75,000* and is between *either:*

(1) Citizens of different states

or (2) Citizens of a state against citizens of foreign states or countries

or (3) Citizens of different states, with additional parties from different states or countries or (4) Citizens of one state (or different states) against citizens of a foreign state acting as a π (pursuant to 28 USC § 1603(a))

(b) If the final judgment is $75,000 or less, the court may impose costs on π.

(c) "Citizenship" for the purposes of § 1332/§ 1441

(1) a corporation shall be deemed to be a citizen of any State by which it has been incorporated and of the State where it has its principal place of business; and

(2) the legal representative of the estate of a decedent shall be deemed to be a citizen only of the same State as the decedent, and the legal representative of an infant or incompetent shall be deemed to be a citizen only of the same State as the infant or incompetent.

1. Corporate citizenship is considered both:
   a. The corporation's state of incorporation
   and b. The corporation's principal place of business[1]
2. Insurance company's citizenship is:
   a. Its state of incorporation
   and b. Its principal place of business
   and c. The state of the insured person (customer) if the insurance company is not joined as a Defendant.
3. Executors/trustees are citizens of the state of the decedent/beneficiary, with regard to related claims.
4. Aliens are citizens of the state where they are domiciled (per § 1332(a)), if they reside there with the intention of becoming a permanent resident of U.S.

* * *

[1] Exception: In any action against an insurance carrier where the insured is not a named defendant, the insurance company is deemed a citizen of both:
a. the State in which the insured is a citizen, and
b. any State by which the insurer has been incorporated
c. the State where it has its principal place of business

D. OBJECTING TO JURISDICTION

Relevant Rule: Rule 12

Rule 12. Defenses and Objections; When and How; Motion for Judgment on the Pleadings; Consolidating and Waiving Defenses; Pretrial Hearing

(a) Time frame for parties to respond

(1) Answers, Complaints and Counterclaim replies

(A) Answer and Complaint: Unless a federal statute supersedes, the *Answer* must be served:
   (i) *If Summons served:* the answer must be served within 20 days after service (extended if out-of-state).
   (ii) *If Service waived:* the answer must be served within 60 days after request for waiver is *sent* (90 if outside of the U.S.).

(B) Answer to a Cross-claim: If the Answer is in response to a Cross-claim, π has 20 days from the date the Cross-claim was served.

(C) Response to a Counterclaim: The π shall reply to a Counterclaim:
   1. Within 20 Days after service of Defendant's answer
   2. Within 20 Days after service of a court order, if π's reply is ordered by the court (unless the order directs otherwise)

Extension for United States

(2) If the United States is a party, it shall have 60 days after the United States Attorney is served to respond.

(3) If an officer or employee of the United States is sued in his individual capacity (for acts or omissions while performing his duties on behalf of the United States), he has 60 days after he is served, or after the United States Attorney is served (whichever is later).

(4) Exceptions to time limit: The time limitations above will not apply in the following cases:

(A) *If a Court denies the motion or postpones disposition* — the Answer is due within 10 days after Court notifies of decision to proceed or (B) *If a Court grants motion for a more definite statement*—the Answer is due within 10 days after receipt of π's revised pleadings

(b) How presented:

i. All Defenses must be made in answer, *except for*:
   (1) Motion for lack of Subject Matter Jurisdiction
   (2) Motion for lack of Personal Jurisdiction
   (3) Motion for improper venue
   (4) Motion for insufficiency of process
   (5) Motion for insufficiency of service of process
   (6) Motion for failure to state a valid claim upon which relief can be granted
   (7) Motion for failure to join a party under Rule 19

ii. The above defenses are made in a pre-answer motion.

iii. Where no response to a Pleading is required, the above defenses may be made at trial.

iv. There is no waiver by joining a defense with other defenses or objections.

(c) Motion for judgment on the pleadings may be made after the pleadings if it does not delay the trial.

(d) Implied motion for Summary Judgment

1. A 12(b)(6) motion is treated as a motion for Summary Judgment (Rule 56) if:
   a. The 12(b)(6) motion is made (failure to state a claim).
   and b. Matters outside the pleading are presented to the court (which are not excluded by the court).
2. In such a case, all parties shall be given a reasonable opportunity to present all material pertinent to such a motion (Rule 56).

(e) Motion for more definite statement:

1. This motion may be made if π's pleadings are too vague/ambiguous so that Defendant cannot reasonably frame a response.
2. The motion must point out the defects in π's pleadings.
3. If granted, the π must re-plead within 10 days of the notice of motion (otherwise the court may strike pleadings or make any other order).

(f) Motion to strike

- This may be done by
  (1) The court's own motion
  or (2) A party's motion made before answering (or 20 days after being served, if no Answer is allowed)

- The court may order something stricken from the pleadings if it contains:
    1. Insufficient defenses
    2. Redundancies
    3. Immaterialities
    4. Scandalous matter

(g) Consolidating defense—

(1) A party can join motions under this rule with any other motions available to the Defendant.

(2) If this motion is made, any available Rule 12(b) defenses that are omitted will be deemed to be waived (unless allowed by 12(h)(2) or (3)).

(h) Waiver or preservation of defenses—

(1) Objection to

a. Lack of Personal Jurisdiction (Rule 12(b)(2))

or b. Improper Venue (Rule 12(b)(3))

or c. Insufficiency of Process (Rule 12(b)(4))

or d. Insufficiency of Service (Rule 12(b)(5)) will be **waived if:**

(A) Omitted from Consolidated motions (12(g)) (i.e., if you make one, you must make all)

or (B) Omitted from:

(i) A Rule 12 Motion

or (ii) A Responsive Pleading or a Rule 15(a) amendment

(2) Other motions

- Other motions are made
    (A) In any Rule 7(a) pleading
    (B) In a 12(c) Motion
    (C) At trial
- This includes:
    a. Failure to state a valid Claim (Rule 12(b)(6))
    b. Failure to Join a third party under Rule 19 (Rule 12(b)(7))
    c. Failure to State a Legal Defense

(3) Motion for Lack of Subject Matter Jurisdiction (Rule 12(b)(1)) may be made AT ANY TIME (even after judgment).

(i) Preliminary hearings on any motions (under 12(b)(1)-(7)) shall be granted upon the request of any party, unless the judge decides to defer the hearing until trial.

IV. REMOVAL TO FEDERAL COURT

OVERVIEW

- If a Federal Court would have Subject Matter Jurisdiction over a case, the Defendant may remove the case from state court to a federal court.
- Purpose: To prevent prejudice to Defendant in π's home state (in a diversity case)
- "πs and Defendants shall have the option to choose Federal Courts for cases within the Federal Jurisdiction"
- **Exception**: If **any** Defendant resides in the forum state, the case may not be removed to federal court (e.g., If there are 2 Defendants, and 1 Defendant resides in the forum state, the second Defendant cannot remove)
- If a diversity case has more than 1 Defendant, ALL Defendants must remove the case together
- Requesting removal doesn't create Personal Jurisdiction over the Defendant (i.e., can still argue no PJ after removal)
- Venue Transfer vs. Removal
  - Transfer—Change venue (within the same Jurisdiction)
  - Removal—Change from state court to Federal court

Relevant Rules: 28 U.S.C. §1441, §1445, §1446, §1447

§1441. Cases That Can Be Removed to Federal Court

(a) Removal from state court by Defendant
Whenever federal courts have original jurisdiction, a case may be removed from the state court by the Defendant (but not by the π) to the appropriate federal court in the district of original state forum.

(b) Removable subject matters:

1. Any **federal question** case may be removed without regard to residence of the parties
2. **Diversity cases** may be removed as long as any Defendant is not a citizen of the present forum.

(c) Joinder of cause—When an independent federal question is joined with a non-federal subject matter, the court may choose to either:

1. Split the matters and hear only the federal element of the case

or 2. Hear the entire case

or 3. Remand matters where state law predominates

(d) Foreign state defendant—When a π sues a foreign state, the case may be removed by the foreign state (and tried without a jury; the limitations of § 1446(b) may be enlarged).

(e) Other removable cases—cases under § 1369 (multiparty, multiforum jurisdiction):

(1) § 1369 cases may be removed:

a. Aside from 1441(b), a defendant may remove a case from state court to federal court if:

(A) the action could have been brought in a United States district court under § 1369

or (B) the action could not have been brought to district court originally, but the defendant is a party to a case brought under § 1369 (or that could have been brought under § 1369) and arises from the same incident as the action in State court.

b. Procedure and timing:

(i) § 1446 procedures must be followed.

(ii) A notice of removal may also be filed before trial of the state court action within 30 days after the defendant first becomes a party to a federal court case under § 1369 and that case arises from the same incident as the state court case.

(iii) A notice of removal may also be filed before trial of the state court action at a later time with leave of the federal court.

(2) Damage hearings remanded to state court:

a. If a case is removed under this section and the court required additional hearings on damages, the federal court shall remand the damages hearing to the state court.

b. Exception: If the court finds that the action should be kept:

i. for the *convenience of parties and witnesses*

and ii. in the *interest of justice.*

(3) Effective date of remand to state court:

a. Effective date: 60 days after the district court's liability determination and decision to remand.

b. Appeals. An appeal on the liability decision may be taken during that 60-day period (to the Circuit court), in which case the remand is not effective until the appeal is done (after the remand becomes effective, the liability issue can no longer be appealed or reviewed).

(4) Appealing a remand decision: The federal court's decision to remand a damages hearing to state court cannot be appealed or reviewed.

(5) For purposes of this section and §§ 1407, 1697, and 1785, a case removed under this subsection is considered a § 1369 action.

(6) Nothing here restricts the district court's power to transfer or dismiss a case on the ground of inconvenient forum.

(f) No need to re-file: The federal court to which a case is removed may still hear a case that the state court had no jurisdiction over (the case need not be dismissed and re-filed in federal court).

§ 1445. Non-Removable Cases

The following cases may not be removed:

(a) Railroad cases (pursuant to 45 USC § 51-60)

(b) Common carriers if the amount is *greater than or equal to* $10,000 (pursuant to 45 USC § 11707)

(c) State Worker's Compensation law cases

§ 1446. Procedure for Removal

(a) Filing—Must file pursuant to Rule 11, with a:

(1) Short statement of the grounds for removal
(2) Copy of process and pleadings
(3) Copy of orders served upon the Defendant

(b) Limitations

1. Must file within 30 days after (the shorter of):
   a. Defendant's receipt of π's initial pleadings
   b. Service of the summons, if pleadings are not required to be served
2. If π amends the pleadings (making the case removable), the Defendant may file for removal within 30 days after π's amended pleadings are filed and delivered.

* * *

(d) Promptly after filing, the Defendant shall give written notice to all parties and shall file a copy with the clerk. Once the state court is notified, the state court *automatically* loses control.

(e) If a Defendant has actual custody of process issued by the state court, the district court shall issue its writ of habeas corpus, and the marshal shall take the Defendant into his custody, and deliver a copy of the writ to the clerk of the state court.

§ 1447. Procedure After Removal

(a) A court may do "anything" to bring all parties before it.

(b) District court may:

1. Require the party asking for removal to file all records of the state court proceedings with the district court clerk.

and 2. Cause all records to be brought before it by having the state court issue a Writ of Certiorari.

(c) **Motion to remand** (for any defect in removal procedure)

1. A motion to remand (back to state court) may be made by π.
2. The motion must be within 30 days of the § 1446 filing of notice.
3. If the district court lacks subject matter jurisdiction at any time before judgment, the case may be remanded to state court.
4. Orders remanding a case back to the state may require payment of expenses associated with removal.
5. The state court shall proceed with the case once the district court clerk mails a certified copy of the order of remand.

(d) An order to remand is not appealable (unless removed pursuant to § 1443).

(e) If, after removal, the π joins other Defendants that destroy subject matter jurisdiction (i.e., no more complete diversity), the court may:

1. Deny the joinder

or 2. Remand the case to state court

V. PENDANT JURISDICTION

OVERVIEW

- When a case is moved to a Federal Court under § 1441 and the federal claim is dropped (or because "Interpleader" of a third party dissolves Diversity), the court may remand the case to the state court or dismiss it — *without prejudice*
  - § 1367 allows the court to retain federal jurisdiction if the federal question is dropped, as long as the Diversity requirements are still met.
  - Courts have the discretion to remand or keep a "*Pendant Jurisdiction Case*" based on:
    - Judicial efficiency — economy
    - Conveniences
    - Fairness
    - Comity (prevents state prejudice against π)

Relevant Rules: 28 U.S.C. § 1367

§ 1367. Supplemental Jurisdiction

(Over subsequent parties or actions)

(a) "Supplemental jurisdiction" — includes jurisdiction over any claims *related* to the claims in a case which form the *same case or controversy* (including joinder or intervention of claims).

(b) Supplemental-diversity jurisdiction — When courts have Subject Matter Jurisdiction based only on diversity, complete diversity must be continued for all counterclaims against third parties.

(c) Court's discretion — A Court may decline Supplemental Jurisdiction if:

1. The claim raises a novel or complex issue of state law.

or 2. The claim is *"substantially"* predominant over the original [federal] claim.

or 3. The court dismissed all claims having Subject Matter Jurisdiction.

or 4. Exceptional circumstances compel the federal court to decline jurisdiction.

(d) Statute of limitations — is tolled while

1. The supplemental claim is pending

or 2. For a period of 30 days after its dismissal *unless* state law provides for a longer tolling period.

(e) "State" includes the District of Columbia, Puerto Rico, and any other U.S. territory.

VI. VENUE

OVERVIEW

Once it is decided that the federal court system can hear a case, it must be decided which particular courts within that system can hear the case.

- Venue rules are mostly statutory and may differ in different types of cases with a special statute (e.g., FTC cases and Federal Securities claims)
- The general Federal Venue Statute (§ 1391) established venue for claims not covered by a special statute.
- Proper venue depends on the type of SMJ the Federal Court has:
  - **Diversity jurisdiction**: In a diversity jurisdiction case, proper venue will be:
    1. Where the Defendant resides (if all Defendants reside in one state)

    or 2. Where Substantial events occurred or where the subject property is located (i.e., there is enough property/activity to ensure a relationship between the cause of action and the Court)

    or 3. Any district that has personal jurisdiction over the Defendants when the action is brought (if there is no other district) ("Fallback Provision")
  - **Federal question**: In a diversity jurisdiction case, proper venue will be:
    1. Where the Defendant resides (if all Defendants reside in one state)

    or 2. Where Substantial events occurred or where the property is located (i.e., there is enough property/activity to ensure a relationship between the cause of action and the Court)

    or 3. In any district where Defendant may be found ("Fallback Provision")
- **Corporate defendants**: Any district where they are subject to Personal Jurisdiction (i.e., minimum contact must be established)
- πs often choose districts based on the type of jury (e.g., large cities tend to give greater awards than suburbs, how judges are assigned, and other factors).
- **Waiving venue** (§ 1406/Rule 12)
  - A Rule 12(b)(3) motion for improper venue must be made *either*:
    1. *Before the answer is sent*

    or 2. *In the answer itself*
  - § 1406 prevents jurisdiction from being destroyed if the parties do not object to venue.
- **Forum non conveniens** (§ 1404)
  - A party can *transfer* a case from one District Court to another for convenience of the parties or witnesses.
  - A Case may be transferred only to a court "*where it might have been brought originally*"
  - Transfer discretionary— A District Court is not forced to hear a case when the original court agrees to transfer a case to it.
  - The π's choice of forum shall *rarely be disturbed*, but the court must waive venue if the forum prejudices Defendant.

- Factors considered to dismiss a case for forum non conveniens:
- If the "*ends of justice*" strongly militate in favor of removing
- If there is an *alternative* forum in the U.S. or the Defendant consents to go elsewhere
- Other factors:
  - Parties' residences
  - Situs of cause of action
  - Location of witnesses
  - Economic burden of increased litigation
  - Ease of access to sources of proof
  - Enforceability of judgment
  - Public policy
    - Court congestion
    - Interest to the state/district
    - Public vs. private interests
- If π or Defendant makes Motion to Transfer Venue, the original state's law still applies
- Favorability of laws is not considered in Forum Non Conveniens, unless the new forum would be completely inadequate (e.g., if the new forum would be in Iran).

- **Diversity and venue**
  - Defendants must reside in the same state if the Defendants' residence will be the basis of establishing proper venue.
  - If Defendants reside in different states, π must sue in the district where substantial actions related to the case occurred.
  - If most events occurred outside the US, then:
    - π may bring the suit wherever there is common Personal Jurisdiction over all Defendants

    or • π may bring 2 separate cases (one for each Defendant)

Relevant Rules: 28 U.S.C. §1391, §1392, §1404, §1406 Rule 12(b)(3), Rule 12(g), Rule 12(h)

§1391. Venue

(a) **Diversity case:** If a case has federal jurisdiction based solely on diversity, it may be brought:

1. In the district court where any Defendant resides, if all Defendants reside in same state.

or 2. In the district court where *substantial* events or property is located.

or 3. If no other district can hear the case, then it may be heard wherever all Defendants are subject to personal jurisdiction at the commencement of the action (if no such place is available, the parties must bring separate suits).

(b) Jurisdiction not based solely on diversity: Suits involving a **federal question** (as defined in § 1331) may be brought:

1. In the district court where any Defendant resides, if all Defendants reside in same state

or 2. In the district court where *substantial* events or property is located

or 3. If no other district is available, then the suit may be brought wherever any one Defendant may be found.

(c) Corporate venue:

1. Wherever a corporation is subject to personal jurisdiction at commencement of the action (any district where "contacts" would give the corporation personal jurisdiction (under the "minimum contacts test")).
2. If none available, look to the district with the most "*significant*" contacts.
3. If there is no one particular district in the state in which the company has enough contacts for personal jurisdiction, but the state as a whole "qualifies" (under the "minimum contacts test"), the entire state is considered to have personal jurisdiction over the Defendant corporation.

(d) Venue of an alien: An alien may be sued in any district.

(e) Venue for an officer or employee of the U.S.

(1) Where a Defendant resides (if all Defendants reside in the same state).
(2) Where *substantial* events or property exist
(3) If no real property is involved, then where the π resides

(f) Venue for a suit against a foreign state (as defined in § 1603(a)):

(1) Where *substantial* events or property exist
(2) Where the vessel or cargo is situated
(3) Wherever the agency is licensed to do business (or actually does business)
(4) If the action is brought against a foreign state: In the D.C. District Court

(g) Venue for a suit where jurisdiction based on § 1369 (multiparty, multiforum jurisdiction):

1. Any district in which any defendant resides

or 2. Any district in which a *substantial* part of the accident (on which the case is based) took place

§ 1392. Multiple Districts

If Defendants reside or have property located in more than 1 district, π can bring the action in any of those districts.

§ 1404. Change of Venue

(a)

i. Change of venue may be made for the following reasons:
   1. Convenience of parties

   or 2. Convenience of witnesses

   or 3. *"In the interest of justice"*

ii. A district may transfer a case to any other district where the case *may have been brought*.

or (b) Both parties may consent to change venue (subject to the court's discretion)

(c) A district court may order any civil action to be tried at any place within the division in which it is pending.

(d) Definitions:

E-Z Definition:
1. **"District Court"** includes U.S. District Court for the District Court for the Canal Zone.
2. **"District"** includes the territorial jurisdiction of that court.

§ 1406. Waiver of Venue

(a) If venue is wrong, the district court may:

1. Dismiss the case

or 2. Transfer the case to an appropriate district

(b) Even if a party does not make a timely and sufficient objection to venue, jurisdiction <u>will not</u> be destroyed (See Rule 12 for bringing a motion for improper venue).

(c) Definitions:

E-Z Definition:
1. **"District Court"** includes U.S. District Court for the District Court for the Canal Zone.
2. **"District"** includes the territorial jurisdiction of that court.

Rule 12(b)(3). Objecting to Venue

A Motion for Improper Venue need not appear in the answer.

Rule 12(g). Consolidating Defense

(1) A party can join motions under this rule with any other motions available to the Defendant.

(2) If this motion is made, any available Rule 12(b) defenses that are omitted will be deemed to be waived (unless allowed by 12(h)(2) or (3)).

Rule 12(h). Waiver or Preservation of Defenses

(1) Objection to

a. Lack of Personal Jurisdiction (Rule 12(b)(2))
or b. Improper Venue (Rule 12(b)(3))
or c. Insufficiency of Process (Rule 12(b)(4))
or d. Insufficiency of Service (Rule 12(b)(5)) will be **waived** if:
(A) Omitted from Consolidated motions (12(g)) (i.e., if you make one, you must make all)
or (B) Omitted from:
(i) A Rule 12 Motion
or (ii) A Responsive Pleading or a Rule 15(a) amendment

(2) Other motions

- Other motions are made
  (A) In any Rule 7(a) pleading
  (B) In a 12(c) Motion
  (C) At trial
- This includes:
  a. Failure to state a valid Claim (Rule 12(b)(6))
  b. Failure to Join a third party under Rule 19 (Rule 12(b)(7))
  c. Failure to State a Legal Defense

(3) Motion for Lack of Subject Matter Jurisdiction (Rule 12(b)(1)) may be made AT ANY TIME (even after judgment).

VII. PLEADINGS

A. GENERAL RULES OF PLEADINGS

OVERVIEW

- **Detail of pleadings:**
  - Pleadings should briefly state claims
  - Many courts want more detailed pleadings
    - To reduce litigation/discovery costs
    - To make a Motion to Dismiss easier to bring
- **Orders:** Courts may:
  - Order the party to make a more definite statement (8(e))
  - Dismiss the claim for *failure to state a claim* (12(b)(6))—but only when it is *beyond a doubt* that π has no chance of winning.
- **Burdens of proof for conditions:**
  - Condition subsequent—Defendant has burden of proving any condition subsequent
  - Condition precedent—π has burden of proving any condition precedent

1. *Specificity:*
   - Requirements for pleadings have become more liberal. Specificity is no longer needed.
     - Party need not state the actual legal claim; he may use colloquial language to describe the type of action (e.g., "You're liable because your actions were reasonably foreseeable" is sufficient to assert Proximate Causation).
     - The party must show that the facts set forth a claim
   - Basic requirements—Must include:
     - **Enough information to notify the other party what to expect the suit to be so as to allow him to properly prepare an answer.**
     - Allegations of fault and causation
     - A valid claim—such that if all facts in the complaint were true, the pleader would win
     - Specificity may be beneficial in speeding up the action (e.g., Settlement, summary judgment, etc.)
2. ***Special matters***:
   - Special matters require more detailed pleadings:
     - Special matters include:
       - Civil Rights cases
       - Preexisting conditions or things difficult for **Defendants** to foresee
       - Fraud cases (securities)
   - Circumstances of special matters must be pleaded so that they provide a *factual foundation* for otherwise conclusory allegations, *especially* in hard-to-prove fraud cases (e.g., scienter is a state of mind)

- **Fraud cases:** Special "*particularity*" standard is imposed in fraud cases. Level of required specificity is much higher than in ordinary cases:
  - Factual foundation necessary
  - *Rationale*: Distrust that people will bring frivolous/false suits.
- Special damages (Rule 9(g))
  - Must be pleaded in the complaint
  - Especially needed if a PREEXISTING CONDITION must be proven in a particular claim (e.g., must prove that Mark had a history of seizures, and drove without taking the required medication to prevent such seizures)

3. ***Alternative pleadings:***

   Mutually exclusive alternative pleadings are allowed (e.g., Stephanie didn't do it; but if Stephanie did do it, she's insane) if:
   - π is unsure of the facts, yet can ultimately find them
   - Key witnesses are unavailable (e.g., they are dead)
   - Complete justice can be accomplished only with such pleadings

4. ***Answer:***
   - A party has 20 Days after the complaint was served to answer it (extended for out of state service)
     - Alternatives:
       - Deny
       - Deny knowledge or information sufficient to form a belief as to the truth of the allegation ("DKI")
       - Admit
       - Disputing facts—partial admittance
       - Affirmative defense—admitting to the allegations, yet including a "but" clause (usually claiming contributory fault)
       - Counterclaim—Defendant presents claims against third parties
       - Implead—bring in a third party
   - Denying for lack of knowledge or Information:
     - "DKI" is considered a denial.
     - It is insufficient (even in Good Faith) if the Defendant has control over obtaining the knowledge necessary for determining validity of an allegation.
     - Rule 11 "honesty" provisions apply. Thus, a "DKI" is not appropriate if Defendant "*should have known*" of a particular fact.
     - If DKI is inappropriate, the court may consider it an admission.

Relevant Rules: 7, 8, 9, 10

Rule 7. Pleadings Allowed; Form of Motions and Other Papers

(a) Pleadings: Allowable pleadings include:

(1) The Complaint
(2) The Answer
(3) A Reply to a Counterclaim
(4) An Answer to a Cross-claim
(5) A third-party complaint (if that party was not an original party under Rule 14)
(6) A third-party answer (if a third-party complaint was served)
(7) A Reply to an answer or third-party answer (allowed only if the court orders)

(b) Motions and other papers

(1) Requirements for an application for an order:
  (A) Must be made in writing:
    1. Writing requirement will be fulfilled if the motion is stated in a written notice of the hearing of the motion.
    2. Writing requirement is not necessary if a motion is made at a hearing or trial.
  (B) Shall state grounds for motions with "*particularity*"
  (C) Shall state relief sought
(2) All rules regarding form of pleadings and captioning (numbering) of rules apply.

Rule 8. General Rules of Pleading

(a) Claims for relief—must contain:

(1) A Short plain statement of jurisdiction (unless the court already has it)
(2) A Short and plain statement that the Pleader is entitled to relief
(3) Relief sought ("demand for judgment") *Alternative types of relief may be demanded*

(b) Defenses; form of denials

(1) For responses:
  (A) the Pleader shall state (in plain and short terms) defenses to each claim asserted
  and (B) admit or deny the allegations
(2) Denials must respond to the substance of the denied allegations.

(3) <u>Types of denials which a Pleader may make</u>:
  - a. *Specific denial*—applying only to parts of the pleadings
  - or b. *Complete denial*—applying to entire complaint
  - or c. *General denial*—applying to the entire complaint, except paragraphs specified

(4) If the Pleader intends to deny only a part of an allegation, he shall specify what is true and deny only the remainder.

(5) If the Pleader is without sufficient knowledge or information (to admit or deny) the Pleader may so state (a.k.a. "D.K.I."). In such a case, the court will consider it as if the Pleader *denied* the allegations.

(6) Effect of failure to deny
  - a. Any denials omitted are deemed to have been admitted, unless:
    - i. A responsive pleading was not required
    - or ii. The omission involved a dispute of the amount of damages claimed
  - b. Any allegations to which no answer is required (or allowed) shall be taken as denied.

(c) Affirmative defenses

(1) <u>Types of affirmative defenses:</u>

- Accord and Satisfaction
- Arbitration and Award
- Assumption of Risk
- Contributory Negligence
- Discharge in Bankruptcy
- Duress
- Laches
- License
- Res Judicata
- Waiver
- Estoppel
- Failure of Consideration
- Fraud
- Illegality
- Injury
- Injury by fellow servant
- Payment
- Release
- Statute of Frauds

(2) If the Pleader makes a mistake and puts Counterclaims as affirmative defenses, the court may treat it as if it were without mistakes.

(d) Consistency of pleadings—concise and direct

(1) In general: Each allegation shall be Direct and Concise (no technical forms of pleadings/motions required).

(2) Alternative statements:
  - a. Claims may be in one count or defense, or as separate ones
  - b. A relationship between the claims is not necessary

c. If one statement is improper, it does not negate the entire pleading (i.e., only the improper allegation will be negated).

(3) Inconsistent statements: A Pleader may state as many separate claims as it wants in the pleadings

(e) Construction of pleadings: Pleadings shall be construed so as to "*do justice.*"

Rule 9. Pleading Special Matters

(a) Capacity

(1) Other than to show jurisdiction, there is no need to allege:
 (A) capacity to sue
 (B) authority to sue as a representative
 (C) an organized association's legal existence

(2) If a party wants to raise a capacity issue, it must do so in a *specific negative* allegation (which must be stated with particularity (i.e., with a specific factual foundation)).

(b) Fraud, mistake, condition of mind—

1. Accusations of fraud, mistake—must be stated with *particularity* (i.e., with a specific factual foundation).
2. Accusations of malice, intent, knowledge, and conditions of mind—may be alleged *generally.*

(c) Conditions Precedent:

1. A Denial that a Condition Precedent has not been fulfilled must be stated with *particularity.*
2. An allegation that a Condition Precedent was performed may be alleged *generally.*

(d) Official document or act—It is sufficient to simply say that it was done in compliance with the law.

(e) Judgment—Domestic or foreign court judgments are sufficient to aver a judgment or decision. There is no need to describe the jurisdiction of the court.

(f) Time and place—Allegations of time and place are material.

(g) Special damages—must be specifically stated.

(h) Admiralty and maritime claims

(1) **How designated.**

a. If a claim is both an admiralty or maritime claim and also a claim on some other ground, the pleading may designate the claim as an admiralty or maritime claim

b. This designation would apply for purposes of:
   1. Rule 14(c) — Third-Party Practice in Admiralty or Maritime Cases
   2. Rule 38(e) — Jury trials in Admiralty or Maritime Cases
   3. Rule 82 — Jurisdiction and Venue in Admiralty or Maritime Cases
   and 4. The Supplemental Rules for Admiralty or Maritime Claims and Asset Forfeiture Cases

c. If a claim is only an admiralty or maritime claim, it is considered one for all of the above purposes (whether or not designated one).

(2) **Designation for appeal.** A case that includes an admiralty or maritime claim within this subdivision (h) is an admiralty case within 28 U.S.C. § 1292(a)(3).

Rule 10. Form of Pleadings

(a) Captions; names of parties

i. Every pleading requires a caption with:
   1. Name of court
   2. Title of action
   3. File number (docket number)
   4. Type of pleading (see 7(a); e.g., answer, complaint)
   5. Name of first party on each side

ii. If the pleading is a **complaint** it must *also* include the names of <u>*all*</u> parties.

(b) Separate statements

1. All allegations (claims/defenses) shall be made in NUMBERED paragraphs.
2. Each paragraph shall be limited to a single set of circumstances (or whenever needed for clarity).
3. In later paragraphs or pleadings, paragraphs may be referred to by paragraph number.

(c) Adoption by reference:

1. Statements in a pleading may be adopted by reference in:
   a. Other parts of the pleadings
   or b. In different pleadings
   or c. In motions
2. An exhibit is a part of a pleading for all purposes

B. AMENDED AND SUPPLEMENTAL PLEADINGS

OVERVIEW

- Courts usually allow amendments to pleadings (15(a)) unless the adverse party can show that he will be prejudiced (e.g., the Statute of Limitations would have barred the claim).
- The opposing party has the burden of showing that he will be prejudiced.
- Each party has one opportunity, *as of right,* to amend pleadings.
- Subsequent amendments must be requested from the court ("*Motion for leave to amend*") within 20 days after service of the pleadings.
- Parties may consent to try issues not in the pleadings. They may also "imply" consent by addressing the issue outside the pleadings (at which point the issue is considered as if it were in the pleadings).
- **STATUTE OF LIMITATIONS AND RELATION BACK** (See Rule 15(c)):
  - The "*Relation Back Doctrine*" moves the effective date of the "action/amendment" back to the date of the original pleadings (within the statute of limitations).
  - Requirements:
    - Notice must be given to all potential Defendants
    - The Defendant may not be prejudiced (i.e., it *should have known* about the complaint/problem)
    - The Burden rests on the party opposing the "Relation Back" to show Prejudice
  - **Application**—The Relation Back Doctrine applies only if:
    - Notice of the claim is given to the party
    - or • If misnamed Parties were used
      - Relation Back will be allowed if a Master-Servant or Invitor-Invitee relationship exists
    - or • If the parties are joint tortfeasors (then they must be individually named and informed before the Statute of Limitations runs out)
  - Some states allow "Doe" pleadings (e.g., the pleadings say Mark Smith v. Doe)
- **Acceptable notice:**
  - The Statute of Limitations may be extended with the *Court's discretion* if the Defendant is aware that the claim is being made (or should have known that it is being made) against it before the Statute of Limitations runs out;
  - If the Defendant is a complete stranger to the case, the Statute of Limitations runs as normal

Relevant Rule: 15

Rule 15. Amended and Supplemental Pleadings

(a) Amendments:

(1) Parties have a *right* to 1 amendment:
- (A) Before the answer or responding pleading is served.
- (B) In a non-responsive pleading, 20 days after the pleading is served.

(2) Otherwise, amending party must:
- a. Request a *"leave of court"* to amend the pleading (Court must consent when *"justice so requires"*)
- or b. Obtain written consent from the adverse parties

(3) Answering amended pleadings—must be done within the *longer of:*
- a. 10 days after service of the amendment
- or b. The time remaining within the original 20-day response period (from the initial pleading)

(b) Amendments during or after trial

(1) Objections to issues during trial
- a. If a party objects to amendments, new evidence, or issues not explicitly included in pleadings, the court may still grant/allow if it will *promote justice* (and the other party cannot show prejudice).
- b. The court may grant a continuance to allow the objecting party to meet the evidence.

(2) Issues tried by consent
- a. Issues *expressly* or *impliedly* consented to by parties are considered to have been raised in pleadings (although they never were).
- b. Parties may make a *Motion to Amend* the Pleadings (to conform to the evidence) at any time, even after judgment.
- c. Failure to amend does not affect the result of the trial on that issue.

(c) Relation back of amendments:

(1) Amendments will be considered to relate back to date of the original pleading if:
- (A) Permitted by the law providing for the Statute of Limitations in the case
- or (B) They are related to the original claims (i.e., arising out of the same conduct, transaction, or occurrence)
- or (C) There were misidentified parties in original claim. Such amendments will relate back to date of pleading only upon reasonable notice if:

(i) A Party has received notice of the action and will not be prejudiced in maintaining a defense on the merits.

and (ii) The Party knew or should have known that the action would have been taken against her, *but for* the fact that there was a mistake as to her actual identity.

(2) **Notice to the United States.** When the U.S. (or an officer or agency of the U.S.) is added as a defendant by amendment, 15(c)(1)(C)(i) and (ii) are satisfied if process was delivered or mailed to the U.S. Attorney, the U.S. Attorney General, or to the officer or agency.

(d) Supplemental pleadings:

1. Upon Motion, Pleadings may be amended for events occurring *after* service of the original pleadings if:
   a. Reasonable notice is given

   and b. The terms are just
2. Supplemental Pleadings must set forth the transactions or events that have happened since the date the original pleading was drafted.
3. Permission to supplement a pleading may be granted, even though the original pleading has a defective statement claiming relief or defense.
4. If the court deems it advisable, it may order the opposing party to respond within a specified time.

C. DEFENSES AND OBJECTIONS

Relevant Rule: 12

Rule 12. Defenses and Objections; When and How; Motion for Judgment on the Pleadings; Consolidating and Waiving Defenses; Pretrial Hearing

(a) Time frame for parties to respond

(1) Answers, Complaints, and Counterclaim replies

(A) Answer and Complaint: Unless a federal statute supersedes, the *Answer* must be served:

(i) *If summons served:* the answer must be served within 20 days after service (extended if out of state).

(ii) *If service waived:* the answer must be served within 60 days after request for waiver is *sent* (90 if outside of the U.S.).

(B) Answer to a Cross-claim: If the Answer is in response to a Cross-claim, π has 20 days from the date the Cross-claim was served.

(C) Response to a Counterclaim: The π shall reply to a Counterclaim:

1. Within 20 Days after service of Defendant's answer
2. Within 20 Days after service of a court order, if π's reply is ordered by the court (unless the order directs otherwise)

Extension for United States

(2) If the United States is a party, it shall have 60 days after the United States Attorney is served to respond.

(3) If an officer or employee of the United States is sued in his individual capacity (for acts or omissions while performing his duties on behalf of the United States), he has 60 days after he is served, or after the United States Attorney is served (whichever is later).

(4) Exceptions to time limit: The time limitations above will not apply in the following cases:

(A) *If a Court denies the motion or postpones disposition*—the Answer is due within 10 days after Court notifies of decision to proceed

or (B) *If a Court grants motion for a more definite statement*—the Answer is due within 10 days after receipt of π's revised pleadings

(b) How presented:

i. All Defenses must be made in answer, *except for*:
   (1) Motion for lack of Subject Matter Jurisdiction
   (2) Motion for lack of Personal Jurisdiction
   (3) Motion for improper venue
   (4) Motion for insufficiency of process
   (5) Motion for insufficiency of service of process
   (6) Motion for failure to state a valid claim upon which relief can be granted
   (7) Motion for failure to join a party under Rule 19

ii. The above defenses are made in a pre-answer motion.

iii. Where no response to a Pleading is required, the above defenses may be made at trial.

iv. There is no waiver by joining a defense with other defenses or objections.

(c) Motion for judgment on the pleadings may be made after the pleadings if it does not delay the trial.

(d) Implied motion for summary judgment

1. A 12(b)(6) motion is treated as a motion for summary judgment (Rule 56) if:
   a. The 12(b)(6) motion is made (failure to state a claim).
   and b. Matters outside the pleading are presented to the court (which are not excluded by the court).
2. In such a case, all parties shall be given a reasonable opportunity to present all material pertinent to such a motion (Rule 56).

(e) Motion for more definite statement:

1. This motion may be made if π's pleadings are too vague/ambiguous so that Defendant cannot reasonably frame a response.
2. The motion must point out the defects in π's pleadings.
3. If granted, the π must re-plead within 10 days of the notice of motion (otherwise the court may strike pleadings or make any other order).

(f) Motion to strike

- This may be done by
  (1) The court's own motion

or (2) A party's motion made before answering (or 20 days after being served, if no Answer is allowed)

- The court may order something stricken from the pleadings if it contains:
  1. Insufficient defenses
  2. Redundancies
  3. Immaterialities
  4. Scandalous matter

(g) Consolidating defense—

(1) A party can join motions under this rule with any other motions available to the Defendant.

(2) If this motion is made, any available Rule 12(b) defenses that are omitted will be deemed to be waived (unless allowed by 12(h)(2) or (3)).

(h) Waiver or preservation of defenses—

(1) Objection to

a. Lack of Personal Jurisdiction (Rule 12(b)(2))

or b. Improper Venue (Rule 12(b)(3))

or c. Insufficiency of Process (Rule 12(b)(4))

or d. Insufficiency of Service (Rule 12(b)(5)) will be **waived if:**

(A) Omitted from Consolidated motions (12(g)) (i.e., if you make one, you must make all)

or (B) Omitted from:

(i) A Rule 12 Motion

or (ii) A Responsive Pleading or a Rule 15(a) amendment

(2) Other motions

- Other motions are made
  - (A) In any Rule 7(a) pleading
  - (B) In a 12(c) Motion
  - (C) At trial
- This includes:
  - a. Failure to state a valid Claim (Rule 12(b)(6))
  - b. Failure to Join a third party under Rule 19 (Rule 12(b)(7))
  - c. Failure to State a Legal Defense

(3) Motion for Lack of Subject Matter Jurisdiction (Rule 12(b)(1)) may be made AT ANY TIME (even after judgment).

(i) Preliminary hearings on any motions (under 12(b)(1)-(7)) shall be granted upon the request of any party, unless the judge decides to defer the hearing until trial.

D. SANCTIONS FOR IMPROPER PLEADINGS

OVERVIEW

- <u>Rule 11 Duties</u>:
  - **Duty to investigate**: π's attorney has the duty to investigate the legitimacy of a claim before filing/signing a pleading.
  - **Duty to mitigate**: If π is suing for lawyers' fees, he has a duty to mitigate by <u>*attempting to dismiss*</u> the case early on.
- <u>Requirements for sanctions</u>
  - π attempts to bring a *frivolous suit*

  or • π brings insubstantial claims to court
- The court can impose Rule 11 sanctions even if π moves to dismiss the case, since π's dismissal does not terminate the Court's power over the case (see Rule 41).
- <u>Review of Rule 11 decisions</u>:
- Appellate Courts should use either:
  - Abuse of Discretion standard to see if the evidence is <u>grossly</u> misinterpreted

  or • Error of Law Standard
- The Appellate Court does not dispute whether the District Court was correct in determining facts applicable to Rule 11.
- Only attorneys' fees incurred while the case is in the District Court are recoupable (not appellate fees)

Relevant Rule: 11

Rule 11. Signing Pleadings, Motions, and Other Papers; Representations to the Court; Sanctions

(a) Signature

1. Signature must be made <u>by the lawyer</u>; if there is no lawyer, the pleader must sign.
2. The signer must include his address and telephone number and email address.
3. There is no need to accompany pleadings with an affidavit (unless specifically provided for by another rule or statute).
4. If the signature is missing, the court may strike the pleadings, unless it is signed promptly after such omission is brought to the pleader's attention.

(b) Representations to court

A signature implies that, to best of the signer's knowledge, with *reasonable inquiry*, the pleading is:

(1) Made with a proper purpose — not to harass or cause unnecessary cost or delay

and (2) Warranted by *existing law* (or a non-frivolous argument to change existing law)

and (3) Well-grounded in fact — likely to be reasonably supported by facts

and (4) Based on evidence — Denials of factual contentions are based on evidence or reasonably based on lack of belief/information.

(c) Sanctions — If Rule 11(b) is violated, the court may impose sanctions to lawyers/signers:

(1) **In general**.

(2) **Motion for Sanctions** *((A) in the Pre-December 2003 Rule).*

(A) **By motion**:

1. Motion for Sanctions must be made separately from other motions.
2. The motion must state violation of Rule 11(b).
3. The motion may be filed only if the pleading is not corrected within 21 days of service.
4. The court may award the winner reasonable expenses and fees incurred in making or opposing the motion.
5. Law firms will be held jointly liable — *absent exceptional circumstances*.

(3) **On Court's initiative**: If the Court initiates the sanctions (by Order to Show Cause), the burden of proof will fall on the pleader to show that it is not in violation.

(4) Nature of sanctions: Sanctions shall be limited to what is "*sufficient to deter repetition*" of the conduct. This may include:

a. Non-monetary damages (e.g., Equitable damages)

b. Penalties paid to the court

c. Payment of another party's expenses/lawyers' fees

(5) Limitation of sanctions: Money damages are not awarded for:

(A) Violations of 11(b)(2) (pleading not warranted by law) against represented party

(B) When initiated by Court (Rule 11(c)(1)(B)), unless the Court issues an Order to Show Cause *before* either:

1. A Voluntary Dismissal (made by or against a party (or attorney) to be sanctioned)

or 2. A Settlement of Claims (made by or against a party (or attorney) to be sanctioned)

(6) Order: Court shall prescribe conduct and basis for sanction

(d) Inapplicability to discovery—Rule 11 does not apply to:

1. Disclosures
2. Discovery requests
3. Responses
4. Objections
5. Motions subject to provisions in Rules 26–37

E. CLASS ACTIONS

Relevant Rules: 23, 23.1, 23.2

Rule 23. Class Actions

(a) Prerequisites to a class action — one or more members of a class may sue or be sued as representative parties IF:

(1) "Numerosity": The class is so large that the joinder of all members is impracticable.

and (2) "Commonality": There is a common question of law or fact involved.

and (3) "Typicality": Claims or defenses of the representative parties are typical of the rest of the class.

and (4) "Adequacy": The Representative parties will adequately and fairly protect the class's interests.

(b) Class actions maintainable: 23(a) must be satisfied and *either:*

(1) Separate actions by individual members would create a risk of

(A) *Inconsistent/Varying adjudications*, which would establish incompatible standards of conduct for the opposing party (mostly used in property actions, nuisance, or reward cases)

or (B) Adjudication for an individual member which would *substantially* impair or impede other members from taking action or protecting themselves (mostly for declaratory judgments, injunctions)

or (2) The opposing party has acted similarly adverse to the entire class

or (3) i. The court finds that (mostly for damages)

a. The facts common to class are *predominate over* the facts specific to each individual

and b. A class action would be the best way for *fair and efficient* adjudication

ii. Pertinent consideration which court must weigh:

(A) The *Interest of members* to individually control their own cases

(B) The *Extent and nature of litigation* involved

(C) The *Desirability of concentrating the litigation* in a particular forum

(D) The *Difficulties likely to be encountered* in managing the class action (e.g., expenses)

(c) Order determining whether class action should be certified:

(1) The court order for certification
   (A) When a person sues or is sued as a class representative, the court *must* determine (by order) whether to certify as a class action.
   (B) The order must:
      i. Define the class
      ii. Define the class claims, issues, or defenses
      iii. Appoint "class counsel" under Rule 23(g)
   (C) A Rule 23(c)(1) order may be altered or amended before final judgment.

(2) Notice requirements[2]
   (A) *For 23(b)(1) or (2) classes:* The court may direct appropriate notice to the class.
   (B) *For 23(b)(3) classes:*
      i. The Court *must* direct the best notice under the circumstances.
      ii. Notice must advise each member (in plain and easy language):
         (i) The nature of the case
         (ii) The class definition
         (iii) The class claims, issues or defenses
         (iv) That a member may appear through a lawyer if she desires
         (v) That the Court will exclude the member from the class upon a member's request (before the specified date)
         (vi) How to request exclusion
         (vii) The binding effect of a judgment on the class (under Rule 23(c)(3))

(3) Judgment:
   (A) *Judgments in Class Actions under (b)(1) and (b)(2)*—These judgments apply to all people whom the court finds to be members of the class.
   (B) *Judgments in Class Actions under (b)(3)*—These judgments apply to all people whom the court finds to be members of the class if:
      1. The members received appropriate notice of the action

[2] In 2003 the notice provisions to Rule 23 were substantially revised.

and 2. The members <u>did not</u> request exclusion from the class

(4) <u>Particular issues</u>: A class action may be brought with respect to particular issues only

(5) Subclasses: A class may be subdivided into subclasses (each subclass shall be treated as a separate class)

(d) Orders in conduct of actions:

(1) In general: The court may issue orders to:

(A) Prescribe measures to prevent due repetition or complication

(B) Require specific methods of notice.

1. The objective would be to protect class members and to conduct the case fairly.
2. Notice includes notice of:
   (i) any step in the case
   (ii) the proposed extent of the judgment
   (iii) the class members' opportunity to:
   - inform the court whether they consider the representation *"fair and adequate"*
   - to intervene and present claims/ defenses
   - to otherwise come into the case

(C) Impose conditions on representative parties

(D) Require that pleadings be amended to represent class

(E) Deal with similar procedural matters

(2) Combining and amending orders:

a. A Rule 23(d)(1) order may be combined with a Rule 16 order

b. Such orders may be *altered or amended* as the court sees fit

(e) Settlement, dismissal, or compromise—The court must approve any settlements (or dismissals), subject to the following procedures

(1) <u>Notice</u>: The court *must* direct notice to all members who would be bound by the settlement (or dismissal).

(2) <u>Hearing</u>: The court needs to have a hearing (to determine if the settlement is *fair, reasonable, and adequate*) before approving a settlement that binds class members.

(3) <u>Agreements made in connection with a settlement</u>: Parties seeking approval of a settlement must file a statement showing any agreement made in connection with the proposed settlement.

(4) <u>New opportunity for exclusion</u>: If a case was previously certified under 23(b)(3), the court may condition approval of a settlement on a new notice to the class members to opt out of the class

(even though they got notice already and did not request exclusion).

(5) Objections to settlements requiring approval:
   a. Who May Object: Any class member
   b. Withdrawing Objections: May only be done with Court's approval

(f) Appeals:

1. A court of appeals may permit an appeal from a district court order that grants or denies class action certification.
2. Time: Application for an appeal must be made within 10 days after entry of the order denying or granting the certification.
3. Stay of proceedings: An appeal does not stay the District Court proceedings unless ordered by either:
   a. The district court judge
   b. The court of appeals

(g) Class counsel

(1) Appointing class counsel: A court that certifies a class must appoint "class counsel" (unless a statute provides otherwise)
   (A) Mandatory criteria: The court *must* consider:
      (i) The attorney's work done in identifying or investigating potential claims in the case,
      (ii) The attorney's experience in:
         1. class actions
         2. other complex litigation, and
         3. claims of the type asserted in the action,
      (iii) The attorney's knowledge of the applicable law, and
      (iv) The resources the attorney will commit to representing the class
   (B) Discretionary criteria: The court may consider any other matter pertinent to whether counsel will *"fairly and adequately"* represent the interests of the class.
   (C) Other court directions: The court may direct potential class counsel to:
      1. provide information on any subject pertinent to the appointment
      2. propose attorney fee (and costs) terms
   (D) Attorney's fees awards: The court order appointing counsel may include provisions about the award of fees or costs (dealt with in Rule 23(h).
   (E) The court may make "further orders" in connection with the appointment.

(2) Standard for appointing class counsel

1. When There Is One Applicant: The court may appoint that applicant only if the applicant qualifies under Rule 23(g)(1)(B) and (C).
2. When There Is More Than One Applicant: The court *must* appoint the best applicant.

(3) Interim counsel: The court may designate interim counsel to act for the would-be class (before determining whether to certify the action as a class action).

(4) Duty of class counsel: "Class counsel must fairly and adequately represent the interests of the class."

(h) Attorney fees award. In a certified class action, the court may award reasonable attorney fees and costs (authorized by law or by agreement of the parties) as follows:

(1) Motion for award of attorney fees.

a. An attorney must make a motion for fees and costs under Rule 54(d)(2).
b. Notice of the motion must be served on all parties.
c. Motions made by class counsel must be directed to the class members in a *reasonable manner*.

(2) Objections to motion. The following people may object to the motion for fees:

a. A class member
b. Any party from whom payment is sought

(3) Hearing and findings.

a. The court *must* make findings of fact and conclusions of law on the motion (following Rule 52(a))
b. The court may hold a hearing

(4) Reference to special master or magistrate judge. The court may refer issues related to the amount of the award to a special master or to a magistrate judge (as provided in Rule 54(d)(2)(D)).

Rule 23.1. Derivative Actions

(a) Prerequisites

1. This rule applies in a derivative action brought by one or more shareholders to enforce a right of a corporation
2. Derivative action may not be maintained if it appears that π does not adequately represent the interests of class (shareholders, members, and other similarly situated members).

(b) Pleading requirements: Shareholders must prepare (and verify) a complaint that:

(1) Alleges that the π was a shareholder

a. At the time of the transaction π is complaining about

or b. After the transaction, and π's shares devolved on the π by operation of law

and (2) Alleges that the action is not a collusive one to confer jurisdiction in a Federal Court, in which it otherwise may NOT have such jurisdiction

and (3) Alleges with particularity that:

(A) the efforts (if any) made by π to obtain a remedy directly with the corporate directors/officers/shareholders

(B) The reasons why π's efforts to remedy the situation failed

(c) Settlement, dismissal, and compromise

1. The court *must* approve proposed settlements
2. Class representatives must notify the class of any settlement (notification to be given in a manner proposed by court)

Rule 23.2. Actions Relating to Unincorporated Associations

1. This rule applies in a derivative action brought by one or more shareholders to enforce a right of a corporation.

2. Cases brought by or against unincorporated associations may be maintained only if it appears that the representatives will fairly and adequately represent the entire class.

3. Procedures during the case:

   a. The court may issue any order that corresponds with Rule 23(d).
   b. The procedure for settlement, voluntary dismissal, or compromise must correspond with the procedure in Rule 23(e).

VIII. PRETRIAL CONFERENCE

Relevant Rule: 16

Rule 16. Pretrial Conferences

(a) Objectives: A Court may order (at its discretion) that parties appear for a conference to:

(1) Expedite disposition of a case

or (2) Establish early controls, so that the case is not "protracted" from lack of management

or (3) Discourage wasteful pre-trial activities

or (4) Improve the quality of trial with better preparation

or (5) Facilitate Settlement of the case

(b) Scheduling and planning

(1) **Contents of the order:** The Judge (or Magistrate) shall enter a Scheduling Order

(A) After receiving the parties' 26(f) report

or (B) After consulting with the parties (at a scheduling conference or by phone, mail, etc.)

(2) **Timing for the scheduling order:**

a. The Order shall be made ASAP, after the parties' Rule 26(f) report is received (or after a phone or other conference with the parties)

b. The Order must be made no later than:

- 120 days after the complaint has been served

and • 90 days after Defendant has made an appearance

limiting the time to:

(3) **Contents**

(A) Required contents

- Time to Join other parties
- Time to Amend Pleadings
- Time to File Motions
- Time to Complete Discovery (outside deadline)

(B) Optional contents

(i) Modifications of the 26(a) and 26(e)(1) Disclosure Times

(ii) Modifications of the extent of discovery

(iii) Dates for pre-trial conferences and trial

(iv) *Any other appropriate matters*

(4) **Modification of scheduling order:** The Schedule may only be modified by *both:*
   a. The court's permission
   and b. Showing of good cause

(c) Attendance and matters for consideration at a pre-trial conference— Participants may consider and take action regarding:

(A) Attendance

1. At least one of each party's attorneys must be present at any pre-trial conference, and must have the authority to:
   a. Enter into stipulations
   b. Make admissions (regarding matter anticipated to be discussed)
2. The court may require that a party or representative be present or *reasonably available* (for example, by phone) to consider settlement.

(B) Matters for consideration

(A) Formulation/Simplification of Issues to eliminate frivolous claims
(B) Necessity/Desirability of amending pleadings
(C) Possibility of obtaining Disclosure/Admissions to reduce factual disputes
(D) Avoidance of unnecessary proof of evidence and limitations of evidence (pursuant to Federal Rules of Evidence)
(E) Appropriateness/Timing of a Rule 56 Summary Judgment Motion.
(F) Control/Scheduling of Discovery (Rule 26 and Rules 29-37)
(G) Pre-trial Matters:
   i. Identifying Witnesses/Documents
   and ii. Preparing a schedule for
      - Exchanging pre-trial briefs
      - Further conferences
      - and Trial
(H) Referring matters to a Magistrate
(I) Settlement and use of ADR (Alternate Dispute Resolution)
(J) Form or Substance of the pre-trial order
(K) Disposition of pending motions
(L) Adopting special procedures for specific complex issues (or unusual proof problems)
(M) Orders for separate trials (per Rule 42(b))
(N) Orders to present certain evidence early (to facilitate early judgments (pursuant to Rule 50(a) and 52(c))

(O) Orders establishing a reasonable time limit for presenting evidence
(P) Other matters to facilitate a "just, speedy, and inexpensive" disposition of the case

(d) Pre-trial orders

1. After each conference, an order shall be filed, reciting the action taken at the conference.
2. Orders may be modified only by a subsequent order.

(e) Final pre-trial conference and orders

1. A Final Pre-trial Conference may be held.
2. It should be held as close to the trial date as reasonably possible.
3. It should include a trial plan and a discussion of evidence.
4. At least one trial attorney per party must appear.
5. Orders after a Final Pre-Trial Conference may be modified only to prevent *manifest injustice.*

(f) Sanctions

(1) In general: Rule 37 sanctions may (by the court or by motion) be invoked if a party or attorney:
(A) Does not appear at a conference
(B) Comes unprepared to participate in the conference (or does not participate in good faith)
(C) Fails to obey a scheduling order

(2) Imposing fees and costs
a. The court *must* order the reimbursement of reasonable expenses (this includes attorneys' fees) incurred because of a violation of this rule
b. The award of expenses and fees may be made against:
- the party
- the attorney
- or both

c. This award may be made <u>instead of</u> or <u>in addition to</u> any other sanction.
d. <u>Exceptions</u>:
i. If the noncompliance was "substantially justified"
ii. If other circumstances make the award of expenses "unjust."

IX. DISCOVERY

A. DISCOVERY PRINCIPLES AND BASIC METHODS

OVERVIEW

1. ***Disclosure***
   - Automatic disclosure: Rule 26(a) requires disclosure of certain types of materials without waiting for a Discovery request. This includes:
     - Witness information
     - Copy or description of documents/electronic information
     - Damage Computation
     - Insurance information
   - Scope of discovery: All information sought must be:
     - Directed for trial
     - To establish a foundation of knowledge
   - Types and methods of discovery: Discovery can be obtained through:
     - Interrogatories
     - Depositions
     - Demands for Documents, Electronic Information, or for Inspection
     - Physical and mental Examinations
     - Requests for Admission
2. ***Limitations and protective orders***
   - A court can limit Discovery (e.g., number of requests, length of depositions) on the basis of burden or that the request is "unreasonably duplicative."
   - Objections to Discovery requests must specifically state:
     - Why or how the request is burdensome

     and • On what grounds it is objected to (per Rule 26(c))
   - Courts often use a Balancing Test in deciding whether to grant Protective Orders:

     Interests of court in discovery

     v.

     Interests encroached upon party seeking protection
   - Tax Returns are not privileged, but have a "heightened protection" (like Work Product)
   - Upon Good Cause, a court may restrict dissemination of information *Only* if it is acquired through Discovery and *could not* be obtained from other sources.
3. ***Work-product doctrine***
   - A Party may obtain the work product of an adversary only if it can prove (with facts/circumstances):
     - That such information is *either*:

- No longer available

or - Unduly burdensome to re-obtain

and - There is a substantial need for the information

- "*Substantial need*" and "*Undue burden*" tests may be used only when written testimony is received and information does not contain mental impressions.
- Communications to counsel—can be obtained only if their essence is recorded; and only in *extremely rare cases*, since they clearly represent the lawyer's *privileged mental process*.
- "*Work product*" includes material containing:
  - Mental Impressions
  - or - Conclusions
  - or - Opinions
  - or - Legal theories
- The Work-product rule may be waived when the **main issue of the case regards**:
  - Activities of Council
  - or - Litigation
  - or - Discovery Information
- Demand for information obtained by surveillance should be granted (although the court has discretion).

4. ***Expert testimony:***
   - Rule 26(b)(4) allows parties to obtain testimony of all witnesses expected to appear at trial.
   - Non-testimonial witnesses: Adverse parties may only obtain the testimony of witnesses not expected to appear at trial, if the adverse party can show "Exceptional circumstances"
   - Changes in Testimony
     - All changes in testimony must be disclosed to the other party before trial (Rule 26(e))
     - Changed testimony cannot be used, *unless*:
       - It is supplemented with updated information
       - and - *Notice* exists (i.e., Parties know or reasonably should know of changes in testimony)
5. ***Discovery costs***
   - Each party bears its own discovery costs
   - If Discovery is protested with *good cause*, the court may charge the adverse party if it loses.
   - When using π's employees as witnesses (from out of state), Defendant must *either*:
     - Pay for π's employee's travel expenses
     - or - Go to the State where the employee is located

Relevant Rules: 26, 27, 28, 29, 30, 31, 32, 33

Rule 26. Duty to Disclose; General Provisions Governing Discovery

(a) Required disclosures—Methods to discover:

(1) Initial disclosure[3]

(A) A party must provide (without waiting for a discovery request):

(i) **People** (name, address, phone (if available), and subject of the information) *likely to have discoverable information* that the disclosing party may use (this does not include people with information that will be used only to impeach other testimony)

(ii) Relevant **Documents, electronic information, and tangible things** (or a description and location, by category) that are in the possession, custody, or control of the party, and that the disclosing party may use (this does not include information that will be used only to impeach other testimony)

(iii) **Computation of damages,** *unless* privileged or protected

(iv) **Insurance agreements** which may indemnify or pay part of judgment

(v) Exceptions: The Initial Disclosure rules *do not apply*:

1. In cases specified in Rule 26(a)(1)(E) (added December 1, 2000)
2. If the parties stipulate otherwise
3. If the court orders otherwise

(B) **Exemptions from initial disclosure:**

(i) Action for review on an administrative record

(ii) Forfeiture action (in rem) arising from a federal statute

(iii) Petition for habeas corpus (or other proceeding to challenge a conviction or sentence)

(iv) Action brought *pro se* by a person in the custody of the U.S. (or a state)

---

[3] In 2000, Rule 26(a)(1) was amended to add certain exemptions to the Initial Disclosure requirements. The rule was also narrowed to require only information that the disclosing party may use to support its position. The timing was also changed to provide for 14 days instead of 10 days, to provide time for parties joining the case late, and to provide time for objections to the Initial Disclosure rule.

(v) Action to enforce or quash an administrative summons or subpoena
(vi) Action by the U.S. to recover benefit payments
(vii) Action by the U.S. to collect on a student loan guaranteed by the U.S.
(viii) Ancillary proceedings (ancillary to proceedings in other courts)
(ix) Action to enforce an arbitration award

(C) Timing (in general):
1. Disclosures shall be made within 14 days after the meeting of the parties (pursuant to Rule 26(f))
2. A different time may be set by stipulation or court order.
3. If a party objects to Initial Disclosures (generally) during the Rule 26(f) conference and in the Rule 26(f) Plan, the court sets the time for disclosures after deciding on the objection.

(D) Timing (for parties joined later): If a party is served or joined after the Rule 26(f) conference, Initial Disclosures must be made within 30 days after being served or joined (unless otherwise stipulated or ordered).

(E) Basis for initial disclosure; unacceptable excuses: All *"reasonably available"* information must be submitted. It is not a valid excuse that:
1. Investigations are not fully complete
or 2. Opponents' discovery is insufficient
or 3. Opponents failed to submit discovery

(2) Disclosure of expert testimony:

(A) A party must disclose the identity of all expert witnesses who may be used at trial (to present evidence under Rules 702, 703, and 705 of the Federal Rules of Evidence)

(B) Experts must submit and sign a written report containing:
(i) A complete statement of *all* opinions which may be expressed at trial and the basis and reasons for the expert's opinion
and (ii) Data and information on which the opinion is based
and (iii) Exhibits to be used to support the opinion
and (iv) Qualifications of the expert (including all publications within the past 10 years)
and (v) A listing of all previous cases in which the expert had testified (*either* at trial or deposition)
and (vi) Compensation to be paid for the study or testifying

(C) The **due date** of expert disclosures is (unless the court changes):
  (i) Initial expert testimony: At least 90 days before trial
  (ii) Rebutting expert testimony (responding to initial testimony): Within 30 Days of the initial expert disclosure
(D) Supplementing the disclosure: The parties must supplement these disclosures when required under Rule 26(e)

(3) Pretrial disclosures
  (A) For any evidence to be used at trial, a party shall disclose and *promptly* file with the court:
    (i) The **name**, **address**, **phone number** of each witness and the subject matter of their testimony (if not already provided), separately indicating which witnesses may appear at trial and which may not.
    (ii) **Designation** of witnesses whose testimony is expected to be by deposition.
    (iii) Appropriate **identification** of each document and exhibit, and summaries of evidence.
  (B) Other disclosure rules:
    1. Pretrial disclosure must be submitted at least 30 days before trial.
    2. Within 14 days after pretrial disclosure, a party may file a list disclosing:
      (i) Any objections to the use of depositions
      (ii) Any objections to the admissibility of materials (with a reason for the objection)
    3. If objections are not made before 14 days, they are deemed to be waived, unless excused for *good cause.*

(4) Form of disclosure; filing—All disclosures shall be:
  a. In writing
  and b. Signed
  and c. Served
  and d. Promptly filed in court

(b) Discovery scope and limits

Note: This rule is subject to limitations that the court may impose (under the rules).

(1) Scope in general
  a. A party may obtain discovery regarding any matter that is:
    1. Not privileged
    and 2. Relevant to the claim or defense of any party

b. "Relevant" information need only to appear *reasonably calculated* to lead to the discovery of admissible evidence; it does not necessarily have to be admissible.

c. Relevant information can include information about:
   i. Books, documents, or other tangible things
   or ii. The identity of people with knowledge of any discoverable matter

d. The court may also order discovery of any matter "relevant to the subject matter involved in the lawsuit," but only for **good cause.**

e. All discovery is subject to the limitations of Rule 26(b)(2)(B)

(2) Limitations

(A) Optional limitations:

1. Courts (and not Local Rules[4]) can set limits on the length and number of depositions and the number of interrogatories.
2. Local Rules or Courts may set limits on the number of Requests for Admissions (Rule 36).

(B) Required limitations: Discovery shall be limited if the court determines (see subsection (c) below for how the Court makes this determination) that:

(i) The discovery sought is:
   a. unreasonably cumulative or duplicative
   or b. obtainable from a more convenient or less expensive source

or (ii) The party making the request has had an opportunity to already get the information throughout discovery in the case.

or (iii) The burden or expense of the proposed requests outweighs the likely benefit. The court should consider:

- The needs of the case
- The amount in controversy
- The parties' resources
- How important the issue at hand is
- How important discovery is in resolving the issue.

*(C) The court may act either on its own initiative (after giving notice) or pursuant to a motion to limit discovery (see Rule 26(c)).

---

[4] There is no need because national limits are set by Rules 30, 31, and 32.

(3) Trial preparation: Materials (work product)

(A) Disclosure: Normally, work product is not discoverable. A party may obtain discovery gathered by another party only if he can show:

(i) That they are within the scope of 26(b)(1)

and (ii) There is a need, meaning:

1. A *"substantial need"* for the materials to prepare his case

and 2. That he cannot obtain the *"substantial equivalent"* of the materials without *"undue hardship"*

(B) Disclosure is limited to materials themselves. Courts will protect opinions or conclusions (e.g., conclusions, theories of recovery, strategies, etc.).

(C) Previously made statements:

1. If a party "previously made a statement" concerning the action or subject matter, she must turn it over to a requesting party.
2. If the other party denies materials—The party seeking discovery may:

a. Move for a court order to obtain the other party's materials.

and b. Apply for expenses incurred in relation to the motion (under Rule 37(a)(5)).

E-Z Definition:
A "**previously made statement**" is:

(i) A written statement signed or adopted by the person making it

(ii) A recorded transcript or recording of an oral statement by the person making the "showing"

(Rule 26(b)(3)(C)(i) and (ii))

(4) Trial preparation; obtaining expert opinions:

(A) Expert who may testify:

1. Depositions of any person identified as an expert may be taken and may be used at trial.
2. If an Expert Disclosure Report is required (by Rule 26(a)(2)(B)), the deposition shall be conducted *after* the report is received.

(B) Experts employed only for trial preparation:

1. A party may not discover known facts, or opinions of another party's experts (via deposition or interrogatory) who are not expected to be used at trial

2. Exceptions:
   (i) As provided in Rule 35(b) (Mental and Physical Examinations: Examiner's Report)
   or (ii) If the requesting party shows *exceptional circumstances* that make it impractical to obtain the expert information himself (i.e., by hiring his own expert).

(C) Payment: The court shall require the party requesting the information to pay the following (unless *manifest injustice* will result):
   (i) A reasonable fee to the expert for her time spent in responding to Rule 26(b)(4)(A) or (B) discovery requests.
   and (ii) A reasonable portion of the expert's fee to the other party for the expert opinions obtained by him under Rule 26(b)(4)(B) only (not (A)).

(5) Claims of privilege or protection of trial-preparation materials.

(A) **Information withheld.** When a party claims privilege or a trial-preparation objection
   (i) the party has to make the claim *expressly*
   (ii) the party has to describe the nature of the documents (or communications or things) in a way that will enable other parties to assess whether or not privilege exists (without revealing the information itself).

(B) **Information produced.**
   1. Notice: If privileged information or protected work product is produced, the party producing it must send a notice to the opposing party.
   2. Return of documents:
      a. After being notified, a party:
         i. must promptly return, sequester, or destroy the specified information (and any copies)
         ii. may not use or disclose the information until the claim is resolved.
         iii. may promptly present the information to the court (under seal) for a ruling on the claim.
      b. If it's too late: If the receiving party disclosed the information before being notified, it must take reasonable steps to get it back.

c. Preservation of returned information: All information must be preserved (by a producing party) after return, until the court rules on the claim.

. . .

d. The receiving party may promptly present the information to the court (under seal) for a determination of the claim.

(c) Protective orders:

(1) In general.

i. Requirements for requesting a Protective Order:
   a. Motion for protection must be made
   b. Showing of Good Cause
   c. Certification of Good-Faith Effort or attempt to settle the matter without the court

ii. A court may make any order *which justice requires* to protect any party from:
   a. Annoyance
   or b. Embarrassment
   or c. Oppression
   or d. Undue burden or expense

iii. Controls which courts may use to protect parties include *one or more of the following*:
   (A) That disclosure or discovery is not to be had
   (B) Disclosure or discovery may be had only on *specified terms and conditions (i.e., time and place)*
   (C) Discovery may be had by a *certain method*
   (D) Discovery scope may be limited to *certain matters*, prohibiting inquiry into other matters
   (E) Designating in whose presence discovery is conducted
   (F) Sealing depositions and allowing them to be opened by court order only
   (G) Trade secrets or confidentiality is not to be revealed, or to be revealed in a specified manner
   (H) Parties file simultaneous specified documents and information in sealed envelopes to be opened with a court order

(2) Ordering discovery. If a motion for a protective order is denied (in whole or partially), the court may, *on just terms,* order that any party (or third party) provide or permit discovery.

(3) Awarding expenses. Rule 37(a)(5) applies.

(d) Sequence and timing of discovery[5]

(1) Timing: Unless the court allows, or the parties agree, a party may not seek discovery from any source until after a conference of the parties (pursuant to Rule 26(f)).

(2) Sequence:

- **Normal sequence**
  - (A) The methods of discovery may be used in any order
  - (B) Discovery by one party does not require another party to delay discovery
- **Changing the sequence:** A party may move for a change of sequence and timing based on:
  - i. Injustice
  - or ii. Inconvenience of parties
  - or iii. Inconvenience of witnesses

(e) Supplementing disclosures and responses

(1) In general: A party who responded to a discovery request is required to supplement it with new information if:

(A) The party learns that the disclosed information/interrogatories are *incomplete* or *incorrect*, and new information has not been made known to the other parties during discovery (or in subsequent writings)

or (B) as ordered by the court.

(2) Expert witness:

a. For a Rule 26(a)(2)(B) expert report, the party must supplement both:

i. The expert's report

and ii. Information given during the expert's deposition

b. The time limit for these additions or changes is the time Rule 26(a)(3) pretrial disclosures are due.

(f) Meeting of parties:

(1) Conference timing:

a. The parties shall confer at least 21 days before scheduling a Rule 16(b) conference or order

b. A court order may exempt the meeting

(2) Conference content; parties' responsibilities:

a. Parties shall consider:

1. The nature and basis of claim
2. Their defenses

[5] By amendment in 2000, Rule 26(d) and (f) limit the authority of Local Rules to allow discovery before a 26(f) conference, and to exempt a case from conference altogether. Also, the amendment requires only a "conference," and not necessarily a face-to-face meeting.

3. Possibilities for a prompt settlement
4. Discussing 26(a)(1) disclosures
5. Disclosure arrangements and the creation of a discovery plan
6. Issues relating to preserving discoverable information

b. All attorneys or parties (if *pro se*) are required to set up the conference and to make a *good faith* effort to reach an agreement.

c. A discovery plan must be submitted within 14 days after the conference.

d. A court may order that the parties/attorneys attend the conference in person.

(3) Discovery plan: Discovery plan shall include:

(A) What permitted changes should be made to 26(a) disclosures and when 26(a)(1) disclosures will be made

and (B) What subjects need discovery (and due dates and whether they should be done in phases)

and (C) any issues relating to disclosure or discovery of electronic information, including the form or forms in which it should be produced[6]

and (D) any issues relating to privilege or work product, including whether to ask the court to include any agreement the parties may have made on how to assert claims of privilege or work product after production[7]

and (E) any new limitations or changes in the limitations on discovery imposed by the FRCP or local rules

and (F) any other orders under Rule 26(c) (Protective Orders) or 16(b) or (c) (Scheduling Orders) that should be entered by the court

(4) Expedited schedule: If necessary, the court may (by local rule):

(A) *The Conference:* Decrease the 21-day limit for the conference so that the Rule 16(b) conference occurs closer to the 26(f) conference

or (B) *The Written Plan:*

1. Decrease the 14-day limit for the written plan

or 2. Excuse the written plan

or 3. Require an oral report on the discovery plan at the Rule 16(b) conference

---

[6] This subsection (C) was added by the December 2006 amendments.

[7] This subsection (D) was added by the December 2006 amendments.

(g) Signing of disclosures, discovery requests, responses, and objections

(1) Signature required; effect of signature:

i. Every 26(A)(1) or (3) disclosure must be signed by at least one attorney (or by the party if not represented) to be valid (recognized by the court).
ii. The signature should include the signer's name and address and e-mail address.
iii. The signature is a certification that to the *best of his knowledge, information, and belief* (formed after reasonable inquiry):
   (A) For disclosure: The disclosure is complete and correct (as of the time it was made).
   (B) For discovery requests: Every discovery request, response, or objection is:
      (i) Consistent with good faith and existing law (including these rules) or a *non-frivolous* argument to extend, modify, or reverse an existing law
      (ii) Has a proper purpose — it is not used for purposes such as harassment, delay, or to increase costs of litigation
      (iii) Is not unreasonable or unduly burdensome or expensive when considering:
         1. The needs of the case
         and 2. The discovery already obtained in the case
         and 3. The amount in controversy
         and 4. The importance of the issues at stake in the litigation

(2) Failure to sign:

a. An unsigned request, response, or objection will be stricken (unless it is signed promptly after the omission is brought to the party's attention)
b. A party need not respond to an unsigned request.

(3) Sanctions:

a. If rules are violated, appropriate sanctions (such as in Rule 11) will be imposed, either by:
   i. The court's own initiative
   or ii. Motion by the opposing side
b. Sanctions may include an order to pay the amount of the reasonable expenses incurred because of the violation, including *reasonable attorneys' fees.*

Rule 27. Depositions to Perpetuate Testimony

(a) Before an action is filed

(1) *Petition*—A person desiring to obtain testimony of any matter before a case is filed may file a petition showing:
   - (A) That the petitioner expects to be a party to a valid cause of action, but is unable to bring it as of yet
   - (B) The subject matter of the expected action and the petitioner's interest in the action
   - (C) The facts the petitioner hopes to establish with the proposed testimony
   - (D) The reasons for desiring to obtain testimony
   - (E) The names and descriptions of expected adverse parties (and their locations)
   - f. The names of the people to be examined (to testify)
   - g. The subject matter of the testimony expected to be elicited
   - h. A request for an order authorizing the petitioner to take depositions as testimony

(2) *Notice and service*
   - **a. Notice.**
     1. After the petition is filed, the petitioner shall serve upon any expected adverse parties the following:
        - A copy of the petition
        - A notice stating the time and place of the hearing
     2. The notice must be served at least 20 days before the hearing.
   - **b. Service.**
     1. Rule 4 Service applies.
     2. The notice may be served either inside or outside the district or state.
     3. If service cannot be made with *due diligence* on an expected adverse party, the court may order other service (e.g., service by publication)
     4. If a party were not served under Rule 4 and is not otherwise represented, the court *must* appoint an attorney to represent and to cross-examine the deponent on that person's behalf.
     5. Rule 17(c) ("Infants or Incompetent Persons") applies if any expected adverse party is a minor or is incompetent.

(3) <u>*Order and examination*</u>—If the court believes that delay of the testimony will cause an injustice, the court will:

a. Make an order designating or describing people who may testify

b. Specify the subject matter to be examined

c. Specify the method of testimony (Deposition or Interrogatories)

(4) <u>*Using the deposition*</u>—A deposition may be used as testimony if:

a. The action is related to the subject matter of the deposition

and b. It would be admissible evidence in the court of the state in which the deposition was taken.

(b) Pending appeal

(1) In general: If a case is pending appeal, but there is a chance it will return to the district court, a party may request "leave" to take depositions for use in the event of further proceedings in the district court.

(2) Motion: A <u>motion for leave to take deposition</u> must be filed, including:

(A) The names and addresses of people to be examined and the substance of testimony expected to be elicited

and (B) The reasons for requesting advance testimony

(3) Court order:

a. If the court finds that perpetuating the testimony may prevent a failure or delay of justice, the court may:

i. permit the depositions to be taken

and ii. may issue orders (e.g., those authorized by Rules 34 and 35).

b. The depositions may be taken and used like any other district court case deposition.

(c) Perpetuation by action—"This rule does not limit the power of a court to entertain an action to perpetuate testimony."

Rule 28. Persons Before Whom Depositions May Be Taken

(a) Within the United States

(1) In general: Depositions may be taken before *either:*

(A) An officer "authorized to administer oaths by U.S. law"

or (B) A person appointed by the court

(2) E-Z Definition:

"Officer": In Rules 30, 31, and 32, "Officer" includes a person:
a. appointed by the court under this Rule 28
or b. designated by the parties under Rule 29(a).

(b) In foreign countries

(1) In general: Depositions may be taken *either:*
(A) Under any applicable treaty or convention
or (B) Under a letter of request (no need to be "rogatory")
or (C) On notice with an oath administrator authorized by U.S. law or the foreign country's law
or (D) With a person commissioned by the court

(2) Issuing a letter of request or a commission. A letter of request, a commission, or both may be issued:
(A) on appropriate terms after an application and notice of it; and
(B) without a showing that taking the deposition in another manner is impracticable or inconvenient.

(3) Form of a request, notice, or commission.
a. The letter (if used according to a treaty or convention) must be captioned as set forth in the treaty or convention.
b. A letter of request may be addressed "To the Appropriate Authority in [name of country]."
c. A deposition notice or a commission must name (by name or title) before who the deposition is to be taken.

(4) Letter of request—admitting evidence.
a. The following <u>are not</u> reasons for excluding evidence obtained in response to a letter of request:
- it is not a verbatim transcript
- the testimony was not taken under oath
- any similar departure from the requirements for U.S. depositions.

(c) Disqualification: A deposition may not be taken by any interested party, which includes

1. A fiduciary, attorney, employee, or relative of a party or the attorney
or 2. Someone financially interested in the action

Rule 29. Stipulations About Discovery Procedure

Unless the court otherwise mandates, parties may agree *in writing* to:

(a) Provide for depositions, which may be taken before any person, at any time or any place and (b) Modify the FRCP's discovery procedures and limitations (except extending time limits that could affect the discovery cutoff, motions, or trial, which may only be extended with court approval)

Rule 30. Depositions by Oral Examination

(a) When leave required for depositions:

(1) Without leave: A party may normally take depositions of anyone *without* leave of court.

(2) With leave: Leave of court is only required if:

(A) If the parties cannot agree and:

(i) The proposed deposition will result in more than 10 depositions (under Rule 30 or 31) by a party.

or (ii) The Person to be examined has already been deposed.

or (iii) A party requests to take a deposition before a Rule 26(f) discovery meeting, *unless a witness is leaving the country and will not be available later.*

or (B) The person to be deposed is in prison

(b) Notice of examination

(1) **Notice in general:**

a. *Notice to take deposition:* The deposing party must give reasonable notice in writing to every other party in the action, stating:

1. The **time and place** the deposition is to be held
2. The **name and address** of each person to be examined (if known)
3. If name not known, a **general description** sufficient to identify the person or a particular class to which the deponent belongs (if the name and address are unknown)

(2) Producing documents (*Subpoena duces tecum*): If a subpoena duces tecum is to be served, notice must include the materials sought to be produced

(3) Method of recording

(A) Method stated in notice:

i. The notice shall state the method of deposition recording.

ii. Depositions may be recorded by sound, video, or stenograph.

iii. The party taking the deposition shall bear the cost of recording.
iv. Any party may request a transcript of a deposition *((b)(2) in pre-December 2007 rule).*

(4) By remote means:
a. Upon written agreement of the parties or court order, a party may use a telephone or other "remote electronic means" (e.g., fax) to take a deposition.
b. Depositions will be considered to have been taken where the deponent is located.

(5) Officer's duties
(A) Before the deposition
1. Depositions shall be conducted before a court-appointed officer (unless the parties agree otherwise)
2. A deposition must begin with:
(i) The officer's name and business address
and (ii) The date, time, and place of the deposition
and (iii) The name of the deponent
and (iv) The administration of deponent's oath
and (v) An identification of all persons present
(B) Conducting the deposition
1. If the deposition is not recorded stenographically, the officer shall repeat items (A)(i), (ii) and (iii) at the beginning of each new tape.
2. The appearance or demeanor of a deponent cannot be distorted via camera or recording techniques (e.g., disguising voice).
(C) After the deposition: At the end of the deposition, the officer shall:
1. Say that the deposition is complete
and 2. Explain who will take custody of the record
and 3. Discuss any pertinent matters

(5) Production of documents
Notice to a party deponent may be accompanied by a Rule 34 request for documents and tangible things (which are to be brought to the deposition).

(6) Depositions of organizations
a. A party may name a corporation, business or governmental agency as a deponent and reasonably describe the matters to be examined.
b. The organization must:
1. Designate one or more officers, directors, or managers to testify on its behalf
2. Describe what each deponent will testify about

c. A subpoena is used to notify a non-party organization
d. An organization's representative shall testify to *"all matters known or reasonably available to the organization."*

(c) Examination and cross examinations

(1) Examination and cross examination:
a. The Examiner of a witness may proceed as provided for in the FRE Rules 103 and 615 for trial
b. The officer should put the witness under oath and record the testimony.

(2) Objections:
a. All objections regarding the following shall be noted on the record (but the deposition proceeds):
i. To the officer's qualifications
ii. The manner of the recording
iii. The evidence presented
iv. Any other aspect of the examination proceeding
b. An objection must be stated:
i. concisely
and ii. in a nonargumentative and nonsuggestive manner
c. A person may instruct a deponent not to answer only in the following cases:
i. when necessary to preserve a privilege
ii. to enforce a court-ordered limitation
or iii. to present a Rule 30(d)(3) motion to terminate or limit the deposition.

(3) Participating through written questions
a. If written depositions are used, questions are delivered to the deposing officer and read to the deponent.
b. The answers are given to the officer, who records them.

(d) Duration; sanction; option to terminate or limit[8]

(1) Duration:
a. A deposition is limited to <u>1 day</u> of <u>7 hours</u>.
b. The court or parties (by stipulation) may change the time limit.
c. <u>Extra time</u> must be allowed if:
i. Extra time is needed for a *fair examination,* **or**
ii. The deponent (or some other person or circumstance) impedes or delays the examination

[8] In 2000, 30(d) was amended to limit depositions to 1 day of 7 hours, unless otherwise ordered or stipulated. 30(f), below, was amended to delete the provision allowing a deposition to be filed with the court.

(2) Sanction: The court may impose sanctions on deponents that impede or needlessly delay a deposition.

(3) Motion to terminate examination:

(A) Grounds: At any time during a deposition, a party or deponent may move to terminate the examination or change its scope.

Grounds for motion:

1. The deposition is being conducted in bad faith
2. The deposition is unreasonably embarrassing, annoying, or oppressive

(B) Order:

1. The court has discretion to make changes or terminate the deposition.
2. The deposition is then suspended until the court has time to review the motion.

(C) Award of expenses: Rule 37(a)(5) applies.

(e) Review by witness

(1) Review; statement of changes: If a party or deponent asks to *review* depositions before their completion, the deponent will have 30 days after receiving the transcript to:

(A) Review the transcript

and (B) List the changes in a statement with the reasons for each change, and sign the statement.

(f) Certification and delivery; exhibits; copies of the transcript or recording; filing

(1) Certification and delivery:

a. The officer must certify that the deposition was made under oath and was accurately transcribed

b. The certification must be:

i. In writing,

and ii. Sealed in an envelope

and iii. Marked with the case name and the deponent's name

and iv. Sent to an attorney who must protect it against loss, destruction, or tampering

(2) Documents and tangible things:

(A) Originals and copies

a. Any copies of documents and things produced shall be marked and attached to the deposition.

b. Copies of depositions shall be sent to any requesting parties; anyone may inspect the exhibits as well.

c. If the producing party wants to keep the originals, he may:
   (i) offer copies to be marked and attached and to be used as originals (provided all parties had a fair opportunity to compare the copies with the originals)
   or (ii) give all parties a fair opportunity to inspect and copy the originals after the exhibits are marked (and then the originals are deemed as if attached to the deposition)

(B) Order regarding the originals: Any party may make a motion asking that the originals be attached to the deposition until final disposition of the case.

(3) Copies of the transcript or recording

a. The officer shall retain stenographic notes or copies of the deposition recording.

b. Any party or deponent is entitled to a copy of the transcript, provided they pay *reasonable charges*.

(4) Notice of filing: The party taking the deposition shall give prompt notice of filing to all other parties.

(g) Failure to attend a deposition or serve a subpoena: Any party may recover reasonable expenses (including attorney's fees) for attending a deposition if:

- They expected the deposition to be taken

and • They attend (in person or by counsel)

and • The noticing party either:

   (1) Does not attend and proceed with the deposition.
   or (2) Fails to serve a subpoena on a non-party witness, who therefore does not attend.

Rule 31. Depositions by Written Questions

(a) Notice of serving questions

(1) Without leave: A party may normally use *written questions* for its deposition without leave of court

(2) With leave: Leave of court is only required if:

(A) The parties cannot agree and:
   (i) the proposed deposition will result in more than <u>10</u> depositions (under Rules 30 and 31) by a party.
   or (ii) the person to be examined has already been deposed.

or (iii) a party makes a request to take the deposition before the Rule 26(f) discovery meeting.

or (B) The person to be deposed is in prison.

(3) Service; required notice: If a party wants to use *written questions* for its deposition, he must serve them to *every* party, stating:

a. The name and address of the person to answer them (if known)

b. If the name is unknown, a description sufficient to describe the person or class of which he is a part.

c. The name and title of the officer taking the deposition.

(4) Questions directed to an organization: The following may be deposed by written questions under Rule 30(b)(6):

a. a public or private corporation

b. a partnership

c. an association

d. a governmental agency

(5) Questions from other parties:

a. Within 14 days of service of questions, a party may serve **cross-questions** to all other parties.

b. Within 7 days of being served cross-questions, a party may serve **redirect-questions** to all other parties.

c. Within 7 days of redirect-questions, a party may serve **re-cross-questions** upon all other parties.

d. Courts may change the above times for cause shown.

(b) Delivery to the officer; officer's duties: All questions and notices shall be copied and given to the recording officer, who then:

(1) asks the questions and takes the deponent's testimony

and (2) prepares and certifies the deposition

and (3) sends the deposition to the party, attaching a copy of the questions and the notice

(c) Notice of Completion or filing.

(1) ***Completion.*** The party who noticed the deposition must notify all other parties when it is completed (so that they may make use of the deposition).

(2) ***Filing.*** The party filing must promptly give notice of the filing to all other parties.

Rule 32. Using Depositions in Court Proceedings

(a) Use of depositions

(1) In general: Depositions (if admissible under the FRE) may be used in court against a party provided:

(A) The party was present at time of the deposition or had reasonable notice of the deposition and (B) The portions being used would be admissible (under the FRE) if the deponent was actually testifying

and (C) Rule 32(a)(2) through (8) allow use of the deposition

(2) Impeachment and other uses: The deposition may be used by any party to:

a. contradict or impeach the testimony of a deponent as a witness

or b. for other purposes allowed by the FRE.

(3) Deposition of party, agent, or designee: An adverse party may use a deposition for any purpose provided that the person deposed was the party's officer, director, managing agent, or Rule 30(b)(6) or 31(a)(4) designee.

(4) Unavailable witness: As personal testimony of a non-party to be used by any party for any purpose, if the court finds that:

(A) The witness is dead

or (B) The witness is too far (more than 100 miles from the place of trial, or outside of the U.S.), unless it appears that the witness' absence was procured by a party

or (C) The witness is sick or imprisoned

or (D) A party offering the deposition is unable to procure attendance of the witness by subpoena

or (E) It is "in the interest of justice" *(upon motion with notice)*

(5) Limitations on use:

(A) Deposition taken on short notice: Depositions cannot be used if:

1. The party it's being used against had less than 11 days' notice of the deposition

and 2. The party promptly moved for a Rule 26(c)(1)(B) protective order (not to be deposed or to change the time or place)

and 3. The motion was still pending when the deposition was taken

(B) Unavailable deponent; party could not obtain an attorney: Depositions taken without leave of court (under Rule 30(a)(2)(A)(iii) cannot be used if:

a. The party it's being used against shows that after getting notice of the deposition it could not get an attorney

and b. The party used *diligent* efforts to get an attorney.

(6) Using part of a deposition: If only part of the deposition is used as evidence, an adverse party may require the remainder to be shown for fairness.

(7) Substituting a party: Substituting a party (under Rule 25) has no effect on the right to use a deposition previously taken.

(8) Deposition taken in earlier action: May be used, whether taken in a state or federal case, provided:

a. All of the following are true:
- the deposition was lawfully taken
- and the deposition was filed in the prior case (if required)
- The later case involves the same subject matter
- The later case is between the same parties (or their representatives or successors)

or b. The FRE allow it

(b) Objections to admissibility:

1. Objections may be made at any time during a trial or hearing as if objecting to the live testimony of the witness.
2. This rule is subject to Rules 28(b) and 32(d)(3).

(c) Forms of presentation

1. Depositions may be given in transcript or non-transcript form, unless the court orders otherwise.
2. In a jury trial, if any party requests, any deposition offered (other than for impeachment) <u>must</u> be in transcript form if available (the court may order otherwise for *good cause* shown).

(d) Effect of errors in depositions

(1) <u>Notice</u>: All errors shall be deemed waived unless written objection is served promptly after the party gave notice.

(2) <u>The officer's qualification</u>: Disqualification of an Officer—waived unless:

(A) An objection is made before the deposition

(B) An objection is made promptly after learning of the officer's disqualification

(3) <u>Taking of the deposition</u>:

(A) *Objection to Competence, Relevance, or Materiality*—not waived unless the objection would have definitely caused the deposition to be removed.

(B) *Objection to an Error or Irregularity*—waived if:

(i) it relates to:
- how the deposition was taken
- or the form of a question or answer
- or the oath/affirmation
- or a party's conduct
- or other matters that might have been corrected at that time.

(ii) not made promptly <u>at</u> the deposition.

(C) *Objection to a Written Question*—waived unless objected to within 5 days after the date that the last authorized questions were served.

(4) Completion/return of deposition, *transcribed, certified, filed*—waived unless a motion to suppress is made within a *reasonable time* (from when *due diligence* would have discovered it).

Rule 33. Interrogatories to Parties

(a) In general

(1) Number

a. A party may not serve more than 25 separate interrogatories

b. Leave of court is needed if a party wants to serve more than 25 interrogatories

(2) Scope

a. An interrogatory may relate to anything that falls under Rule 26(b).

b. An interrogatory may ask for an opinion (that relates to fact) or the application of law to fact

c. A court may order that a party may wait until certain discovery is complete, or until a pretrial conference or until some other time before answering an interrogatory.

(b) Answers and objections

(1) Responding party: The interrogatory should be answered by:

(A) The party to whom directed

(B) An officer or agent (if the party is a company or agency)

(2) Time to respond:

a. Within 30 Days after they were served.

b. The court may change this time limitation, or parties may agree to new limits (under Rule 29).

(3) Answering each interrogatory:

a. Each question, unless it is objected to, must be answered:

1. Separately
2. Fully
3. In Writing
4. Under Oath

(4) Objections:

a. If questions are objected to, the objecting party shall state all objections and answer those questions that are not objectionable.

b. Grounds for objections must be stated with specificity.

c. Any objection not *timely* stated is waived unless *good cause* is shown.

(5) **Signature:**

a. Answers must be signed by the person writing them

b. Objections—must be signed by the attorney making them

(c) Use at trial: An interrogatory response may be used to the extent allowed by the FRE.

(d) Option to produce business records: The answering party may offer (instead of a written answer) a business record which is responsive, provided:

- **Responsiveness of record.** The answer may indeed be derived from the business record or an audit of the business record(s)

and • **Burden of research.** The burden of getting the answer is *substantially* the same for the party serving the interrogatory as for the answering party.

- The responding party does both of the following:
  (1) Identifying the record with specificity: Specifies the relevant record in *sufficient detail* to permit the asking party to find and identify it (as quickly as the answering party would have found it).
  and **(2) Opportunity to inspect:** Gives the asking party a *reasonable opportunity* to see the records and copy or summarize them.

B. PRODUCTION OF DOCUMENTS

OVERVIEW

- This discovery device includes electronic information as well as documents and other things.
- Requests should be specific and the responses or objections should correspond to the requests.
- Documents need not be in the possession of a party. They may be only in CONTROL or CUSTODY
- Procedure for Production of International Entities:
  - The U.S. party must draft a Letter Rogatory
  - The letter must be sent to the Central Authority of the Foreign Country
  - The Letter must be forwarded to a "Domestic" court in the Foreign Jurisdiction
  - The Foreign court must send an Order of Discovery to the International party
  - **Problem:** Many countries have many more discovery limits, and can deny Americans access to information.

Relevant Rule: 34

Rule 34. Producing Documents and Tangible Things, or Entering onto Land, for Inspection and Other Purposes

(a) In general:

(1) **Produce documents (and electronic information) for inspection:**

1. A party may request another party to:
   (A) Produce any document or electronic information in its *possession, custody, or control.*
   (B) Permit the requesting party to inspect, test, or sample any tangible thing in its *possession, custody, or control.*
2. The data or item produced must be translated into usable form by the responding party.
3. This rule only applies to things that fall within the scope of Rule 26(b).

E-Z Definition:
"Documents" and "Electronically-stored Information" include:

- writings
- drawings
- graphs

- charts
- photographs
- sound recordings
- images
- other data or data compilations stored in *any medium*

(Rule 34(a)(1)(A))

(2) **Entry upon land.**

1. A party may also request entry onto land or other property in the *possession or control* of the responding party for the following purposes:
    - inspection and measuring
    - surveying
    - photographing
    - testing and sampling
2. This rule applies to the property or any item on the property.
3. This rule applies only to things that fall within the scope of Rule 26(b).

(b) Procedure

(1) Contents of the request: The request must:

(A) State each item or category of items (must be stated separately) to be inspected with *"reasonable particularity"*

(B) Describe the manner in which the inspection will be done and set a reasonable time and place for inspection

(C) State the form in which electronic information is to be produced

(2) Responses and objections:

(A) Time to respond: Within 30 Days (subject to change by the court or agreement of the parties—see Rule 29 ("Stipulations")) of the request.

(B) Responding to each item: The responding party must state which items are permitted and which are objected to (and reasons for any objections).

(C) Objections: If a party has a partial objection to a category of things being demanded, the responding party should allow inspection of the unobjectionable portion.

(D) Responding to a request for production of electronic information: The responding party should set forth the proposed manner of production, whether:

a. The manner demanded for the production of electronic information is objected to;

or b. The demanding party did not specify what form she wants the information (in the objection, the responding party must specify a preferred form)

(E) Producing the documents or electronic information:

(i) Documents must be produced:

- as they are kept in the usual course of business or
- organized and labeled to correspond with the categories in the request.

(ii) Form For Producing Electronic Information—Absent a specific method demanded, information must be produced:

- as it is *ordinarily maintained*

or
- in a form that is *reasonably usable*

(iii) Electronic Information needs only to be produced in one form.

(c) Non-parties—may be compelled to produce documents under Rule 45.

C. PHYSICAL/MENTAL EXAMINATIONS

OVERVIEW

- Examinations may be required only of PARTIES.
- Prerequisites for exam:
  - Must show <u>Good Cause</u> for requiring an exam
  - The exam must correlate to a fact *in controversy*
- An attorney may accompany clients to examinations as long as they do not interfere with the exam.
- The only basis for the exclusion of an attorney is a "*compelling showing of need.*"

Relevant Rule: 35

Rule 35. Physical/Mental Examinations

(a) Order of examination

(1) In general: The requesting party must:
 a. Make a motion for a court order
 b. Show that the physical condition (including blood group) is <u>*in controversy*</u>
 c. Have the examination done by a suitably licensed or certified examiner

(2) Motion and notice; contents of the order
 (A) Must give notice to all parties and show *good cause* for the physical or mental examination
 (B) Must specify the:
  a. Examiner
  b. Time and place of examination
  c. Manner and conditions of examination
  d. Scope of examination

(b) Examiner's report

(1) Request by the party or person examined: A party may request a report of the examination and the party must deliver a copy together with all prior findings

(2) Contents: The examiner's report must:
 a. be in writing
 b. set out the examiner's findings, including:
  - diagnoses
  - conclusion
  - and the results of any tests

(3) **Request by the moving party:**
   a. The moving party may request and receive similar reports of all other (earlier or later) examinations of the same condition.
   b. If the party (who controls the person examined) shows that it could not obtain the reports, they do not have to be produced.

(4) **Waiver of privilege:** By requesting a report or taking an examiner's testimony, the examined party waives the privilege to get another examiner to testify for her.

(5) **Failure to deliver a report:** The court may order that a party deliver the examination report (and if it's not provided, the court can exclude the testimony).

(6) **Scope:**
   a. This provisions agrees to examinations held by the parties' agreement.
   b. This section does not preclude conducting an examination under other rules.

D. ADMISSIONS

OVERVIEW

- Admissions are obtained to *eliminate* disputed facts in trial, while interrogatories and depositions only constitute *evidence* from which to argue facts.
- A party who obtains an Admission does not waive his right to rely on that information if the adverse party attempts to present evidence "overlapping" or "exceeding" the admission (e.g., that damages are greater than admitted).

Relevant Rule: 36

Rule 36. Requests for Admission

(a) Scope and procedure

(1) Scope: A party may serve upon another party a written request for an admission (within the scope of Rule 26(b)(1) and for the pending action only) regarding:
   (A) statements of opinion or fact, the applicability of law to fact, and the truth of opinions
   (B) the genuineness of any documents described

(2) Form; copy of a document
   a. Each matter must be separately stated.
   b. A request to admit the genuineness of a document must have a copy of the document attached (unless made available before).

(3) Time to respond; effect of not responding: If no answer or objection is received within 30 Days (can be changed by agreement of the parties or by the court) of the request for admission, a party is considered to admit the allegation.

(4) Answer:
   a. Admissions and denials must be specific to the related questions.
   b. A party may not give "lack of knowledge and information" as a reason for not answering a request, unless:
      i. The party has made a reasonable inquiry
      and ii. There is not enough information to enable the party to admit or deny.

(5) Objections: If an objection is made, the reasons shall be stated in detail.

(6) Motion regarding the sufficiency of an answer or objection:

a. The requesting party may make a motion regarding the sufficiency of an answer/objection.

b. If the court does not like an objection, it can order that an answer be made (and if it is not made, the court presumes an admission).

c. The court may wait until a pretrial conference (or some other time before trial) before making a final decision.

d. Award of Expenses: Rule 37(a)(5) applies.

(b) Effect of admission; withdrawing or amending it

1. Any admissions are *conclusively established*, unless the court grants a motion to withdraw or amend the admission.
2. Admissions are made only in regard to the pending action (i.e., cannot be used in other cases).
3. Amendments or withdrawals may be permitted on a showing that the "*presentation of the merits of the action*" would be promoted and if the opposing party cannot show that he will be prejudiced.

E. SANCTIONS

OVERVIEW

- Rule 37 Sanctions should be imposed when the adverse party or the court can show that a delay/refusal of discovery was due to *either*:
  - Willfulness
  - or • Bad Faith
  - or • Any fault of party/deponent
- Inability to answer is <u>not</u> grounds for Rule 37 sanctions.
- <u>Sanctions include</u>:
  - Dismissal
  - Default Judgment
  - Admission
  - Monetary penalties
- Dismissals and default judgments are very <u>rare</u>; most Courts refuse to grant them because a party will often suffer for his attorney's inadequacy.

Relevant Rule: 37

Rule 37. Failure to Make Disclosure or Cooperate in Discovery; Sanctions

(a) Motion for order compelling disclosure or discovery

(1) In general: A party may move for an order compelling disclosure or discovery, provided:

a. The motion is made notice to other parties and all affected persons.

b. The motion must include a certification that the moving party conferred in a good faith attempt to get the discovery without court action.

(2) Appropriate court:

a. *Where action pending*—motion required where deponent is a party

b. *Where deposition is pending*—motion required if deponent is not a party

(3) Specific motions:

(A) <u>To compel disclosure</u>: If a party fails to disclose (under 26(a)), a party may make a <u>motion to compel disclosure</u>.

(B) <u>To compel a discovery response</u>:

1. If a deponent refuses to answer, a party may make a motion for an <u>order compelling an answer</u>.

2. This includes:
   (i) Failure of a deponent to answer a question
   (ii) Failure of a corporation to make a 30(b)(6) or 31(a)(4) designation
   (iii) Failure of a party to answer an interrogatory
   (iv) Failure of a party to permit inspection

(C) Related to a deposition: If a deponent refuses to answer, a party may make a motion for an order compelling an answer.

(4) Evasive or incomplete disclosure, answer or response: An evasive answer is considered failure to answer for these purposes.

(5) Payment of expenses; protective orders:

(A) If the motion is **granted**, or disclosure is made after the motion is filed:
1. The party/deponent must pay reasonable fees spent to make the motion.
2. The court does not award fees and expenses if:
   (i) the moving party did not attempt to resolve the issue prior to court intervention
   or (ii) The nondisclosure was *substantially justified*
   or (iii) Other circumstances make such an award *unjust*

(B) If the motion is **denied**, and the motion is not *substantially justified*, the party making the motion must pay reasonable fees spent to oppose the motion.

(C) If the motion is denied in part and granted in part:
1. expenses may be reasonably apportioned
2. the court may grant a protective order (under Rule 26(c)).

Note: All sanctions and awards under (A) through (C) above must give an opportunity to be heard.

(b) Failure to comply with a court order

(1) Sanctions in district where deposition is taken—Failure to be sworn or provide an answer is considered contempt in that court.

(2) Sanctions in district where action is pending

(A) *For not obeying a discovery order,* the court may:
   (i) Conclude that matters sought to be discovered by a party are to be found in that party's favor

(ii) Refuse to allow the disobedient party to support or oppose designated claims or defenses
(iii) Strike a pleading
(iv) Stay proceedings until the order is obeyed
(v) Dismiss the action (in whole or in part)
(vi) Strike a pleading
(vii) Hold the disobedient person in contempt of court (unless it is in regards to a Rule 35 examination)

(B) *For not producing a person for examination,* the court may apply (b)(2)(i)-(vi), above, *unless* the party shows that it cannot produce the person for examination

(C) *Payment of expenses*—The court may require the opposing party to pay reasonable attorney's fees resulting from his disobedience, *unless* the court finds the disobedience *substantially justified* or an award would otherwise be *unjust.*

(c) Failure to disclose, to amend an earlier response, or to admit[9]

(1) Failure to disclose or amend (i.e., information required under Rule 26(a)):

a. The non-disclosing party is not allowed to use the undisclosed information as evidence at trial or at a hearing.

b. Sanctions may be imposed if:

i. There is no *substantial justification* not to disclose the information

and ii. The failure to disclose was harmful

c. This applies to a failure to disclose, and also to a failure to amend a prior response (pursuant to Rule 26(e)).

d. The court may also impose other sanctions, including:

(A) Payment of reasonable expenses and/or attorneys' fees caused by the failure
(B) Informing the jury of the failure to disclose
(C) Any action authorized under Rule 37(b)(2)(A)(i)-(vi).

(2) Failure to admit (i.e., under Rule 36): If a party refuses to admit to the authenticity of a document and another party proves its authenticity, the court *must* impose fees spent to prove the document's validity, *unless:*

(A) The request was objectionable under Rule 36(a)
or (B) The admission sought was of no substantial importance

---

[9] In 2000, 37(c) was amended to include failure to disclose and failure to amend a prior response (as required by Rule 26(e)(2)) as sanctionable.

or (C) The party failing to admit had reasonable grounds to believe that he would prevail on that matter

or (D) Other good reason is shown

(d) Party's failure to attend its own deposition, serve answers to interrogatories, or respond to a request for inspection—subjects a party to Rule 37(b) sanctions.

(1) In General

(A) *Motion; grounds for sanctions.* The court may, on motion, order sanctions if:

(i) a party (or a person designated under Rule 30(b)(6) or 31(a)(4)) fails to appear for that person's deposition, after being served with proper notice

or (ii) a party, after being properly served with interrogatories (Rule 33) or a request for inspection (Rule 34), fails to serve its answers, objections, or written response.

(B) *Certification.* The moving party must certify that good faith attempts to resolve the discovery issues were attempted before court intervention.

(2) Unacceptable excuse for failing to act. A Rule 37(d)(1)(A) failure is not excused because the request was objectionable, *unless* the party failing to act has a Rule 26(c) motion for a protective order pending.

(3) Types of sanctions.

a. Sanctions may include anything listed in Rule 37(b)(2)(A)(i)-(vi).

b. Instead of or in addition to these sanctions, the court *must* require the party or attorney (or both) to pay the reasonable expenses (including attorneys' fees) caused by the failure, *unless*:

i. the failure was *substantially justified*

or ii. other circumstances make an award of expenses *unjust*.

(e) Subpoena of a person in a foreign country—abrogated

(e) Lost electronic information—A court may not (unless there are *"exceptional circumstances")* impose Rule 37 sanctions on a party for not providing electronic information which was lost as a result of the "routine, good-faith operation" of the electronic information system.

(f) Failure to participate in framing a discovery plan—If a *good faith* effort is not made to agree on a 26(f) discovery plan, reasonable attorney's fees to bring the plan to court will be imposed (after an opportunity to be heard).

X. SUMMARY JUDGMENT

OVERVIEW

- Summary Judgment may be requested by either party to prevent a case from going to trial.
- Summary Judgment may be granted only if there is no question of fact to be determined.
- If Summary Judgment is requested, the judge will adjudicate the case based on the applicable law and the facts as stated in the pleadings.
- **Burden of proof:**
  - The party moving for a Summary Judgment bears the burden of proving that there is no evidence to support the non-moving party's case.
  - The non-moving party has the burden of showing that there remains a *genuine issue of material fact* that would have to be decided by a fact finder at trial.
  - Summary judgment is appropriate if only a question of law remains to be decided (i.e., the judge will make a decision as a *matter of law* since there is no need to find facts at trial).
- **Evidence:**
  - Significant probative evidence: Whenever a "fair-minded" jury could return a verdict for the non-moving party, the case should go to trial.
  - Evidence will be viewed in a light most favorable to the non-moving party.
  - The non-moving party may not rely on allegations in the pleadings to defend against summary judgment (i.e., it needs "specific facts"—and not "allegations" to defend the motion).
- **Discovery:**
  - The court is obligated to give the non-moving party an adequate opportunity for discovery (to obtain such specific facts as required to oppose the Motion for Summary Judgment).
  - A Rule 56(f) Affidavit to extend the time for discovery must specify what the party expects to obtain from discovery, and why such information hasn't yet been obtained.

Relevant Rule: 56

Rule 56. Summary Judgment

(a) By a claiming party: A party may move for summary judgment (with or without supporting affidavits) *after* either:

1. 20 days from commencement of the action

or 2. Service of a motion for summary judgment ("SJ") by the adverse party

(b) By a defending party: May move for summary judgment at *any time* (with or without supporting affidavits).

(c) Serving the motion; proceedings

1. A Motion for SJ must be served to the adverse party at least 10 days before the scheduled hearings.
2. The adverse party may serve opposing affidavits *at any time* before the hearing.
3. Summary judgment must be based upon:
    a. Pleadings
    b. Depositions
    c. Interrogatories
    d. Admissions
    e. Affidavits
4. Summary judgment shall be rendered if, based on the above:
    a. There is no *genuine issue of any material fact* shown (discretionary)
    and b. The moving party is entitled to judgment *as a matter of law.*

(d) Case not fully adjudicated on the motion

(1) Establishing facts
    a. If only part of the case is adjudicated, the court shall determine which facts remain at issue for trial.
    b. The Judge shall file an order establishing the "adjudicated facts" and how they affect the amount in controversy.

(2) Establishing liability

Summary judgment may be granted on **liability** alone, even if there is a genuine issue on the **amount of damages.**

(e) Affidavits; further testimony:

(1) In general
    a. Must include personal knowledge of facts (admissible under the Federal Rules of Evidence)
    b. Shall show that the affiant is competent to testify
    c. The court may permit the affidavit to be supplemented by depositions, interrogatories, or other affidavits.

(2) Opposing party's obligation to response:
    a. The adverse party must set forth *specific facts* showing that there is a genuine issue for trial (cannot rely on pleadings).
    b. If the adverse party cannot show that there is a genuine issue, SJ shall be entered against her *if appropriate* (given an opportunity for discovery).

(f) When affidavits are unavailable If a party opposing a motion for SJ can show in its affidavit that it cannot obtain affidavits containing facts *essential* to justify its opposition to SJ, then the court may:

(1) Deny the motion
or (2) Order a continuance to permit affidavits to be obtained (or other depositions or discovery to be had)
or (3) Make any just order

(g) Affidavits submitted in bad faith (to delay the proceeding)

1. A party making an improper affidavit shall pay the other party's reasonable expenses (including attorney fees) associated with the motion for SJ.
2. The offending party or attorney may be guilty of contempt.

XI. THIRD-PARTY CLAIMS

A. IMPLEADER AND JOINDER

OVERVIEW

- Process for determining necessity of joinder
  - Courts look to see if a party can be joined under Rule 19(a)
  - If no Personal Jurisdiction can be established over the third party, the court must determine whether
    - To proceed with the case anyway (without joining the third party)

    or
    - To dismiss case (if the third party is indispensable to the case)
- *The rule is not to be applied in a rigid manner, but should, instead, be governed by the particularities of the individual case.*
- A party in a Joint & Several liability action is merely a "*Permissive Party*" not a Compulsory one.
- Claim preclusion:
  - All claims related to the action must be joined (or else are forfeited)
  - Unrelated claims may be brought, but they are not precluded from future litigation.

Relevant Rules: 13, 14, 18, 19, 20, 21, 42

Rule 13. Counterclaims/Cross-claims

(a) Compulsory Counterclaims

(1) A "*Compulsory Counterclaim*" must be raised and:
  (A) Includes any claim "arising out of" the initial action *(i.e., they must arise out of the "same transaction or occurrence")*
  (B) Does not include adding third parties not subject to the court's jurisdiction

(2) Exceptions: The Counterclaim must be stated in the pleading *unless:*
  (A) The claim is already subject to another pending action
  (B) The Defendant brings the suit by attachment or process without the Court's jurisdiction.

(b) Permissive Counterclaim is any claim against an opposing party (not a new party) whether or not related to the case.

(c) Relief sought in Counterclaim—Counterclaims may seek more relief or different relief than the original claims that the opposing party had sought.

(d) Counterclaims against the U.S.—These rules do not enlarge the present limits (fixed by statute) of asserting Counterclaims against the U.S. government.

(e) Post-pleading Counterclaims—may be presented as a counterclaim in a "supplemental pleading," if the Court allows.

(f) Omitted Counterclaim—a pleader may obtain leave of court to Counterclaim by amending the pleading, only if it is omitted by

1. Oversight
or 2. Inadvertence
or 3. Excusable neglect
or 4. *When justice so requires.*

(g) Cross-claims against a co-party—are usually considered permissive.

1. Guarantors Same Transaction: May allow Cross-claim against a co-party for a claim either:
    a. *Arising out of the same transaction or occurrence* of *either*:
        1. The original action
        or 2. A Counterclaim
    or b. Relating to any property subject to the original action
2. Indemnity: Cross-claims may include a claim to a co-party to indemnify the claimant for all or part of the liability arising out of the action.

(h) Joinder of additional parties—parties may be joined in Counterclaims and Cross-claims (pursuant to Rules 19 and 20).

(i) Separate trials; separate judgments—Judgment on a Cross-claim or Counterclaim may be made in accordance with Rule 54(b) (even if the claims of the opposing party have been dismissed or otherwise disposed of) if:

1. A Court orders separate trials pursuant to Rule 42(b)
and 2. The Court has jurisdiction to do so.

Rule 14. Third-Party Practice

(a) When Defendant may bring a third party

(1) Making third-party claims:
- At any time after the commencement of a case, the Defendant may become a "third-party π" by serving a Complaint

on a third party (who is not in the original action). This happens when the Defendant feels that the third party is liable to *indemnify* the Defendant for any judgment (e.g., insurance company or surety).

- If the Defendant serves the third party no later than 10 days after serving its original Answer, no "leave of court" is needed to serve the third party. After 10 days, the Defendant must get "leave of court" by filing a motion with notice to all parties.
- The third party is then known as a "Third-Party Defendant" and the Defendant is known as a "Third-Party Plaintiff."

(2) The third-party defendant must
  (A) assert all defenses
  (B) assert all compulsory (Rule 13(a)) counterclaims against the defendant or cross-claims (Rule 13(g)) against any other defendant
  The third-party defendant may:
  (B) *(cont'd)* assert all permissive (Rule 13(b)) counterclaims against the defendant
  (C) assert defenses against the plaintiff's claim
  (D) assert counterclaims against the plaintiff if they arise out of the same transaction as the plaintiff's claims against the defendant

(3) π may claim against the third-party defendant if the claim arises out of the same transaction as the claim against the defendant

(4) Any party may move to:
  a. Strike third-party claim
  or b. Sever the claim
  or c. Separate trial

(5) A third party may bring in a fourth party who may also be liable to the Defendant or the third party (Note: Complete diversity is not needed for third party.)

(6) Admiralty and maritime claims
  a. If the third-party complaint is within admiralty jurisdiction, may be *in rem* against:
    - a vessel
    - cargo
    - or other property subject to admiralty cases *in rem*
  b. Terminology: In these cases:
    - The word "Summons" (in the Rules) applies to the Warrant of Arrest
    - The words "Plaintiff/Defendant" (in the Rules) applies to any person asserting a claim (See Admiralty Rule C(6)(a)(1)).

(b) When π may bring a third party: When a claim is made against the π (like, for example, a counterclaim), the π may bring in a third party just as the Defendant (under Rule 14(a)).

(c) Admiralty and maritime claims

(1) When a plaintiff brings an admiralty or maritime claim (within the meaning of Rule 9(h)), a defendant (or claimant) may bring in a Third-Party defendant for contribution or indemnity, or otherwise on account of the same transaction or occurrence.

(2) If the defendant demands judgment in the plaintiff's favor against the third-party defendant, the third-party defendant must defend under Rule 12 against both the plaintiff's claim and the defendant's third-party claim, and the case goes forward as if the plaintiff had sued both the third-party defendant and the third-party plaintiff.

Rule 19. Required Joinder of Parties

(a) Persons to be joined (if feasible)

(1) Required party

1. Requirements:
   - a. Joined parties must be subject to Personal Jurisdiction
   - and b. Joinder cannot destroy SMJ (diversity)
2. A third party MUST be joined if:
   - (A) *Complete relief* cannot be accorded among the present parties without joining the third party
   - or (B) The third party claims a *related interest* in the action, and its absence from the suit may:
     - (i) Impair or Impede its ability to protect that interest.
     - or (ii) Leave any of the present parties subject to double liability or inconsistent verdicts

(2) Joinder by court order

- a. The court *must* order a required party to be joined.
- b. If a third party refuses to be a π, he may, upon the Court's discretion, be made:
  - i. A Defendant
  - or ii. An *Involuntary* π

(3) Venue: If a third party objects to venue, and his presence makes venue improper, the joinder will be dismissed (and the entire case itself will also be dismissed if third party is considered an "*indispensable party*").

(b) When joinder is not feasible

1. The court may determine that a third party is needed and dismiss the case if he cannot be joined.
2. A party is needed if, in "*in equity and good conscience*," the case should not proceed without him.
3. **Factors considered:** (to determine if a third party is needed in the case):
   (1) The Extent of prejudice to the existing parties that the third party's absence may bring
   (2) The Extent that prejudices may be avoided or reduced by other means, like:
      (A) protective provisions in the judgment
      (B) shaping the relief
      or (C) other measures
   (3) The Adequacy of judgment without the third party
   (4) Whether the π will have an adequate remedy if the case were dismissed for nonjoinder.

(c) Pleading the reasons for nonjoinder. A party must state (in his claim):

(1) the name of any person who must be joined if feasible but is not joined (if the name is known)
and (2) the reasons for not joining that person.

(d) Exception for class actions. This rule is subject to Rule 23 (Class Actions).

Rule 20. Permissive Joinder of Parties

(a) Persons who may join or be joined

(1) Plaintiffs—Plaintiffs may sue together in the same case:
   i. They may sue jointly, severally, or in the alternative
   ii. They must assert a claim which *both*:
      (A) Arises out of the same transaction or occurrence (or series of transactions or occurrences)
      and (B) Has a question of law or fact common to all co-parties in the action
(2) Defendants—Defendants may be sued together in the same case:
   i. This includes property subject to a case in rem
   ii. They must be subject to a claim which *both*:
      (A) Arises out of the same transaction or occurrence (or series of transactions or occurrences)
      and (B) Has a question of law or fact common to all co-parties in the action

(3) Extent of relief: There is no need for all plaintiffs or defendants to seek all claims of relief being claimed in the action; judgment will be made according to each party's rights or liabilities.

(b) Protective measures—The court may order separate trials or make *other such orders* to prevent:

1. A party from being embarrassed

or 2. Delay

or 3. Prejudice

or 4. A party from incurring undue expense from the inclusion of a third party, if no claims exist between the parties.

Rule 21. Misjoinder and Nonjoinder of Parties

1. Misjoinder is NOT a ground for dismissal of a case.
2. Parties may be dropped or added at any stage of the action by:

   a. Motion

   or b. Courts initiative

3. Any claim against a party may be severed and proceeded with separately (see Rule 42).

Rule 18. Joinder of Claims

(a) Joinder of claims—A party may join *as many* independent or alternate claims as it has against an **opposing** party. These include:

1. Original claims
2. Counterclaims
3. Cross-claims
4. Third-party claims

(b) Joinder of remedies—Whenever a claim is dependent on the outcome of a claim in another action, the two cases may be joined into a single action.

Rule 42. Consolidation; Separate Trials

(a) Consolidation of cases—If cases involve a common question of law or fact, a court may:

(1) Order a joint hearing or trial of any issue in the action

or (2) Order a complete consolidation of the cases

or (3) May make orders to avoid costs or delay

(b) Separate trials — A court may split any claims for any of the following reasons:

1. For convenience
2. To avoid prejudice
3. To expedite and economize

B. INTERVENTION

OVERVIEW

- When a party wants to join a case, he should make a Rule 24 **Motion for Intervention**.
- A party seeking to intervene must prove that he has a "*significantly protectable interest*" in the action in order to have a RIGHT to intervene (otherwise intervention is in the court's discretion).
- Requirements for establishing a "*significantly protectable interest*":
  - The person demonstrates a legal interest in the action to intervene as of *right*
  - The right requires a direct, substantial legally protectable interest in the proceedings.
  - The person need not show that he has a legal or equitable interest in jeopardy, but must show he had a "protectable interest" in the litigation's outcome.
  - There must be a direct effect on a *legally cognizable* interest (as opposed to contingent or remote).
  - It requires consideration of all the competing and relevant interests raised by an Application for Intervention.
  - The person's rights and duties are affected by the legislature's disposition.
  - The court may consider any significant *legal effect* of an applicant's interests. A court is not limited to consequences of a strictly legal nature.
- Amicus Curiae Briefs — are briefs of non-parties in a pending suit
  - Often non-parties with an indirect interest in the suit (i.e., they'll be affected by the precedent of the case at bar) write Amicus Curiae briefs to the court (instead of participating in action) (e.g., Bank X may write an Amicus Curiae brief in a suit between Bank A and B involving a ruling on the effects of the FDIC on banks in a suit)
  - Courts often look for outside opinions (e.g., lobby groups, federal agencies, etc.)
  - Request to file Amicus Curiae Briefs must be granted before the brief can be filed
- Sometimes non-parties want to become parties instead because they have a much greater interest in the outcome of the suit (i.e., the suit or legal outcome will directly affect them).

Relevant Rule: 24

Rule 24. Intervention

(a) Intervention of right

i. Anyone may intervene (upon timely motion) in a case when:
   (1) A federal statute allows (unconditionally)
or (2) The Applicant claims a *direct* interest in a *related property or transaction* subject to adjudication, but only if:
   a. The moving party's interest isn't already properly represented in the case.
   or b. The moving party has a direct "*significantly protectable*" interest at stake and not intervening will impair/impede the applicant's ability to protect that interest.

Note: A party may not intervene if Complete Diversity will not be maintained.

(b) Permissive intervention

(1) In general: Anyone may intervene (upon timely motion) in a case when:
   (A) A federal statute allows (conditionally)
or (B) The moving party's claim is related to the main action by question of law or fact

(2) By a government officer or agency: A federal or state officer or agency may intervene (upon timely motion) in a case when the party's claim or defense is based on:
   (A) That officer's or agency's statute or executive order
or (B) Any regulation, order, requirement, or agreement made under the statute or executive order

(3) Delay or prejudice: The court has discretion, and should weigh any delays & prejudices to the original parties (resulting from the intervention).

(c) Procedure—notice and pleading required:

1. The Intervening party shall serve a *Motion to Intervene* (per Rule 5).
2. Requirements of motion to intervene—the motion must:
   a. State the grounds for intervention
   and b. Be accompanied by a pleading describing the claim or defense (that intervention is being sought for).

C. INTERPLEADER

OVERVIEW

- Interpleader is a case between Stakeholders and Claimants (Not πs and Defendants).
- Interpleader allows joinder of related claims in one action, to avoid inconsistent judgments.
- Interpleader usually involves "replevin," where claimants all want a particular piece of property, which the stakeholder has.
- Note: The Stakeholder can also be a claimant (and a Defendant in a previous action, who brings this action as a stakeholder-claimant)
- Forum shopping—Sometimes interpleader is unfair, because it changes the forum that the original πs chose.
- As an alternative remedy, courts may enjoin parties, forbidding them to receive anything greater than what was *originally* at stake (so as not to have inconsistent verdicts). The enforcement of the judgment will go to the court where the interpleader would have been held.
- Complete diversity is not needed between parties of an interpleader from different states (only Minimal Diversity, i.e., so it's okay if the stakeholder and claimants are from the same state, so long as 1 person in the action is diverse).
- There is no need for claims to be "reduced to judgment" before a third party may be impleaded.

Relevant Rules: 22, 28 U.S.C. § 1335, § 1397

Rule 22. Interpleader

("Rule Interpleader"—requires complete diversity)

(a) Grounds

(1) By a Plaintiff: Interpleader is appropriate if a π might be exposed to double liability.

a. Interpleader may take place, even though:

(A) There is no common origin of causes or are not identical—but are adverse and independent cases

or (B) The plaintiff denies liability to any claimant

(2) By a Defendant: A defendant may also interplead (by cross-claim or counterclaim) if he might be exposed to double liability.

(b) Relation to other rules and statutes: This remedy does not supersede 28 USC § 1335, § 1397, or § 2361

§ 1335. Interpleader

("Statutory Interpleader"—minimal diversity allowed)

(a) The district court has original jurisdiction over a civil action of interpleader if:

(1) Subject Matter Jurisdiction exists:

a. The controversy is <u>*greater than or equal to* $500</u>

and b. **Minimal Diversity**: At least 2 parties (not all) need diversity of citizenship (as defined in 28 USC 1332(a) or (d))

and (2) "Stakeholder" posts a bond (or deposits the property in the court)

(b) Interpleader may take place, although

1. There is no common origin among the titles or claims of the conflicting claimants

or 2. The actions are not identical, but are adverse and independent actions.

§ 1397. Interpleader Venue

A § 1335 interpleader action may be brought in a judicial district where *greater than or equal to* one <u>claimant</u> resides.

XII. JURY

A. RIGHT TO JURY TRIAL

OVERVIEW

- A Party has a right to a jury trial in cases in **law** (not **equity**) that is protected by the Seventh Amendment of the Constitution.
- When **law** and **equity** cases are combined in one action, the court must decide whether or not *each issue* should go to a jury. Any issue that is "legal" in nature should go to the jury.
- The court decision is based on:
  - The custom of ruling the issue in question (whether it has been in law or equity)
  - The remedy sought (money or injunction)
  - The practical abilities and limitations of juries (not considered as much)
- The court should err on the side of allowing a jury trial.
- Waiving right to a jury
  - A party will waive its right to a jury if it fails to make a timely demand (10 days from service of pleading)
  - A court may order a jury trial by *Motion, or its own initiative* if a demand is not made.
  - Waiver by contract may be effective if:
    - It is *knowingly* and *intentionally* waived
    - The Party seeking waiver must prove that the contract was both voluntary and informed.
    - Courts look at:
      - Length of the contract
      - Bargaining power between the parties
      - Past business relationships
      - Probability that parties understood the waiver of their right to a jury.

Relevant Rules: 38, 39

Rule 38. Right to a Jury Trial; Demand

(a) Preserved right—The rights of a jury trial guaranteed by the Seventh Amendment of the Constitution shall be preserved to parties "*inviolate*."

(b) Demand—Any party may demand a jury trial on any issue protected by the Constitution or a federal statute, by:

(1) Serving a written "demand" on other parties

and (2) Filing the demand (pursuant to Rule 5) no later than 10 days from service of the last pleading directed to such issue.

(c) Specification of issues:

1. In the demand, the party may specify which issues it wants to be tried by a jury. Otherwise, trial by jury is assumed to be demanded for all issues.
2. If a party specifies only some issues, then the other party has <u>10 days</u> (unless the court shortens) to serve a "demand" for other issues she wishes to be tried by a jury.

(d) Waiver

1. Failure to serve and file (pursuant to this rule) constitutes a waiver of the right to a jury.
2. Once a demand is made, it may be withdrawn only if <u>both parties consent</u>.

(e) Admiralty Claims—These rules do not apply.

Rule 39. Trial by Jury or Court

(a) When demand is made: When a jury trial is demanded, the trial shall proceed as a jury action *unless:*

(1) The parties both consent on record (either in writing or on oral record in a hearing).

or (2) Upon motion or the court's own initiative, the court finds that a right to a jury trial on all or some of the issues does not exist under the Constitution or any federal statute (e.g., the issue arises out of equity).

(b) When no demand is made:

1. If no jury demand is made, the case shall be tried by the court.
2. If a party neglects to make a demand, the court (upon motion) has *discretion* to allow a jury trial, if it finds that such a demand might have been made.

(c) Advisory jury and trial by consent: For cases not triable as of right by jury:

(1) The court may try an issue with an *advisory jury* (by motion or on its own initiative).

(2) The court may allow a jury if both parties agree. <u>Exception</u>: cases against the U.S. in which a statute provides for trial *without* a jury.

B. VERDICTS

OVERVIEW

- General Verdict—A "Yes" or "No" decision, without an explanation for the jury's conclusion
- Special Verdicts—often used along with **special interrogatories** to track the jury's thought pattern (making it easier to determine the verdict's validity)
  - Judges retain broad discretion in determining whether or not to use special verdicts/interrogatories.

Relevant Rules: 51, 49

Rule 51. Instructions to Jury; Objections; Preserving a Claim of Error

(a) Requests.

(1) At or before the close of evidence: A party may file (and should give copies to every other party) written requests for jury instructions. This may be done:

i. at the close of the evidence

or ii. at an earlier reasonable time that the court directs

(2) After the close of evidence:

(A) Requests dealt with in Rule 51(a)(1): A party may file requests on issues that could not *reasonably* have been anticipated earlier, and

(B) All Requests: The court may allow any untimely request on any issue.

(b) Instructions.

(1) Informing the parties: The court *must* inform the parties of its proposed instructions and proposed action on the requests before instructing the jury and before final jury arguments;

(2) Allowing objections on the record:

- The court *must* allow the parties to object on the record before the instructions are given
- The court *must* allow the objections to the proposed instructions to be made out of the jury's hearing

(3) When to instruct the jury: The court may instruct the jury at any time after trial begins (but before the jury is discharged).

(c) Objections.

(1) ***How to make:*** Objections to an instruction (or failure to instruct) must be made on the record

(2) ***What:*** Objection must state *distinctly* the objection and the grounds

(3) ***When to make:***

(A) If a party has been informed of an instruction before the jury is instructed and before final jury arguments (as provided by Rule 51(b)(1)): Objections must be made pursuant to Rule 51(b)(2).

(B) If a party has not been informed of an instruction before the time for objection in Rule 51(b)(2): Objections must be made *promptly* after learning about the instruction or request (whether it will be given or refused).

(d) Assigning error; plain error.

(1) **Assigning error.**

(A) Instruction given: A party may assign error if she made a proper objection under Rule 51(c)

(B) Failure to give an instruction: A party may assign error if:

1. She made a request under Rule 51(a), and
2. She also made an objection under Rule 51(c) (unless the court made a definitive ruling on the record rejecting the request, in which case a 51(c) objection is not necessary)

(2) **Plain error.** Only if *substantial rights* are affected, a court may consider a plain error that has not been preserved under Rule 51(d)(1), above.

Rule 49. Special Verdict; General Verdict and Questions

(a) Special verdicts:

(1) In general: The court may require a jury to return only a **special verdict.**

1. The special verdict must be in the form of a special written finding upon each issue of fact.
2. The court may submit to the jury:

(A) Written questions susceptible of absolute or other brief answers

or (B) Written forms of the several special findings which could properly be made from the evidence or pleadings or (C) Other methods of submitting issues (as it deems appropriate)

(2) Instructions: The court shall give the jury instructions as necessary to facilitate a jury decision.

(3) Issues not submitted:

a. If the court omits any issue of fact for the jury to decide, the parties must demand submission *before the jury retires.*

b. Those issues omitted and not demanded may be decided by the court.

c. If the court makes no finding, it is considered to have made a finding consistent with its special verdict judgment.

(b) General verdict

(1) In general:

a. The court may submit forms for a **general verdict** accompanied by *written* interrogatories on issues of fact necessary to decide a general verdict.

b. The court shall give appropriate instructions to help the jurors make their decision.

(2) Verdict and answers consistent: When the general verdict and written answers are consistent, appropriate judgment shall be made.

(3) Answers inconsistent with the verdict: When answers are consistent with each other, yet one or more answer is inconsistent with the general verdict, the judge may:

(A) Affirm jury's verdict and enter judgment in accordance with their answers (and not the general verdict).

or (B) Send the jury back for further considerations

or (C) Order a new trial

(4) Answers are inconsistent with each other and inconsistent with the general verdict: The judge shall:

1. Send the jury back for further considerations

or 2. Order a new trial

XIII. JUDGMENT

A. JUDGMENT AS A MATTER OF LAW

OVERVIEW

- This rule applies only to Jury Trials
- A motion for Judgment as a Matter of Law (a.k.a. "Directed Verdict") may be considered before a case goes to the jury.
- The court may grant the motion, deny the motion, or submit the case to the jury and reserve decision on the legal issues raised.
- If the case goes to the jury, a party may move for Judgment Notwithstanding the Verdict ("JNOV") after the jury has submitted its verdict.
- **The Test**:
  - A Directed Verdict may be granted if there is no *legally sufficient* evidentiary basis for a reasonable jury to find for the non-moving party.

Relevant Rule: 50

Rule 50. Judgment as a Matter of Law in a Jury Trial; Related Motion for a New Trial; Conditional Ruling

(a) Judgment as a matter of law

(1) The court may do any of the following in a case where the parties were heard and the court finds that there is no *legally sufficient evidentiary basis* for a *reasonable* jury to find for a party on a certain issue:

(A) the court may resolve the issue against the party; and

(B) grant a motion for "judgment as a matter of law" against the party where under controlling law the issue is a prerequisite to the claim.

(2) Motion: A Motion for Judgment as a Matter of Law

a. Must be made *before* the case is submitted to the jury

b. Must specify the judgment sought

c. Must state the applicable law and facts

(b) Renewing motion after trial; alternative motion for new trial

1. Renewal of motion for judgment after trial:

a. If the original motion is denied, the court is deemed to have submitted the case to the jury.

b. The court may later decide the legal issues raised by the motion (which would control the jury finding).

c. The motion may be "renewed" after the verdict by filing and serving a motion within 10 days after judgment is entered (or after the jury is discharged, if the issue was not decided by verdict).

2. Alternative motion for a new trial—The movant may also request a new trial (or join a Rule 59 motion for new trial).
3. Ruling on the renewed motion: The court may:
   (1) Allow the original judgment to stand (if a verdict was returned)
   or (2) Order a new trial
   or (3) Direct entry of judgment as a matter of law

(c) Conditions of granting judgment as a matter of law

(1) If a motion for judgment is granted, the court must also rule on a motion for a new trial (if it was made) as follows:
- The Court must decide whether a new trial should be granted if the judgment is vacated or reversed after the JNOV
- The court *must* describe specific grounds for granting or denying the motion for retrial.

(2) Even if the motion for a new trial is conditionally granted (i.e., if the JNOV is later vacated or reversed), the judgment is still final.
- If the JNOV is later reversed on appeal, the new trial goes forward (unless the appellate court ordered otherwise).
- If the motion for retrial is denied, the denial may be appealed. If the JNOV is later reversed on appeal, the appellate court determines what subsequent proceedings take place.

(d) Time for a losing party's new-trial motion: If judgment as a matter of law has been rendered against a party, that party may serve a motion for a new trial (under Rule 59) no later than 10 days after the judgment was entered.

(e) Denying the motion for judgment as a matter of law; reversal on appeal

1. The successful party may, on appeal, request a new trial, if: the motion was *denied*, and the appellate court finds that the trial court erred in denying the motion for judgment.
2. If the appellate court reverses the trial court's judgment it may also find that:
   a. The appellee is entitled to a new trial
   or b. The trial court shall determine if a new trial should be granted

B. NEW TRIALS

OVERVIEW

- The granting of a new trial is in the court's discretion.
- **Factors Considered**:
  - Was the Verdict Excessive? What was the *maximum amount* supported by the evidence?
  - Were excessive damages caused by "Passion or Prejudice"? Can that be proven?
- Choosing between New Trial and JNOV
  - New Trial—"Passion and Prejudice"—against the *clear weight of evidence*
  - JNOV—impossible for a *reasonable* jury to decide
- New Trial and Remittitur
  - When a party is entitled to a new trial, he has the option of accepting a **remittitur**—a reduction in judgment—instead.
  - Courts will usually prefer a remittitur:
    - Remittitur—can be used for verdicts that give *too much* recovery.
    - New Trial—can be used when issues were affected by "*passion or prejudice*."
  - If a party refuses remittitur and damages issues are clearly independent of liability issues, a new trial (if granted) may be limited to the question of damages.
  - If a court decides to use a remittitur, it must first offer the party a choice between:
    - Accepting a reduction in damages

    or
    - Proceeding with a new trial
  - If remittitur is chosen, the court may not reduce damages below the *"maximum amount supported by the evidence"*
  - Such *maximum award* should be reasonably proportioned to the amount of actual damages.

Relevant Rules: 58, 59, 52

Rule 58. Entering Judgment

(a) Separate document.

- Every judgment (this includes amended judgments) must be on a separate document.
- A separate document is not required for the following orders:
  (1) Deciding a Motion for Judgment After Trial (Rule 50(b))
  or (2) Deciding a Motion to Amend or Make Additional Findings of Fact (Rule 52(b))

or (3) Deciding a Motion for Attorney Fees (Rule 54)
or (4) Deciding a Motion for a New Trial, or to Alter or Amend the Judgment (Rule 59)
or (5) Deciding a Motion for Relief from a Judgment or Order (Rule 60)

(b) Entering judgment (Subject to Rule 54(b)):

(1) **Without the court's discretion:** In the following cases the clerk must (unless the Court orders otherwise), without waiting for the court's direction, *promptly* prepare, sign, and enter the judgment:
(A) when the jury returns a general verdict,
or (B) when the court awards only costs or a sum certain,
or (C) when the court denies all relief

(2) **Court's approval required:** In the following cases the court *must promptly* approve the form of the judgment, and the clerk must then promptly enter it:
(A) when the jury returns a special verdict or a general verdict accompanied by interrogatories
or (B) when the court grants other relief not described in Rule 58(a)(2)

(c) Time of entry: Judgment is considered "entered" (for purposes of these rules):

(1) If Rule 58(a)(1) does not require a separate document: when it is entered in the civil docket under Rule 79(a)

(2) If Rule 58(a)(1) requires a separate document: when it is entered in the civil docket under Rule 79(a) and when any of the following occurs:
(A) when it is set forth on a separate document
or (B) after 150 days from entry in the civil docket.

(d) Request for entry: A party may request that the judgment be a separate document as required by Rule 58(a)(1).

(e) Cost or fee awards:

(1) Taxing of costs or awarding fees may not delay the entry of judgment or extend the time to appeal (except as provided in Rule 58(c)(2)).

(2) When a timely motion for attorney fees is made (under Rule 54(d)(2)), the court may decide that the motion has the same effect (under Federal Rule of Appellate Procedure 4(a)(4)) as a timely Rule 59 motion (New Trial; Amending a Judgment), so long as a notice of appeal has not yet been filed and become effective.

Rule 59. New Trial; Amending a Judgment

(a) In general

(1) Grounds for new trial: A new trial may be granted on all or some of the issues in the following instances:

(A) Trial By Jury — allowed for any reason courts have (until now) allowed a new trial (See Rule 60(b)).

(B) Trial Without a Jury — Allowed for any reason the courts have (until now) allowed a rehearing.

(2) Further action after a non-jury trial: Upon motion for new trial, courts may:

a. Open judgment (if one has been entered)
or b. Take additional testimony
or c. Amend a finding of fact
or d. Amend a finding/conclusions of law
or e. Make new findings of fact or law
or f. Direct entry of a new judgment (or affirm the original judgment)

(b) Time to file a motion for a new trial: The motion must be served no later than 10 Days after entry of judgment.

(c) Time to serve affidavits

1. When a motion for a new trial is based on affidavits, the affidavits shall be served with the motion.
2. The opposing party has 10 Days after service of the motion to serve opposing affidavits (may be extended to no more than 20 days (total) if good cause is shown or the parties agree).

(d) New trial on court's initiative

1. The court may order a new trial on its own initiative, for any reason it may have granted a new trial by motion.
2. The court may order a new trial for reasons not specified in the motion *after* giving notice and an opportunity to be heard.
3. The court *must* specify the grounds for its decision.
4. The court *must* order a new trial no later than 10 days after entry of judgment.

(e) Motion to alter or amend a judgment: Must be served no later than 10 Days after entry of judgment.

Rule 52. Findings and Conclusions in a Non-jury Proceeding; Judgment on Partial Findings

(a) Findings and conclusions by the court

(1) In general:

a. Scope: This rule applies to cases tried without a jury or with an advisory jury.

b. The court shall state *separately* its conclusions of law and its findings of fact.

c. Findings of fact may be stated orally (and recorded) or written in an opinion or memorandum.

d. Judgment shall be entered pursuant to Rule 58.

(2) For an interlocutory injunction: In granting or refusing interlocutory injunctions, the court *must* also specifically state findings of facts and law as grounds for its conclusion.

(3) For a motion: Findings of fact and conclusions of law are not needed for motions under Rule 12 or Rule 56.

(4) Effect of a master's findings: Findings of a master shall be considered findings of the court.

(5) Questioning the evidentiary support: A party may later question the evidence supporting the findings, whether or not he:

- requested findings
- objected to them
- moved to amend them, or
- moved for partial findings.

(6) Setting aside the findings:

a. The findings of fact shall be set aside only if they are *clearly erroneous.*

b. *Due regard* must be given to the trial judge's opportunity to determine a witnesses' credibility.

(b) Amended or additional findings

1. Motion to amend:
   a. A motion for amendment may be made within 10 Days after entry of judgment.
   b. The motion may be made along with a motion for a new trial (pursuant to Rule 59).
2. The court may amend its findings or make additional findings, and change the judgment accordingly.
3. When findings of fact are made by the court, a party may raise a question of sufficiency of the evidence, *without:*
   a. Making a motion to amend
   b. Making a motion for judgment
   c. Raising objections to such findings in the district court

(c) Judgment on partial findings ("Mini-trial" or "Partial Judgment")

1. Scope: This subsection applies to trials heard without a jury.
2. A judge may enter judgment as a matter of law *before* all the evidence is heard if:
   a. A party has been fully heard on certain issues
   and b. The claim or defense is controlled by the issues
   and c. The only way the case could be won is if one particular issue was found in favor of that party
   and d. The court did not find the issue in favor of that party
3. The court may also wait until the close of all the evidence to make its decision.
4. The court shall support its decision as required by Rule 52(a).

C. RELIEF FROM A JUDGMENT OR ORDER

Relevant Rule: 60

Rule 60. Relief from a Judgment or Order

(a) Clerical mistakes, oversights, and omissions in judgments, orders, or other parts of the record:

1. Such errors may be corrected by motion or on the court's initiative
2. Such errors may be corrected any time before an appeal is docketed
3. Once an appeal begins, leave of court is needed for a correction to be made.

(b) Grounds for relief from a final judgment or order: The court may relieve a party or its legal representative from a final judgment, order, or proceeding if:

(1) There was mistake, inadvertence, surprise, or excusable neglect.
or (2) Newly discovered evidence was found, which by *due diligence* could not have been discovered in time to move for a new trial.
or (3) There was fraud, misrepresentation, or other misconduct of an adverse party
or (4) The judgment is void (e.g., jurisdiction is not appropriate).
or (5) *Either:*
- a. The judgment was satisfied
- or b. The judgment has been released or discharged
- or c. A prior judgment, upon which the judgment is based, is reversed
- or d. It is no longer equitable that the judgment should have prospective application

or (6) There exists any other reason justifying relief from the operation of the judgment.

(c) <u>Time to make motion</u>

(1) <u>Timing</u>:
- a. For reasons (1), (2), and (3), a motion must be made within <u>1 year</u> from when the judgment or order was entered.
- b. For reasons (4), (5), and (6), a motion must be made within a <u>*reasonable time*</u> from when the judgment was entered or taken.

(2) Effect on finality: The motion does not affect the judgment's finality or suspend its operation.

(d) Other powers to grant relief. This rule does not limit a court's power to:

(1) entertain an independent action to relieve a party from a judgment, order, or proceeding;

or (2) grant relief under 28 USC § 1655 to a defendant who was not personally notified of the action

or (3) set aside a judgment for fraud on the court.

(e) Bills and writs abolished. The following are abolished: bills of review, bills in the nature of bills of review, and writs of coram nobis, coram vobis, and audita querela.

D. DISMISSAL OF ACTIONS

Relevant Rule: 41

Rule 41. Dismissal of Actions

(a) Voluntary dismissal:

(1) By the plaintiff:

(A) *Without a court order:* A case may be dismissed by the π without a court order by:

(i) filing a notice of dismissal at any time before service of an answer or motion for summary judgment is made (whichever is sooner)

or (ii) filing a stipulation of dismissal signed by all parties who have appeared in the action

(B) *Effect:* Dismissal shall be without prejudice, *unless:*

1. Otherwise stated in the notice
2. The case is filed by a π who has already dismissed the action for the same claim in another court (in which case the notice of dismissal operates as an adjudication upon the merits)

Note: This subsection is subject to Rule 23(e), 23.1(c), 23.2, Rule 66, and any other federal statute.

(2) By court order:

a. Unless dismissed under 41(a)(1), a case shall be dismissed only upon a court order.

b. If a counterclaim has been pleaded by the Defendant prior to service of the π's notice of dismissal then:

1. The case cannot be dismissed if the counterclaim cannot remain as an independent action.
2. π's claim can be dismissed if the counterclaim can remain as an independent action.

c. Dismissal of 41(a)(2) cases is without prejudice.

(b) Involuntary dismissal

1. Defendant may move for a dismissal of any claim if π:

a. Fails to prosecute

or b. Fails to comply with the Federal Rules of Civil Procedure

or c. Fails to comply with any court order

2. Dismissal under 41(b) is with prejudice (and operates as an adjudication on the merits), *unless:*
   a. The dismissal order states otherwise
   or b. The case is dismissed for lack of jurisdiction
   or c. The case is dismissed for improper venue
   or d. The case is dismissed for failure to join a party (under Rule 19)

(c) Dismissal of counterclaims

1. This rule applies to any claims, including:
   a. Counterclaims
   and b. Cross-claims
   and c. Third-party claims
2. If a voluntary dismissal is made by the claimant alone (pursuant to 41(a)(1)(A)(i)), it must be made:
   (1) Before responsive pleadings are served
   (2) Before introduction of evidence (at trial or hearing), if there are no responsive pleadings

(d) Costs of previously dismissed actions—If π previously dismissed a case and is now reinstating it (i.e., bringing a case based on or including the same claim against the same Defendant), the court may:

(1) impose costs for the previously dismissed action
and (2) stay the case until the plaintiff complies

XIV. APPEALS

OVERVIEW

Interlocutory appeals (28 USC § 1292):

- § 1291 gives the Appellate Courts jurisdiction over all "final judgments" of a District Court (ordinarily in Federal Courts, a District Court decision cannot be appealed until the entire case has been adjudicated, i.e. there is a final judgment).
- Exception: When an *immediate* appeal is needed to prevent further, perhaps unnecessary, litigation (e.g., a decision on jurisdiction), an "interlocutory" appeal may be granted.
- Factors weighed in determining whether or not to accept an interlocutory appeal:
  - If the decision would *conclusively* determine the disputed question
  - If it resolves an important and *independent* issue (e.g., whether Personal Jurisdiction exists)
  - If the issue is effectively not reviewable on appeal after final judgment
  - Courts should not look at the burden on the Defendant to later prove that there was an erroneous trial.
  - § 1292 — Gives the Court of Appeals the power to review Special Interlocutory Decisions:
    - **Court of appeals has the power** to hear matters before final judgment occurs when the decision deals with:
      - Injunctions — Interlocutory orders granting, continuing, modifying, refusing, or dissolving injunctions
      - Receivers — Interlocutory Orders appointing receivers
      - Admiralty Cases
    - **Subject matter jurisdiction:**
      - The court has *discretion* to hear all other pre-final-judgment decisions

Relevant Rules: 28 U.S.C § 1291, § 1292

§ 1291. Appellate Jurisdiction

The **appellate court** has jurisdiction of appeals from all final decisions of the district courts.

§ 1292. Interlocutory Decisions

(a) The **appellate court** has the power to hear a case before final judgment when:

(1) Injunctions — There is an interlocutory order granting, continuing, modifying, refusing, or dissolving an injunction

(2) Receivers — There is an interlocutory order appointing a receiver (within the meaning of Rule 9)

(3) Admiralty cases

(b) Judge's request to appeal

1. If not included in (a), a district judge may request an interlocutory order appeal by *writing* to the appellate court within 10 days after her order, if she believes there is a controlling question of law where there is substantial ground for difference of opinion, and an appeal may *materially advance* the ultimate termination of the case.
2. The appellate court has discretion to accept such a request.

(c) U.S. appellate courts have **exclusive jurisdiction** of:

(1) Any case covered by § 1295

and (2) Patent infringement cases which are final, except for an accounting (Where jurisdiction would otherwise lie in the Court of Appeals for the Federal Circuit)

(d) Specific issues:

i. The appellate court has discretion to take a case if:

1. The application for appeal is made within 10 days of an order is entered

and 2. *Either:*

a. The Chief Judge of the Court of International Trade issues a 256(b) interlocutory order.

or b. The Chief Judge of the Court of Federal Claims issues a 798(b) interlocutory order.

or c. Any judge of the Court of International Trade/Court of Federal Claims issues an interlocutory order.

and 3. There is a *substantial ground* for difference of opinion on a controlling question of law.

and 4. An immediate appeal may *materially advance* the termination of the suit.

ii. Applicability

(1) The above rules apply to the Court of International Trade.

(2) The above rules apply to the Court of Federal Claims.

(3) Proceedings do not stay unless the district court or appellate court so orders.

(4) Motion to transfer

(A) The appellate court has exclusive jurisdiction over all of the district court's ordering, granting, or denying of motions to transfer a case (pursuant to 28 USC § 1631).

(B) Actions <u>must</u> be stayed (put on hold) until <u>60 days</u> after the court has ruled upon a motion to transfer to the Court of Federal Claims. The time may be extended until after the appeal is decided (if an appeal is taken).

Part Two

E-Z RULES®

FOR THE FEDERAL RULES OF CIVIL PROCEDURE

and Selected Statutes

CONTENTS FOR THE FEDERAL RULES OF CIVIL PROCEDURE AND SELECTED STATUTES

ARTICLE I
SCOPE OF RULES

Rule 1. Scope and Purpose

a. Applicability: These rules govern the procedure for all civil cases in the U.S. District Courts (with the exceptions stated in Rule 81).

b. Objective and construction: *"To secure the just, speedy, and inexpensive determination of every action and proceeding."*

Rule 2. One Form of Action

There is one form of action known as the *civil action*.

ARTICLE II
COMMENCING AN ACTION; SERVICE OF PROCESS, PLEADINGS, MOTIONS AND ORDERS

Rule 3. Commencing an Action

"A civil action is commenced by filing a complaint with the court."

Rule 4. Summons

(a) Summons form (contents and amendments):

(1) Contents: The Summons must have the following:
- (A) The court and the parties' names
- (B) It must be directed to the defendant
- (C) The name and address of plaintiff's attorney (or the plaintiff if he is unrepresented)
- (D) Specify the time for the Defendant to appear to defend himself (before a default occurs).
- (E) Notify the Defendant that the consequence for failing to appear would be <u>default judgment</u> in favor of π.
- (F) Be signed by the clerk
- (G) Bear the court's seal

(2) Amendments: The court may allow a summons to be amended.

(b) Issuing the summons:

1. After the π files the complaint, he may present the summons to the clerk for a signature and seal.
2. If the summons is in proper form, the clerk must sign, seal, and issue it to the π for service on the Defendant.
3. The clerk will issue as many summonses as there are Ds.
4. π or π's attorney is responsible for delivering the Summons and Complaint to Defendant.

(c) Service:

(1) <u>Plaintiff's obligations:</u>
1. A Summons shall be served together with a copy of the complaint.
2. π <u>is responsible for service</u> (see Rule 4(m) for time limits).
3. π must furnish the process server with the necessary copies of the summons and complaint.

(2) Qualifications to serve:
- Anyone *at least* 18 years old

and • a Non-Party to the suit

(3) U.S. Marshal to serve:
- *may* request a U.S. Marshal or a specially appointed agent to serve.
- π *must* request a U.S. Marshal or a specially appointed agent to serve if the π is proceeding in *forma pauperis* (pursuant to 28 USC § 1915) or as a seaman.

(d) Waiver of Service:

(1) Sending a Waiver of Service Notice:

i. To avoid costs, the π may notify the Defendant of the action with a *"Waiver of Service Notice"* and request that the Defendant waive service of the summons.

ii. Any Defendant who has received a proper Waiver of Service Notice has a duty to avoid unnecessary costs of serving the summons.

iii. If the Defendant refuses to waive good cause, the Defendant must pay the costs of service.

iv. Requirements for Waiver of Service Notice:

(A) **In writing**:

(i) Individuals: Notice must be addressed directly to the Defendant.

(ii) Corporations/associations: Notice must be addressed to either an officer, managing/general agent, or agent appointed by law.

(B) Name the **court** in which the complaint has been filed.

(C) **Copy of Complaint:** The notice must:

1. include a copy of the **Complaint**

and 2. 2 Extra copies of Notice and Request

and 3. Prepaid means of return (e.g., Self-Addressed Stamped Envelope)

(D) **Consequences**—π must specify the consequences of compliance and of failure to comply with request (see official form 1A for text)

(E) **Date**—The date when the waiver request was sent must be specified.

(F) **Time limit**

1. π must inform the Defendant of the time limit by which the Defendant must notify π of his intention to waive service.

2. The time limit must be at least 30 days from the *date sent* for return (60 days if sent to a foreign country).

(G) **First class mail**—π must send the notice by first class mail or other reliable means.

(2) Costs to Defendant for denying waiver: The Defendant will be responsible for the following costs if he does not consent to the waiver of notice:

(A) Cost subsequently incurred in order to effectuate service

and (B) Reasonable costs of any motion needed to collect service costs, including attorney's fees.

(3) Time for answer with waiver: Defendant may wait 60 days after the request is sent to furnish an Answer (90 days if sent to a foreign country). Note: Although the Defendant may send an *answer* after 60 days, the response to the notice of waiver **must** still be sent within 30 days.

(4) Commencement of action with waiver: The action proceeds as normal (except for the time for filing an Answer) and is considered to have started once π has filed the waiver notice with the clerk. No proof of service is needed.

(5) A Defendant who waives service does not waive any objection to *venue* or *jurisdiction* of the court.

(e) **Service on individuals:** If the Defendant does not waive service, π may serve according to:

(1) The state law for service—π may rely on the state law of *either*:

a. The state where the District Court (in which the action is being brought) is located

or b. The state where service is being made

or (2) The federal law for service—π may choose any of the following methods to serve under Federal law:

(A) Personal service—π must personally serve the individual (actual hand delivery).

or **(B) Abode service**—to a resident in Defendant's *usual* place of abode (no business service).

or **(C) Substitute service**—to an authorized agent.

(f) Service upon individuals in a foreign country—Unless waived, service may be made outside of the U.S.:

(1) By any internationally agreed method if it is *reasonably calculated to give notice* (e.g., Hague Convention).

or (2) If no internationally agreed method of service, then:

(A) Service laws of the foreign country

or (B) As directed by a foreign authority (in response to a letter rogatory/request)

or (C) By (unless prohibited by the foreign country):

(i) **Personal service**—delivery to the individual of the summons and complaint

or (ii) **Mail**—registered mail to be dispatched by the court clerk in Defendant's country.

or (3) <u>As directed by forum court</u> (i.e., in the U.S.) as long as it is not prohibited by an international agreement.

(g) Service upon infants/incompetents—According to state law (if outside of U.S., refer to 4(f)).

(h) Service on corporations/associations:

i. <u>Applicability:</u> This subsection applies

a. Unless another federal law provides otherwise.

and b. If the Defendant is *either:*

1. A domestic or foreign corporation

or 2. A partnership

or 3. An unincorporated association subject to suit under a common name

and c. A Waiver of Service has not been obtained and filed.

ii. <u>Service under this subsection shall be effective when:</u>

(1) State law is followed

(A) Rule 4(e)(1) for an individual

(B) Delivering a copy to an <u>*authorized* **General Agent**</u>, <u>**Officer**</u>, or <u>**Manager**</u> (and mailing a copy to the Defendant if the statute so requires).

or (2) If the Defendant is a foreign corporation, and Rule 4(f) is followed

(i) Serving the United States, its agencies, corporations, or employees

(1) <u>Effective Service</u>

(A) Delivering to:

(i) The U.S. Attorney for the forum district or the U.S. Attorney's assistant or clerk

or (ii) Registered or certified mailing to civil process clerk

and (B) Sending a registered or certified mailing to the U.S. Attorney General

and (C) Delivering a copy to an officer or agency, if a U.S. agency or officer is involved

(2) <u>Suits against the officer or agency in their official capacity</u>

1. Serving the United States pursuant to Rule 4(i)(1)

and 2. Sending a copy of the Summons and Complaint by registered or certified mail to the officer, employee, agency, or corporation.

(3) Suits against the officer or agency in their individual capacity

1. Method of service:

a. Serving the United States pursuant to Rule 4(i)(1)

and b. Serving the Officer or Employee pursuant to Rule 4(e), (f), or (g).

2. "Individual capacity"

a. This subparagraph applies to officers and employees sued for acts or omissions while performing their duties on behalf of the United States.

and b. This section applies even if the officer or employee is also sued in his official capacity.

(4) *Reasonable time* is allowed to cure a failure to serve the following parties pursuant to Rule 4(i):*

(A) Anyone sued pursuant to Rule 4(i)(2)(A), so long as the Plaintiff properly served either:

1. The United States Attorney

or 2. The Attorney General of the United States

(B) The United States, where it is sued pursuant to Rule 4(i)(2)(B), so long as the Plaintiff properly served an officer or employee of the United States that is being sued in his individual capacity.

(j) Service upon foreign, state, or local governments:

(1) Foreign state, political subdivision, etc.: Service is made pursuant to 28 USC § 1608.

(2) U.S./state/municipal corporation or organization *either*:

(A) Serve the CEO

or (B) According to state law service

***Summary: "Reasonable Time" to Cure a Failure to Serve**

Failed to Serve	Rule Governing Service	Properly Served
Officer, Employee, Agency, or Corporation	4(i)(2)(A)	U.S. Attorney or Attorney General
United States	4(i)(2)(B)	An Officer or Employee sued in his individual capacity

(k) Territorial limits of effective service

(1) Service of a summons or filing of a 4(e) waiver is sufficient to establish **Personal jurisdiction** if:
 (A) The forum district's state laws allow it.
 or (B) The Defendant is a Joined Party (per Rule 14 and 19) and is served within 100 miles from where the summons was issued
 or (C) It is authorized by a federal statute
(2) Defendant not subject to jurisdiction of any state court: A waiver of service notice or service of a summons is effective to establish personal jurisdiction in a federal case if:
 (A) The Defendant is not subject to the jurisdiction of any state court
 and (B) The exercise of jurisdiction over the Defendant is consistent with the Constitution and laws of the U.S. (e.g., State Minimum Contact is greater than the Constitutional Minimum Contact)

(l) Proof of service (if service is not waived):

(1) If service is not made by a U.S. Marshal, an affidavit of service is required as proof of service.
(2) Foreign countries: Proof of service may be attained:
 (A) According to treaty agreements (if served pursuant to 4(f)(1))
 or (B) With a registered mail receipt—if mailed (pursuant to 4(f)(2), (3))
(3) Validity, amendments
 a. Failure to prove service does not affect validity of service.
 b. A Court may allow proof of service to be amended.

(m) Time limit for service

1. Service must be made within 120 days after filing the complaint.
2. If service is not made in time the case will either be:
 a. Automatically dismissed (without prejudice)
 or b. Service will be demanded within a specified time
3. If π shows *good cause*, the court may extend the time to serve (or the service period).
4. This subsection does not apply to service to Foreign Persons (Rule 4(f)) or Foreign Corporations (see Rule 4(j)(1)).

(n) Seizure of property:

(1) Federal law
 a. A court may have jurisdiction over property if a federal statute so provides.

b. Notice to claimants of the property to be seized shall be sent, *either*:
   1. As provided by the statute
   2. By service of a summons under this rule

(2) State law
   a. If Personal Jurisdiction (in the district where the action is brought) over Defendant cannot be obtained with *reasonable effort* the court may assert "in-rem" jurisdiction by seizing the Defendant's assets that are located in the forum district.
   b. The court must seize property according to the state law (in which the forum district court is located).

Rule 4.1. Serving Other Process

(a) In general.

1. **Who serves:** Other Process must be served by a United States marshal (or deputy marshal) or by specially appointed person.
2. **Where:** The service can be made anywhere within the district court's state.
3. Federal statute can extend those limits.
4. **Proof of service:** Proof of service must be made under Rule 4(l).
5. **When this Rule applies:** This Rule 4.1 does not apply to:
   a. a Rule 4 Summons
   or b. a Rule 45 Subpoena

(b) Enforcing Orders: Committing for civil contempt.

1. A civil contempt order (relating to a decree or injunction made to enforce federal law) may be served and enforced in any district.
2. Any other order in a civil contempt proceeding may be served only:
   a. In the issuing court's state
   or b. Within 100 miles from where the order was issued (but not outside the U.S.).

Rule 5. Serving and Filing Pleadings and Other Papers

(a) Service: When required

(1) Service is required for:
   (A) Every order which is required, by its terms, to be served
   (B) Every pleading made after the initial complaint (*unless* the court orders otherwise because there are many Defendants)

(C) Every paper relating to discovery
(D) Every written motion (*unless* it's being heard *ex parte*)
(E) Every written notice, demand, appearance, offer of judgment, and any *"similar papers"*

(2) Service is not required to parties in default (because they failed to appear) *unless* the π wants to assert a new or additional claim of relief to the defaulting Defendant.

(3) Seizure Cases: In cases begun by seizing property, where no person is named as a Defendant, any service required to be made prior to the filing of the answer, claim, or appearance must be made to the person in custody or possession of the property at the time of seizure.

(b) Making service.[10]

(1) Who to serve:
Service under Rules **5(a)** (Service of pleadings and other papers) and **77(d)** (Notice of orders or judgments) shall be made on a party's attorney (if the party is represented by one) unless the Court orders service on the party directly.

(2) Methods of service (for Rule 5(a) service):
(A) **Delivery by hand** to the person
(B) **Office or Home**:
(i) Office: Leaving it at the person's office with a clerk or other person in charge or in a conspicuous place in the office (if no one is in charge)
(ii) If no office/office is closed: Leaving it at the person's **dwelling house** or **usual place of abode** with someone of *suitable age and discretion* who lives there
(C) **Mail:** Mailing a copy to the person's last known address (service is complete upon mailing)
(D) **Clerk of the Court:** Leaving a copy with the Clerk of the Court (if the person has no known address)
(E) **Electronic means**
Note—failed transmission: If a party learns that an attempted electronic transmission service did not reach the intended person, service is not effective.
(F) **"Any other means"—that are consented to by the party served**

[10] The 2001 amendment to Rule 5(b) (Service and Filing of Pleadings and Other Papers) permitted electronic service on parties who give consent. Under the amendment, electronic service is complete on transmission. Service by electronic means is not effective if the party making service learns that the attempted service did not reach the person served.

E-Z Definition:
"Electronic Means" includes:

a. electronic transmission
b. the court's transmission facilities (if authorized by local rule) *Rule 5(b)(3)*

For (E) and (F), note the following:

1. Written consent by the party served is required

2. When service is complete:

   a. Service by electronic transmission — complete on transmission

   b. Service by other means — complete when delivery is made by the serving party

(c) Serving numerous defendants

(1) (A) A Court may (upon motion or the court's own initiative) exempt a Defendant from service of pleadings/replies to other Defendants.

(B) Consequences of the Court's decision: If the court exempts a Defendant from serving other Defendants, the other Defendants will be deemed to have denied or avoided any:

1. Counterclaims

or 2. Cross-claims

or 3. Affirmative defenses

(C) The filing of the pleadings and service on the π is considered sufficient notice to all other Defendants in the case

(2) A copy of every such order shall be served upon the parties as the court directs.

(d) (1) **Filing:**

a. **What to file:** All papers after the Complaint must be filed with the court, with a certificate of service.

b. **When to file:** The filing must be done within a *reasonable time* after service upon the party.

c. **What not to file:** The following disclosures and discovery materials must not be filed until they are used in the proceeding (or the court orders that they be filed):

- Rule 26(a)(1) Disclosure (Initial Disclosure)
- Rule 26(a)(1) Disclosure (Expert Testimony Disclosure)
- Depositions (and Deposition Notices)
- Interrogatories and Responses (including objections)
- Requests for Documents or Inspection and Responses (including objections)
- Requests for Admission and Responses (including objections)

(2) Method of filing[11]

(A) Filing is normally made by filing papers with the clerk of the court.

(B) The judge may permit the papers to be filed directly with the judge (the judge will then indicate the filing date and give the papers to the clerk).

(3) Electronic filing:

a. A court may permit (by local rule) papers to be filed, signed or verified electronically (the Judicial Conference of the United States may set technical standards).

b. E-filed papers are considered written documents for all purposes.

(4) A Clerk may not refuse to file any paper solely because it is not presented in its proper form.

Rule 5.1. Constitutional Challenge to a Statute—Notice, Certification, and Intervention[12]

(a) Notice by a party. A party that files a pleading, written motion, or other paper that draws into question a federal or state statute's constitutionality must promptly:

(1) File a notice of constitutional question.

- Contents: This should state the question and identify the paper that raises it
- When not required:
  - **(A)** if the United States or any of its agencies, officers, or employees is a party to the suit (in the case of a federal statute being questioned)
  - or **(B)** if the state or any of its agencies, officers, or employees is a party to the suit (in the case of a state statute being questioned)

---

[11] This rule was amended in 1996 to permit electronic filing in district courts under certain circumstances. The amendment permits federal courts to establish local rules to allow documents to be filed, signed, or verified by electronic means, provided those means are consistent with technical standards (if any) established by the Judicial Conference of the United States.

[12] This rule was added December 1, 2006, and requires a party that files a pleading, motion, or other paper that questions the constitutionality of a federal or state statute to promptly file a "notice of constitutional question" and serve it on the United States Attorney General or state attorney general. This ensures that the attorney general is notified of constitutional challenges and has an opportunity to exercise the statutory right to intervene at the earliest possible point in the litigation.

and **(2)** Serve the notice. The notice has to be served with the document in question on the Attorney General of the United States (if a federal statute is challenged, or the state attorney general if it is a state statute) either:
  a. by certified or registered mail
  or b. by sending it to an electronic address designated by the attorney general for this purpose.

(b) Certification by the Court. The court *must* (under 28 USC § 2403) certify to the attorney general that there is a constitutional challenge to a statute.

(c) Intervention; final decision on the merits.

1. **Attorney General's right to intervene.** The attorney general may intervene within 60 days (the court may set a later time) after the earlier of:
   a. When notice of constitutional question is filed
   or b. After the court certifies the challenge.
2. **Court's right to reject challenges.** Before the expiration of the time to intervene, the court can reject the constitutional challenge (but the court may *not* enter a final judgment holding the statute unconstitutional).

(d) No forfeiture. If a party fails to file and serve the notice (or if the court fails to certify the challenge), the constitutional claim or defense is not forfeited so long as the claim was otherwise properly and timely made.

Rule 5.2. Privacy Protection for Filings Made with the Court

(a) Redacted filings

- In court filings, the following must be redacted:
  (1) Social Security Number or Taxpayer ID Number: A court paper may use the last four digits only
  (2) Birthdate: A court paper may use the year only
  (3) A minor's name: The court paper may use the minor's initials only
  and (4) Financial Account Number: The court paper may use the last four digits of the account number only.
- This applies to parties as well as non-parties filing papers.
- The court may order that a document not be redacted.

(b) Exemptions from the requirement to redact

(1) In a forfeiture proceeding, where an account number identifies the property allegedly subject to forfeiture

(2) the record of an administrative or agency proceeding;
(3) the official record of a state-court proceeding;
(4) the record of a court or tribunal, if that record was not subject to the redaction requirement when originally filed;
(5) a Rule 5.2(c) or (d) filing (see below)
and (6) a pro se filing in a case brought under 28 USC §§ 2241, 2254, or 2255 (e.g., Habeas Corpus Writ, Motion to Be Released from Prison on Constitutional Grounds).

(c) Limitations on remote access to electronic files; Social-security appeals and immigration cases

- This subsection applies to the following cases:
  a. A Social Security benefits case
  b. A case relating to an order of removal
  c. A case relating to relief from removal
  d. A case relating to immigration benefits or detention
- Access to an electronic file is authorized as follows:
  (1) <u>Parties and their attorneys</u>—may have remote electronic access to any part of the case file, including the administrative record;
  (2) <u>Other people</u>—may have electronic access to the full record at the courthouse, but may have remote electronic access only to:
    (A) the docket maintained by the court
    and (B) an opinion, order, judgment, or the like (but not any other part of the case file or record).
- The court may order that access be limited or expanded otherwise.

(d) Filings made under seal

- The court may order that a filing be made under seal without redaction.
- The court may later unseal the filing or order the person who made the filing to file a redacted version for the public record.

(e) Protective orders

For good cause, the court may:
(1) require redaction of additional information in a particular case
or (2) limit/prohibit a nonparty's remote electronic access to a document filed with the court in a particular case.

(f) Option for additional unredacted filing under seal

- A person making a redacted filing may also file an unredacted copy under seal.
- The court *must* retain the unredacted copy as part of the record.

(g) Option for filing a reference list

1. Filing a reference list: A filing that contains redacted information may be filed together with a reference list that lists each redacted item and gives a unique identifier for each item.
2. Filing the list under seal: That list is then filed under seal and may be amended as of right.
3. Any reference in the case to a listed identifier will be deemed to refer to the redacted information.

(h) Waiver of protection of identifiers

If a person files one's own information without redaction (and not under seal), that person waives the protection of Rule 5.2(a).

Comment: This new rule, added in 2007, allows redacting of sensitive information like Social Security numbers and birthdates. It also specifically limits remote access to Social Security and immigration electronic case filings (these cases require special attention because of how much sensitive information is in them and because of how many filings there are). Remote electronic access by nonparties is limited in these cases to the docket and the written dispositions of the court (unless the court orders otherwise).

Rule 6. Computing and Extending Time

(a) Computation of any time requirements under these rules:

(1) The period begins the day *after* the act, default, or event occurs.
(2) For periods less than 11 days, weekends and legal holidays are not included in computation.
(3) The last day of the period is included in the computation, *unless*:
  1. The last day is a weekend or legal holiday
  or 2. The time limitation for filing is extended to the first day the office of the clerk is open if:
    a. The office of the clerk is closed
    or b. The office of the clerk is inaccessible due to weather conditions

E-Z Definition
(4) A **"Legal holiday"** is
  (A) New Year's Day, Martin Luther King Jr.'s Birthday, Washington's Birthday, Memorial Day, Independence Day, Columbus Day, Veterans' Day, Thanksgiving Day, Christmas Day
  or (B) Any other day declared by the President or Congress or the District Court's State

(b) Extending time

(1) A Court may use its discretion to extend time periods:
   (A) With or without a motion—if a request is made before the expiration of the original time period.
   (B) Upon motion—after expiration of original time period, if the failure to act was caused by "*excusable neglect*."

(2) A Court is limited in extending time periods to the extent provided in the following rules:
   a. 50(b)
   b. 50(c)(2)
   c. 52(b)
   d. 59(b)
   e. 59(d)
   f. 59(e)
   g. 60(b)

(c) Rescinded

(c) Time period for motions

(1) Written motions and notices of hearing may be served no later than 5 days before the date specified for hearing, *unless*:
   (A) The motion may be heard *ex parte*
   (B) A different time period is specified in the FRCP
   (C) A different time period is set by court order

(2) Service of Affidavits:
   a. Affidavits supporting a motion shall be served with the motion (except as otherwise provided by 59(c)).
   b. Opposing affidavits may be served no later than 1 Day before the hearing (unless permitted by the court).

(d) Additional time after service under Rule 5(b)(2)(B), (C), or (D): Whenever a party is properly served under these provisions, 3 days are *added* to the time limit for responding (holidays, Saturdays, and Sundays are included but if the third day falls on a non-weekday, the following day would constitute the final date to respond).

ARTICLE III
PLEADINGS AND MOTIONS

Rule 7. Pleadings Allowed; Form of Motions and Other Papers

(a) Pleadings:

Allowable pleadings include:

(1) The Complaint
(2) The Answer
(3) A Reply to a Counterclaim
(4) An Answer to a Cross-claim
(5) A third-party complaint (if that party was not an original party under Rule 14)
(6) A third-party answer (if a third-party complaint was served)
(7) A Reply to an answer or third-party answer (allowed only if the court orders)

(b) Motions and other papers

(1) Requirements for an Application for an Order:
 (A) Must be made in writing:
  1. Writing requirement will be fulfilled if the motion is stated in a written notice of the hearing of the motion.
  2. Writing requirement is not necessary if a motion is made at a hearing or trial.
 (B) Shall state grounds for motions with "*particularity*"
 (C) Shall state relief sought
(2) All rules regarding form of pleadings and captioning (numbering) of rules apply.

Rule 7.1. Disclosure Statement[13]

(a) Who must file: Nongovernmental corporate party:

A nongovernmental corporate party to a case in a district court must file 2 copies of a statement that either:

(1) Identifies any parent corporation and any publicly held corporation that owns 10% or more of its stock.
or (2) States that there is no such corporation.

---

[13] The purpose of this Rule, added in 2002, is to get information calculated to determine if a judge should be disqualified from a case on the basis of financial information that a judge may not know or recollect.

(b) Time for filing; supplemental filing

(1) A party must file the Rule 7.1(a) statement with its first **pleading** or **request** addressed to the court (e.g., notice of appearance, pleading, petition, motion)

(2) If any required information in the statement changes, the party must promptly file a supplemental statement.

Rule 8. General Rules of Pleading

(a) Claims for relief—must contain:

(1) A Short plain statement of jurisdiction (unless the court already has it)

(2) A Short and plain statement that the Pleader is entitled to relief

(3) Relief sought ("demand for judgment") *Alternative types of relief may be demanded*

(b) Defenses; form of denials

(1) For responses:
   - (A) the Pleader shall state (in plain & short terms) defenses to each claim asserted
   - and (B) admit or deny the allegations

(2) Denials must respond to the substance of the denied allegations.

(3) Types of denials which a Pleader may make:
   - a. *Specific denial*—applying to only parts of the pleadings
   - or b. *Complete denial*—applying to entire complaint
   - or c. *General denial*—applying to the entire complaint, except paragraphs specified

(4) If the Pleader intends to deny only a part of an allegation, he shall specify what is true and deny only the remainder.

(5) If the Pleader is without sufficient knowledge or information (to admit or deny) the Pleader may so state (a.k.a. "D.K.I."). In such a case, the court will consider it as if the Pleader *denied* the allegations.

(6) Effect of failure to deny
   - a. Any denials omitted are deemed to have been admitted, unless:
     - i. A responsive pleading was not required
     - or ii. The omission involved a dispute of the amount of damages claimed
   - b. Any allegations to which no answer is required (or allowed) shall be taken as denied.

(c) Affirmative defenses

(1) Types of affirmative defenses:

- Accord and Satisfaction
- Arbitration and Award
- Assumption of Risk
- Contributory Negligence
- Discharge in Bankruptcy
- Duress
- Laches
- License
- Res Judicata
- Waiver
- Estoppel
- Failure of Consideration
- Fraud
- Illegality
- Injury
- Injury by fellow servant
- Payment
- Release
- Statute of Frauds

(2) If the Pleader makes a mistake and puts Counterclaims as affirmative defenses, the court may treat it as if it were without mistakes.

(d) Consistency of pleadings — concise and direct

(1) In general: Each allegation shall be Direct and Concise (no technical forms of pleadings/motions required).

(2) Alternative statements:

a. Claims may be in one count or defense, or as separate ones
b. A relationship between the claims is not necessary
c. If one statement is improper, it does not negate the entire pleading (i.e., only the improper allegation will be negated).

(3) Inconsistent statements: A Pleader may state as many separate claims as it wants in the pleadings

(e) Construction of pleadings: Pleadings shall be construed so as to *"do justice."*

Rule 9. Pleading Special Matters

(a) Capacity

(1) Other than to show jurisdiction, there is no need to allege:

(A) capacity to sue
(B) authority to sue as a representative
(C) an organized association's legal existence

(2) If a party wants to raise a capacity issue, it must do so in a *specific negative* allegation (which must be stated with particularity, (i.e., with a specific factual foundation)).

(b) Fraud, mistake, condition of mind—

1. Accusations of fraud, mistake—must be stated with *particularity* (i.e., with a specific factual foundation).
2. Accusations of malice, intent, knowledge, and conditions of mind—may be alleged *generally*.

(c) Conditions Precedent:

1. A Denial that a Condition Precedent has not been fulfilled must be stated with *particularity*.
2. An allegation that a Condition Precedent was performed may be alleged *generally*.

(d) Official document or act—It is sufficient to simply say that it was done in compliance with the law.

(e) Judgment—Domestic or foreign court judgments are sufficient to aver a judgment or decision. There is no need to describe the jurisdiction of the court.

(f) Time and place—Allegations of time and place are material.

(g) Special damages—must be specifically stated.

(h) Admiralty and maritime claims

(1) **How designated.**

a. If a claim is both an admiralty or maritime claim and also a claim on some other ground, the pleading may designate the claim as an admiralty or maritime claim
b. This designation would apply for purposes of:
    1. Rule 14(c)—Third-Party Practice in Admiralty or Maritime Cases
    2. Rule 38(e)—Jury Trials in Admiralty or Maritime Cases
    3. Rule 82—Jurisdiction and Venue in Admiralty or Maritime Cases

    and 4. The Supplemental Rules for Admiralty or Maritime Claims and Asset Forfeiture Cases
c. If a claim is only an admiralty or maritime claim, it is considered one for all of the above purposes (whether or not designated one).

(2) **Designation for appeal.** A case that includes an admiralty or maritime claim within this subdivision (h) is an admiralty case within 28 USC § 1292(a)(3).

Rule 10. Form of Pleadings

(a) Captions; names of parties

i. Every pleading requires a caption with:
    1. Name of court
    2. Title of action
    3. File number (docket number)
    4. Type of pleading (see 7(a); e.g., answer, complaint)
    5. Name of first party on each side

ii. If the pleading is a **complaint** it must *also* include the names of <u>*all*</u> parties.

(b) Separate statements

1. All allegations (claims/defenses) shall be made in NUMBERED paragraphs.
2. Each paragraph shall be limited to a single set of circumstances (or whenever needed for clarity).
3. In later paragraphs or pleadings, paragraphs may be referred to by paragraph number.

(c) Adoption by reference:

1. Statements in a pleading may be adopted by reference in:
    a. Other parts of the pleadings
    or b. In different pleadings
    or c. In motions
2. An exhibit is a part of a pleading for all purposes

Rule 11. Signing Pleadings, Motions, and Other Papers; Representations to the Court; Sanctions

(a) Signature

1. Signature must be made <u>by the lawyer</u>; if there is no lawyer, the pleader must sign.
2. The signer must include his address and telephone number and e-mail address.
3. There is no need to accompany pleadings with an affidavit (unless specifically provided for by another rule or statute).
4. If the signature is missing, the court may strike the pleadings, unless it is signed promptly after such omission is brought to the pleader's attention.

(b) Representations to court

A signature implies that, to best of the signer's knowledge, with *reasonable inquiry*, the pleading is:

(1) Made with a proper purpose—not to harass or cause unnecessary cost or delay

and (2) Warranted by *existing law* (or a non-frivolous argument to change existing law)

and (3) Well-grounded in fact—likely to be reasonably supported by facts

and (4) Based on evidence—Denials of factual contentions are based on evidence or reasonably based on lack of belief/information.

(c) Sanctions—If Rule 11(b) is violated, the court may impose sanctions to lawyers/signers:

(1) In general.

(2) Motion for Sanctions *((A) in the pre-December 2007 Rule)*

(A) **By motion**:

1. Motion for Sanctions must be made separately from other motions.
2. The motion must state violation of Rule 11(b).
3. The motion may be filed only if the pleading is not corrected within 21 days of service.
4. The court may award the winner reasonable expenses and fees incurred in making or opposing the motion.
5. Law firms will be held jointly liable—*absent exceptional circumstances.*

(3) On Court's initiative: If the Court initiates the sanctions (by Order to Show Cause), the burden of proof will fall on the pleader to show that it is not in violation.

(4) Nature of sanctions: Sanctions shall be limited to what is "*sufficient to deter repetition*" of the conduct. This may include:

a. Non-monetary damages (e.g., Equitable damages)
b. Penalties paid to the court
c. Payment of another party's expenses/lawyer's fees

(5) Limitation of sanctions: Money damages are not awarded for:

(A) Violations of 11(b)(2) (pleading not warranted by law) against represented party

(B) When initiated by Court (Rule 11(c)(1)(B)), unless the Court issues an Order to Show Cause *before* either:

1. A Voluntary Dismissal (made by or against a party (or attorney) to be sanctioned)

or 2. A Settlement of Claims (made by or against a party (or attorney) to be sanctioned)

(6) Order: Court shall prescribe conduct and basis for sanction

(d) Inapplicability to discovery—Rule 11 does not apply to:

1. Disclosures
2. Discovery requests
3. Responses
4. Objections
5. Motions subject to provisions in Rules 26–37

Rule 12. Defenses and Objections; When and How; Motion for Judgment on the Pleadings; Consolidating and Waiving Defenses; Pretrial Hearing

(a) Time frame for parties to respond

(1) Answers, Complaints, and Counterclaim replies

(A) Answer and Complaint: Unless a federal statute supersedes, the *Answer* must be served:

(i) *If summons served*: the answer must be served within 20 days after service (extended if out-of-state).

(ii) *If service waived*: the answer must be served within 60 days after request for waiver is *sent* (90 if outside of the U.S.).

(B) Answer to a Cross-claim: If the Answer is in response to a Cross-claim, π has 20 days from the date the Cross-claim was served.

(C) Response to a Counterclaim: The π shall reply to a Counterclaim:

1. Within 20 Days after service of Defendant's answer
2. Within 20 Days after service of a court order, if π's reply is ordered by the court (unless the order directs otherwise)

Extension for United States

(2) If the United States is a party, it shall have 60 days after the United States Attorney is served to respond.

(3) If an officer or employee of the United States is sued in his individual capacity (for acts or omissions while performing his duties on behalf of the United States), he has 60 days after he is served, or after the United States Attorney is served (whichever is later).

(4) Exceptions to time limit: The time limitations above will not apply in the following cases:

(A) *If a Court denies the motion or postpones disposition*—the Answer is due within 10 days after Court notifies of decision to proceed

or (B) *If a Court grants motion for a more definite statement*—the Answer is due within 10 days after receipt of π's revised pleadings

(b) How presented:

i. All Defenses must be made in answer, *except for*:
   (1) Motion for lack of Subject Matter Jurisdiction
   (2) Motion for lack of Personal Jurisdiction
   (3) Motion for improper venue
   (4) Motion for insufficiency of process
   (5) Motion for insufficiency of service of process
   (6) Motion for failure to state a valid claim upon which relief can be granted
   (7) Motion for failure to join a party under Rule 19

ii. The above defenses are made in a pre-answer motion.

iii. Where no response to a Pleading is required, the above defenses may be made at trial.

iv. There is no waiver by joining a defense with other defenses or objections

(c) Motion for judgment on the pleadings may be made after the pleadings if it does not delay the trial.

(d) Implied motion for summary judgment

1. A 12(b)(6) motion is treated as a motion for summary judgment (Rule 56) if:
   a. The 12(b)(6) motion is made (failure to state a claim).
   and b. Matters outside the pleading are presented to the court (which are not excluded by the court).
2. In such a case, all parties shall be given a reasonable opportunity to present all material pertinent to such a motion (Rule 56).

(e) Motion for more definite statement:

1. This motion may be made if π's pleadings are too vague/ambiguous so that Defendant cannot reasonably frame a response.
2. The motion must point out the defects in π's pleadings.
3. If granted, the π must re-plead within 10 days of the notice of motion (otherwise the court may strike pleadings or make any other order).

(f) Motion to strike

- This may be done by
  - (1) The court's own motion
  - or (2) A party's motion made before answering (or 20 days after being served, if no Answer is allowed)
- The court may order something stricken from the pleadings if it contains:
  1. Insufficient defenses
  2. Redundancies
  3. Immaterialities
  4. Scandalous matter

(g) Consolidating defense—

(1) A party can join motions under this rule with any other motions available to the Defendant.

(2) If this motion is made, any available Rule 12(b) defenses that are omitted will be deemed to be <u>waived</u> (unless allowed by 12(h)(2) or (3)).

(h) Waiver or preservation of defenses—

(1) Objection to

a. Lack of <u>Personal Jurisdiction</u> (Rule 12(b)(2))

or b. Improper <u>Venue</u> (Rule 12(b)(3))

or c. Insufficiency of <u>Process</u> (Rule 12(b)(4))

or d. Insufficiency of <u>Service</u> (Rule 12(b)(5)) <u>will be **waived if:**</u>

(A) Omitted from Consolidated of motions (12(g)) (i.e., if you make one, you must make all)

or (B) Omitted from:

(i) A Rule 12 Motion

or (ii) A Responsive Pleading or a Rule 15(a) amendment

(2) Other motions

- Other motions are made
  - (A) In any Rule 7(a) pleading
  - (B) In a 12(c) Motion
  - (C) At trial
- This includes:
  - a. Failure to state a valid Claim (Rule 12(b)(6))
  - b. Failure to Join a third party under Rule 19 (Rule 12(b)(7))
  - c. Failure to State a Legal Defense

(3) Motion for <u>Lack of Subject Matter Jurisdiction</u> (Rule 12(b)(1)) may be made AT ANY TIME (even after judgment).

(i) Preliminary hearings on any motions (under 12(b)(1)-(7)) shall be granted upon the request of any party, unless the judge decides to defer the hearing until trial.

Rule 13. Counterclaims/Cross-claims

(a) Compulsory Counterclaims

(1) A "*Compulsory Counterclaim*" must be raised and:
  (A) Includes any claim "arising out of" the initial action *(i.e., they must arise out of the "same transaction or occurrence")*.
  (B) Does not include adding third parties not subject to the court's jurisdiction.

(2) Exceptions: The Counterclaim must be stated in the pleading *unless:*
  (A) The claim is already subject to another pending action.
  (B) The Defendant brings the suit by attachment or process without the Court's jurisdiction.

(b) Permissive Counterclaim is any claim against an opposing party (not a new party) whether or not related to the case.

(c) Relief sought in Counterclaim—Counterclaims may seek more relief or different relief than the original claims that the opposing party had sought.

(d) Counterclaims against the U.S.—These rules do not enlarge the present limits (fixed by statute) of asserting Counterclaims against the U.S. government.

(e) Post-pleading Counterclaims—may be presented as a counterclaim in a "supplemental pleading," if the Court allows.

(f) Omitted Counterclaim—a pleader may obtain leave of court, to Counterclaim by amending the pleading, only if it is omitted by

1. Oversight
or 2. Inadvertence
or 3. Excusable neglect
or 4. *When justice so requires.*

(g) Cross-claims against a co-party—are usually considered permissive.

1. Guarantors Same Transaction: May allow Cross-claim against a co-party for a claim either:
  a. *Arising out of the same transaction or occurrence* of *either*:
    1. The original action
    or 2. A Counterclaim
  or b. Relating to any property subject to the original action

2. Indemnity: Cross-claims may include a claim to a co-party to indemnify the claimant for all or part of the liability arising out of the action.

(h) Joinder of additional parties—parties may be joined in Counterclaims and Cross-claims (pursuant to Rules 19 and 20).

(i) Separate trials; separate judgments—Judgment on a Cross-claim or Counterclaim may be made in accordance with Rule 54(b) (even if the claims of the opposing party have been dismissed or otherwise disposed of) if:

1. A Court orders separate trials pursuant to Rule 42(b)

and 2. The Court has jurisdiction to do so.

Rule 14. Third-Party Practice

(a) When Defendant may bring a third party

(1) Making third-party claims:

- At any time after the commencement of a case, the Defendant may become a "third-party π" by serving a Complaint on a third party (who is not in the original action). This happens when the Defendant feels that the third party is liable to *indemnify* the Defendant for any judgment (e.g., insurance company or surety).
- If the Defendant serves the third party no later than 10 days after serving its original Answer, no "leave of court" is needed to serve the third party. After 10 days, the Defendant must get "leave of court" by filing a motion with notice to all parties.
- The third party is then known as a "Third-Party Defendant" and the Defendant is known as a "Third-Party Plaintiff."

(2) The third-party defendant must

(A) assert all defenses

(B) assert all compulsory (Rule 13(a)) counterclaims against the defendant or cross-claims (Rule 13(g)) against any other defendant The third-party defendant may: assert all permissive (Rule 13(b)) counterclaims against the defendant

(C) assert defenses against the plaintiff's claim

(D) assert counterclaims against the plaintiff if they arise out of the same transaction as the plaintiff's claims against the defendant

(3) π may claim against the third-party defendant if the claim arises out of the same transaction as the claim against the defendant

(4) Any party may move to:

a. Strike third-party claim

or b. Sever the claim

or c. Separate trial

(5) A third party may bring in a fourth party who may also be liable to the Defendant or the third party (Note: Complete diversity is not needed for third party.)

(6) Admiralty and maritime claims

a. If the third-party complaint is within admiralty jurisdiction, may be *in rem* against:

- a vessel
- cargo
- or other property subject to admiralty cases *in rem*

b. Terminology: In these cases:

- The word "Summons" (in the Rules) applies to the Warrant of Arrest
- The words "Plaintiff/Defendant" (in the Rules) apply to any person asserting a claim (See Admiralty Rule C(6)(a)(1)).

(b) When π may bring a third party: When a claim is made against the π (like, for example, a counterclaim), the π may bring in a third party just as the Defendant (under Rule 14(a)).

(c) Admiralty and maritime claims

(1) When a plaintiff brings an admiralty or maritime claim (within the meaning of Rule 9(h)), a defendant (or claimant) may bring in a Third-Party defendant for contribution or indemnity, or otherwise on account of the same transaction or occurrence.

(2) If the defendant demands judgment in the plaintiff's favor against the third-party defendant, the third-party defendant must defend under Rule 12 against both the plaintiff's claim and the defendant's third-party claim, and the case goes forward as if the plaintiff had sued both the third-party defendant and the third-party plaintiff.

Rule 15. Amended and Supplemental Pleadings

(a) Amendments:

(1) Parties have a *right* to 1 amendment:

(A) Before the answer or responding pleading is served.

(B) In a non-responsive pleading, 20 days after the pleading is served.

(2) Otherwise, amending party must:

a. Request a *"leave of court"* to amend the pleading (Court must consent when "*justice so requires*")

or b. Obtain written consent from the adverse parties

(3) Answering amended pleadings—must be done within the *longer of:*

a. 10 days after service of the amendment

or b. The time remaining within the original 20-day response period (from the initial pleading)

(b) Amendments during or after trial

(1) Objections to issues during trial

a. If a party objects to amendments, new evidence, or issues not explicitly included in pleadings, the court may still grant/allow if it will *promote justice* (and the other party cannot show prejudice).

b. The court may grant a continuance to allow the objecting party to meet the evidence.

(2) Issues tried by consent

a. Issues *expressly* or *impliedly* consented to by parties are considered to have been raised in pleadings (although they never were).

b. Parties may make a *Motion to Amend* the Pleadings (to conform to the evidence) at any time, even after judgment.

c. Failure to amend does not affect the result of the trial on that issue.

(c) Relation back of amendments:

(1) Amendments will be considered to relate back to date of the original pleading if:

(A) Permitted by the law providing for the Statute of Limitations in the case

or (B) They are related to the original claims (i.e., arising out of the same conduct, transaction, or occurrence)

or (C) There were misidentified parties in original claim. Such amendments will relate back to date of pleading only upon reasonable notice if:

(i) A Party has received notice of the action and will not be prejudiced in maintaining a defense on the merits.

and (ii) The Party knew or should have known that the action would have been taken against her, *but for* the fact that there was a mistake as to her actual identity.

(2) **Notice to the United States.** When the U.S. (or an officer or agency of the U.S.) is added as a defendant by amendment, 15(c)(1)(C)(i) and (ii) are satisfied if process was delivered or mailed to the U.S. Attorney, the U.S. Attorney General, or to the officer or agency.

(d) Supplemental pleadings:

1. Upon Motion, Pleadings may be amended for events occurring *after* service of the original pleadings if:
   a. Reasonable notice is given
   and b. The terms are just
2. Supplemental Pleadings must set forth the transactions or events that have happened since the date the original pleading was drafted.
3. Permission to supplement a pleading may be granted, even though the original pleading has a defective statement claiming relief or defense.
4. If the court deems it advisable, it may order the opposing party to respond within a specified time.

Rule 16. Pretrial Conferences

(a) Objectives: A Court may order (at its discretion) that parties appear for a conference to:

(1) Expedite disposition of a case
or (2) Establish early controls, so that the case is not "protracted" from lack of management
or (3) Discourage wasteful pre-trial activities
or (4) Improve the quality of trial with better preparation
or (5) Facilitate Settlement of the case

(b) Scheduling and planning

(1) **Contents of the order:** The Judge (or Magistrate) shall enter a Scheduling order
  (A) After receiving the parties' 26(f) report
  or (B) After consulting with the parties (at a scheduling conference or by phone, mail, etc.)

(2) **Timing for the scheduling order:**
  a. The Order shall be made ASAP, after the parties' Rule 26(f) report is received (or after a phone or other conference with the parties)
  b. The Order must be made no later than:
    - 120 days after the complaint has been served

and • <u>90 days</u> after Defendant has made an appearance limiting the time to:

(3) **Contents**

(A) Required contents

- Time to Join other parties
- Time to Amend Pleadings
- Time to File Motions
- Time to Complete Discovery (outside deadline)

(B) Optional contents

(i) Modifications of the 26(a) and 26(e)(1) Disclosure Times

(ii) Modifications of the extent of discovery

(iii) Dates for pre-trial conferences and trial

(iv) *Any other appropriate matters*

(4) **Modification of scheduling order:** The Schedule may only be modified by *both:*

a. The court's permission

and b. Showing of good cause

(c) Attendance and matters for consideration at a pretrial conference— Participants may consider and take action regarding:

(A) Attendance

1. At least one of each party's attorneys must be present at any pre-trial conference, and must have the authority to:

   a. Enter into stipulations

   b. Make admissions (regarding matter anticipated to be discussed)

2. The court may require that a party or representative be present or *reasonably available* (for example, by phone) to consider settlement.

(B) Matters for consideration

(A) Formulation/Simplification of Issues to eliminate frivolous claims

(B) Necessity/Desirability of amending pleadings

(C) Possibility of obtaining Disclosure/Admissions to reduce factual disputes

(D) Avoidance of unnecessary proof of evidence and limitations of evidence (pursuant to Federal Rules of Evidence)

(E) Appropriateness/Timing of a Rule 56 Summary Judgment Motion.

(F) Control/Scheduling of Discovery (Rule 26 and Rules 29–37)

(G) Pretrial Matters:

i. Identifying Witnesses/Documents

and ii. Preparing a schedule for

- Exchanging pretrial briefs
- Further conferences

and • Trial

(H) Referring matters to a Magistrate
(I) Settlement and use of ADR (Alternate Dispute Resolution)
(J) Form or Substance of the pre-trial order
(K) Disposition of pending motions
(L) Adopting special procedures for specific complex issues (or unusual proof problems)
(M) Orders for separate trials (per Rule 42(b))
(N) Orders to present certain evidence early (to facilitate early judgments) (pursuant to Rule 50(a) and 52(c))
(O) Orders establishing a reasonable time limit for presenting evidence
(P) Other matters to facilitate a "just, speedy, and inexpensive" disposition of the case

(d) Pretrial orders

1. After each conference, an order shall be filed, reciting the action taken at the conference.
2. Orders may be modified only by a subsequent order.

(e) Final pretrial conference and orders

1. A Final Pretrial Conference may be held.
2. It should be held as close to the trial date as reasonably possible.
3. It should include a trial plan and a discussion of evidence.
4. At least one trial attorney per party must appear.
5. Orders after a Final Pre-Trial Conference may be modified only to prevent *manifest injustice.*

(f) Sanctions

(1) In general: Rule 37 sanctions may (by the court or by motion) be invoked if a party or attorney:

(A) Does not appear at a conference
(B) comes unprepared to participate in the conference (or does not participate in good faith).
(C) fails to obey a scheduling order

(2) Imposing fees and costs

a. The court *must* order the reimbursement of reasonable expenses (this includes attorneys' fees) incurred because of a violation of this rule
b. The award of expenses and fees may be made against:
    - the party
    - the attorney
    - or both

c. This award may be made <u>instead of</u> or <u>in addition to</u> any other sanction.

d. <u>Exceptions</u>:

    i. If the noncompliance was "substantially justified"

    ii. If other circumstances make the award of expenses "unjust."

ARTICLE IV
PARTIES

Rule 17. The Plaintiff and Defendant; Capacity; Public Officers

(a) Real party in interest

(1) Designation in general

1. Every case must be prosecuted in the name of the real party in interest, except for the following, who may sue in their own names (without joining the beneficiary):
    - (A) an executor
    - (B) an administrator
    - (C) a guardian
    - (D) a bailee
    - (E) a trustee of an express trust
    - (F) the named party in a contract made for another's benefit
    - (G) a party authorized by statute

(2) Action in the name of the U.S. for another's use or benefit
The U.S. may sue on behalf of a beneficiary if a statute so provides.

(3) Joinder of the real party in interest

a. A case cannot be dismissed because it was not originally brought in the name of the interested party.
b. A Court may dismiss a case if it gave π *reasonable time* for an interested party to *"ratify"* the action (bring it in its name).
c. Once an interested party ratifies an action, the action will be considered to have been commenced at the time the original party brought the action.

(b) Capacity to sue or be sued—Capacity to sue shall be determined:

(1) For an individual: by the law in the party's state of *domicile*
(2) For a corporation: by the law in the state in which it was *organized*
(3) For all other cases: by the law in the state of the District Court (i.e., Forum State) *unless*:
- (A) For a Partnership or Unincorporated Association; it may sue in its common name for cases involving Federal rights (only if it has no capacity to sue under state law)
- (B) 28 USC § 754 and § 959(a) govern the capacity of a receiver appointed by the U.S.

(c) Minors or incompetent persons

(1) *Those with representatives*: The following representatives may sue (or be sued) on behalf of the infant or incompetent:
(A) a general guardian
(B) a committee
(C) a conservator
(D) another (similar) fiduciary

(2) *Those without representatives*: *Infants/Incompetents without general guardians, etc.*: The court shall appoint a representative or *"guardian ad litem"* to represent the infant or incompetent in court.

(d) Public officer's title and name

1. A public officer may be named by title, not name
2. The court may order that the name be added

Rule 18. Joinder of Claims

(a) Joinder of claims — A party may join *as many* independent or alternate claims as it has against an **opposing** party. These include:

1. Original claims
2. Counterclaims
3. Cross-claims
4. Third-party claims

(b) Joinder of remedies — Whenever a claim is dependent on the outcome of a claim in another action, the two cases may be joined into a single action.

Rule 19. Required Joinder of Parties

(a) Persons to be joined (if feasible)

(1) Required party

1. Requirements:
   a. Joined parties must be subject to Personal Jurisdiction
   and b. Joinder cannot destroy SMJ (diversity)
2. A third party MUST be joined if:
   (A) *Complete relief* cannot be accorded among the present parties without joining the third party

or (B) The third party claims a *related interest* in the action, and its absence from the suit may:
  (i) Impair or Impede its ability to protect that interest.
  or (ii) Leave any of the present parties subject to <u>double liability</u> or <u>inconsistent verdicts</u>

(2) Joinder by court order

a. The court *must* order a required party to be joined.

b. If a third party refuses to be a π, he may, upon the Court's discretion, be made:
  i. A Defendant
  or ii. An *Involuntary* π

(3) Venue: If a third party objects to venue, and his presence makes venue improper, the joinder will be dismissed (and the entire case itself will also be dismissed if third party is considered an "*<u>indispensable party</u>*").

(b) When joinder is not feasible

1. The court may determine that a third party is needed and dismiss the case if he cannot be joined.
2. A party is needed if, "*in equity and good conscience,*" the case should not proceed without him.
3. <u>**Factors considered:**</u> (to determine if a third party is needed in the case):
   (1) The Extent of prejudice to the existing parties that the third party's absence may bring
   (2) The Extent that prejudices may be avoided or reduced by other means, like:
     (A) protective provisions in the judgment
     (B) shaping the relief
     or (C) other measures
   (3) The Adequacy of judgment without the third party
   (4) Whether the π will have an adequate remedy if the case were dismissed for nonjoinder.

(c) Pleading the reasons for nonjoinder. A party must state (in his claim):

(1) the name of any person who must be joined if feasible but is not joined (if the name is known)

and (2) the reasons for not joining that person.

(d) Exception for class actions. This rule is subject to Rule 23 (Class Actions).

Rule 20. Permissive Joinder of Parties

(a) Persons who may join or be joined

(1) Plaintiffs — Plaintiffs may sue together in the same case:
- i. They may sue jointly, severally or in the alternative
- ii. They must assert a claim which *both*:
  - (A) Arises out of the same transaction or occurrence (or series of transactions or occurrences)
  - and (B) Has a question of law or fact common to all co-parties in the action

(2) Defendants — Defendants may be sued together in the same case:
- i. This includes property subject to a case in rem
- ii. They must be subject to a claim which *both*:
  - (A) Arises out of the same transaction or occurrence (or series of transactions or occurrences)
  - and (B) Has a question of law or fact common to all co-parties in the action

(3) Extent of relief: There is no need for all plaintiffs or defendants to seek all claims of relief being claimed in the action; judgment will be made according to each party's rights or liabilities.

(b) Protective measures — The court may order separate trials or make *other such orders* to prevent:

1. A party from being embarrassed
or 2. Delay
or 3. Prejudice
or 4. A party from incurring undue expense from the inclusion of a third party, if no claims exists between the parties.

Rule 21. Misjoinder and Nonjoinder of Parties

1. Misjoinder is NOT a ground for dismissal of a case.
2. Parties may be dropped or added at any stage of the action by:
   - a. Motion
   - or b. Court's initiative
3. Any claim against a party may be severed and proceeded with separately (see Rule 42).

Rule 22. Interpleader

("Rule Interpleader"—requires complete diversity)

(a) Grounds

(1) By a Plaintiff: Interpleader is appropriate if a π might be exposed to double liability.

a. Interpleader may take place, even though:

(A) There is no common origin of causes or they are not identical—but are adverse and independent cases

or (B) The plaintiff denies liability to any claimant

(2) By a Defendant: A defendant may also interplead (by cross-claim or counterclaim) if he might be exposed to double liability.

(b) Relation to other rules and statutes: This remedy does not supersede 28 USC § 1335, § 1397, or § 2361

Rule 23. Class Actions

(a) Prerequisites to a class action—one or more members of a class may sue or be sued as representative parties IF:

(1) "Numerosity": The class is so large that the joinder of all members is impracticable.

and (2) "Commonality": There is a common question of law or fact involved.

and (3) "Typicality": Claims or defenses of the representative parties are typical of the rest of the class.

and (4) "Adequacy": The Representative parties will adequately and fairly protect the class's interests.

(b) Class actions maintainable: 23(a) must be satisfied and *either:*

(1) Separate actions by individual members would create a risk of

(A) *Inconsistent/Varying adjudications*, which would establish incompatible standards of conduct for the opposing party (mostly used in property actions, nuisance, or reward cases)

or (B) Adjudication for an individual member which would *substantially* impair or impede other members from taking action or protecting themselves (mostly for declaratory judgments, injunctions)

or (2) The opposing party has acted similarly adverse to the entire class

or (3) i. The court finds that (mostly for damages)

a. The facts common to class are *predominate over* the facts specific to each individual and b. A class action would be the best way for *fair and efficient* adjudication

ii. Pertinent considerations which court must weigh:

(A) The *Interest of members* to individually control their own cases

(B) The *Extent and nature of litigation* involved

(C) The *Desirability of concentrating the litigation* in a particular forum

(D) The *Difficulties likely to be encountered* in managing the class action (e.g., expenses)

(c) Order determining whether class action should be certified:

(1) The court order for certification

(A) When a person sues or is sued as a class representative, the court *must* determine (by order) whether to certify as a class action.

(B) The order must:

i. Define the class

ii. Define the class claims, issues, or defenses

iii. Appoint "class counsel" under Rule 23(g)

(C) A Rule 23(c)(1) order may be altered or amended before final judgment.

(2) Notice requirements[14]

(A) *For 23(b)(1) or (2) classes:* The court may direct appropriate notice to the class.

(B) *For 23(b)(3) classes:*

i. The Court *must* direct the best notice under the circumstances.

ii. Notice must advise each member (in plain and easy language):

(i) The nature of the case

(ii) The class definition

(iii) The class claims, issues, or defenses

(iv) That a member may appear through a lawyer if she desires

(v) That the Court will exclude the member from the class upon a member's request (before the specified date)

(vi) How to request exclusion

(vii) The binding effect of a judgment on the class (under Rule 23(c)(3))

[14] In 2003 the notice provisions to Rule 23 were substantially revised.

(3) Judgment:
   (A) *Judgments in Class Actions under (b)(1) and (b)(2)*—These judgments apply to all people whom the court finds to be members of the class.
   (B) *Judgments in Class Actions under (b)(3)*—These judgments apply to all people whom the court finds to be members of the class if:
      1. The members received appropriate notice of the action
      and 2. The members did not request exclusion from the class
(4) Particular Issues: A class action may be brought with respect to particular issues only
(5) Subclasses: A class may be subdivided into subclasses (each subclass shall be treated as a separate class)

(d) Orders in conduct of actions:

(1) In general: The court may issue orders to:
   (A) Prescribe measures to prevent due repetition or complication
   (B) Require specific methods of notice.
      1. The objective would be to protect class members and to conduct the case fairly.
      2. Notice includes notice of:
         (i) any step in the case
         (ii) the proposed extent of the judgment
         (iii) the class members' opportunity to:
            - inform the court whether they consider the representation *"fair and adequate"*
            - to intervene and present claims/defenses
            - to otherwise come into the case
   (C) Impose conditions on representative parties
   (D) Require that pleadings be amended to represent class
   (E) Deal with similar procedural matters

(2) Combining and amending orders:
   a. A Rule 23(d)(1) order may be combined with a Rule 16 order
   b. Such orders may be *altered or amended* as the court sees fit

(e) Settlement, dismissal, or compromise—The court must approve any settlements (or dismissals), subject to the following procedures

(1) Notice: The court *must* direct notice to all members who would be bound by the settlement (or dismissal)
(2) Hearing: The court needs to have a hearing (to determine if the settlement is *fair, reasonable and adequate*) before approving a settlement that binds class members.
(3) Agreements Made in Connection with a Settlement: Parties seeking approval of a settlement must file a statement showing any agreement made in connection with the proposed settlement.
(4) New Opportunity for Exclusion: If a case was previously certified under 23(b)(3), the court may condition approval of a settlement on a new notice to the class members to opt out of the class (even though they got notice already and did not request exclusion).
(5) Objections to Settlements Requiring Approval:
    a. Who May Object: Any class member
    b. Withdrawing Objections: May only be done with Court's approval.

(f) Appeals:

1. A court of appeals may permit an appeal from a district court order that grants or denies class action certification.
2. Time: Application for an appeal must be made within 10 days after entry of the order denying or granting the certification.
3. Stay of Proceedings: An appeal does not stay the District Court proceedings unless ordered by either:
    a. The district court judge
    b. The court of appeals

(g) Class counsel

(1) Appointing class counsel: A court that certifies a class must appoint "class counsel" (unless a statute provides otherwise)
  (A) Mandatory criteria: The court *must* consider:
    (i) The attorney's work done in identifying or investigating potential claims in the case,
    (ii) The attorney's experience in:
      1. class actions
      2. other complex litigation, and
      3. claims of the type asserted in the action,
    (iii) The attorney's knowledge of the applicable law, and
    (iv) the resources the attorney will commit to representing the class
  (B) Discretionary criteria: The court may consider any other matter pertinent to whether counsel will *"fairly and adequately"* represent the interests of the class.

(C) Other court directions: The court may direct potential class counsel to:

1. provide information on any subject pertinent to the appointment
2. propose attorney fee (and costs) terms

(D) Attorney's fees awards: The court order appointing counsel may include provisions about the award of fees or costs (dealt with in Rule 23(h)).

(E) The court may make "further orders" in connection with the appointment.

(2) Standard for appointing class counsel

1. When There Is One Applicant: The court may appoint that applicant only if the applicant qualifies under Rule 23(g)(1)(B) and (C).
2. When There Is More Than One Applicant: The court *must* appoint the best applicant.

(3) Interim counsel: The court may designate interim counsel to act for the would-be class (before determining whether to certify the action as a class action).

(4) Duty of class counsel: "Class counsel must fairly and adequately represent the interests of the class."

(h) Attorney fees award. In a certified class action, the court may award reasonable attorney fees and costs (authorized by law or by agreement of the parties) as follows:

(1) Motion for award of attorney fees.

a. An attorney must make a motion for fees and costs under Rule 54(d)(2).
b. Notice of the motion must be served on all parties.
c. Motions made by class counsel must be directed to the class members in a *reasonable manner.*

(2) Objections to motion. The following people may object to the motion for fees:

a. A class member
b. Any party from whom payment is sought

(3) Hearing and findings.

a. The court *must* make findings of fact and conclusions of law on the motion (following Rule 52(a))b. The court may hold a hearing.

(4) Reference to special master or magistrate judge. The court may refer issues related to the amount of the award to a special master or to a magistrate judge (as provided in Rule 54(d)(2)(D)).

Rule 23.1. Derivative Actions

(a) Prerequisites

1. This rule applies in a derivative action brought by one or more shareholders to enforce a right of a corporation
2. Derivative action may not be maintained if it appears that π does not adequately represent the interests of class (shareholders, members, and other similarly situated members).

(b) Pleading requirements: Shareholders must prepare (and verify) a complaint that:

(1) Alleges that the π was a shareholder
  a. At the time of the transaction π is complaining about
  or b. After the transaction, and π 's shares devolved on the π by operation of law

and (2) Alleges that the action is not a collusive one to confer jurisdiction in a Federal Court, in which it otherwise may NOT have such jurisdiction

and (3) Alleges <u>with</u> particularity that:
  (A) The efforts (if any) made by π to obtain a remedy directly with the corporate directors/officers/shareholders
  (B) The reasons why π's efforts to remedy the situation failed

(c) Settlement, dismissal, and compromise

1. The court *must* approve proposed settlements
2. Class representatives must notify the class of any settlement (notification to be given in a manner proposed by court)

Rule 23.2. Actions Relating to Unincorporated Associations

1. This rule applies in a derivative action brought by one or more shareholders to enforce a right of a corporation.

2. Cases brought by or against unincorporated associations may be maintained only if it appears that the representatives will fairly and adequately represent the entire class.

3. <u>Procedures during the case</u>:

   a. The court may issue any order that corresponds with Rule 23(d).
   b. The procedure for settlement, voluntary dismissal, or compromise must correspond with the procedure in Rule 23(e).

Rule 24. Intervention

(a) Intervention of right

i. Anyone may intervene (upon timely motion) in a case when:
   (1) A federal statute allows (unconditionally)
   or (2) The Applicant claims a *direct* interest in a *related property or transaction* subject to adjudication, but only if:
      a. The moving party's interest isn't already properly represented in the case.
      or b. The moving party has a direct "*significantly protectable*" interest at stake and not intervening will impair/impede the applicant's ability to protect that interest

Note: A party may not intervene if Complete Diversity will not be maintained.

(b) Permissive intervention

(1) In general: Anyone may intervene (upon timely motion) in a case when:
   (A) A federal statute allows (conditionally)
   or (B) The moving party's claim is related to the main action by question of law or fact

(2) By a government officer or agency: A federal or state officer or agency may intervene (upon timely motion) in a case when the party's claim or defense is based on:
   (A) That officer's or agency's statute or executive order
   or (B) Any regulation, order, requirement, or agreement made under the statute or executive order

(3) Delay or prejudice: The court has discretion, and should weigh any delays & prejudices to the original parties (resulting from the intervention).

(c) Procedure—notice and pleading required:

1. The Intervening party shall serve a *Motion to Intervene* (per Rule 5).
2. Requirements of motion to intervene—the motion must:
   a. State the grounds for intervention
   and b. Be accompanied by a pleading describing the claim or defense (that intervention is being sought for).

Rule 25. Substitution of Parties

(a) Death

(1) Substitution if the claim is not extinguished

a. If a party dies, and his claim is not extinguished, a *Motion for Substitution* may be made by:
   1. Any other party of the suit
   or 2. The successors or representatives of the deceased.

b. A Motion for Substitution must be made within 90 days of record of the party's death.

(2) Continuation among the remaining parties: If there are multiple parties on either side and one party dies, the suit will not be dismissed, and any liability of the claim will remain with the survivors.

(3) Service: Notice of hearing and motion shall be served on all parties and involved non-parties (pursuant to Rule 4 and 5)

(b) Incompetency

1. If a party becomes incompetent, the court may allow the suit to continue in the name of a representative of the incompetent person.
2. A Motion for Substitution must be made within 90 days of record of party's Incompetency.
3. The motion and notice of hearing shall be served on all parties and involved non-parties (pursuant to Rules 4 and 5).

(c) Transfer of interest

1. If there is a transfer of interest:
   a. The original party may continue in the action.
   or b. The transferee may substitute the original party.
   or c. The transferee may be joined with the original party.
   or d. The court may direct that the transferee substitute the original party.
2. Motion for Substitution must be made within 90 days of record of party's transfer.
3. Notice of hearing and motion shall be served on all parties and involved non-parties (pursuant to Rules 4 and 5).

(d) Public officers

a. If a Public Officer acting in a case in an official capacity dies or leaves office, the officer's successor shall automatically be substituted.

b. Further proceedings in the action shall be made in the name of the substituted party.
c. An order of substitution may be entered at any time.
d. Failure to make an order of substitution will *not* affect the substitution.

ARTICLE V
DISCOVERY AND DEPOSITIONS

Rule 26. Duty to Disclose; General Provisions Governing Discovery

(a) Required disclosures—Methods to discover:

(1) Initial disclosure[15]

(A) A party must provide (without waiting for a discovery request):

(i) **People** (name, address, phone number (if available), and subject of the information) *likely to have discoverable information* that the disclosing party may use (this does not include people with information that will be used only to impeach other testimony)

(ii) Relevant **Documents, electronic information, and tangible things** (or a description and location, by category) that are in the possession, custody, or control of the party, and that the disclosing party may use (this does not include information that will be used only to impeach other testimony)

(iii) **Computation of damages,** *unless* privileged or protected

(iv) **Insurance agreements** which may indemnify or pay part of judgment

(v) Exceptions: The Initial Disclosure rules *do not apply*:

1. In cases specified in Rule 26(a)(1)(E) (added December 1, 2000)
2. If the parties stipulate otherwise
3. If the court orders otherwise

(B) **Exemptions from initial disclosure:**

(i) Action for review on an administrative record

(ii) Forfeiture action (in rem) arising from a federal statute

---

[15] In 2000, Rule 26(a)(1) was amended to add certain exemptions to the Initial Disclosure requirements. The rule was also narrowed to require only information that the disclosing party may use to support its position. The timing was also changed to provide for 14 days instead of 10 days, to provide time for parties joining the case late, and to provide time for objections to the Initial Disclosure rule.

(iii) Petition for habeas corpus (or other proceeding to challenge a conviction or sentence)
(iv) Action brought *pro se* by a person in the custody of the U.S. (or a state)
(v) Action to enforce or quash an administrative summons or subpoena
(vi) Action by the U.S. to recover benefit payments
(vii) Action by the U.S. to collect on a student loan guaranteed by the U.S.
(viii) Ancillary proceedings (ancillary to proceedings in other courts)
(ix) Action to enforce an arbitration award

(C) <u>Timing (in general)</u>:
1. Disclosures shall be made within <u>14 days</u> after the meeting of the parties (pursuant to Rule 26(f))
2. A different time may be set by stipulation or court order.
3. If a party objects to Initial Disclosures (generally) during the Rule 26(f) conference and in the Rule 26(f) Plan, the court sets the time for disclosures after deciding on the objection.

(D) <u>Timing (for parties joined later)</u>: If a party is served or joined after the Rule 26(f) conference, Initial Disclosures must be made within <u>30 days</u> after being served or joined (unless otherwise stipulated or ordered).

(E) <u>Basis for initial disclosure; unacceptable excuses</u>: All *"reasonably available"* information must be submitted. It is <u>not</u> a valid excuse that:
1. Investigations are not fully complete
or 2. Opponents' discovery is insufficient
or 3. Opponents failed to submit discovery

(2) <u>Disclosure of expert testimony</u>:
(A) A party must disclose the identity of all expert witnesses who may be used at trial (to present evidence under Rules 702, 703, and 705 of the Federal Rules of Evidence)
(B) Experts must submit and sign a <u>written report</u> containing:
(i) A complete statement of *all* opinions which may be expressed at trial and the basis and reasons for the expert's opinion
and (ii) Data and information on which the opinion is based
and (iii) Exhibits to be used to support the opinion
and (iv) Qualifications of the expert (including all publications within the past 10 years)

and (v) A listing of all previous cases in which the expert had testified (*either* at trial or deposition)

and (vi) Compensation to be paid for the study or testifying

(C) The **due date** of expert disclosures is (unless the court changes):

(i) Initial expert testimony: At least 90 days before trial

(ii) Rebutting expert testimony (responding to initial testimony): Within 30 Days of the initial expert disclosure

(D) Supplementing the disclosure: The parties must supplement these disclosures when required under Rule 26(e).

(3) Pretrial disclosures

(A) For any evidence to be used at trial, a party shall disclose and *promptly* file with the court:

(i) The **name**, **address**, **phone number** of each witness, and the subject matter of their testimony (if not already provided), separately indicating which witnesses may appear at trial and which may not.

(ii) **Designation** of witnesses whose testimony is expected to be by deposition.

(iii) Appropriate **identification** of each document and exhibit, and summaries of evidence

(B) Other disclosure rules:

1. Pretrial disclosure must be submitted at least 30 days before trial.
2. Within 14 days after pretrial disclosure, a party may file a list disclosing:
   (i) Any objections to the use of depositions
   (ii) Any objections to the admissibility of materials (with a reason for the objection)
3. If objections are not made before 14 days, they are deemed to be waived, unless excused for *good cause*.

(4) Form of disclosure; filing—All disclosures shall be:

a. In writing

and b. Signed

and c. Served

and d. Promptly filed in court

(b) Discovery scope and limits

Note: This rule is subject to limitations that the court may impose (under the rules).

(1) Scope in general

a. A party may obtain discovery regarding any matter that is:
   1. Not privileged

   and 2. Relevant to the claim or defense of any party

b. "Relevant" information need only to appear *reasonably calculated* to lead to the discovery of admissible evidence; it does not necessarily have to be admissible.

c. Relevant information can include information about:
   i. Books, documents, or other tangible things

   or ii. The identity of people with knowledge of any discoverable matter

d. The court may also order discovery of any matter "relevant to the subject matter involved in the lawsuit," but only for **good cause.**

e. All discovery is subject to the limitations of Rule 26(b)(2)(B).

(2) Limitations

(A) Optional limitations:

1. Courts (and not Local Rules[16]) can set limits on the <u>length</u> and <u>number</u> of depositions and the number of interrogatories.
2. Local Rules or Courts may set limits on the number of Requests for Admissions (R. 36).

(B) Required limitations: Discovery shall be limited if the court determines (see subsection (c) below for how the Court makes this determination) that:

(i) The discovery sought is:

a. unreasonably cumulative or duplicative

or b. obtainable from a more convenient or less expensive source

or (ii) The party making the request has had an opportunity to already get the information throughout discovery in the case.

or (iii) The burden or expense of the proposed requests outweighs the likely benefit. The court should consider:

- The needs of the case
- The amount in controversy
- The parties' resources

[16] There is no need because national limits are set by Rules 30, 31, and 32.

- How important the issue at hand is
- How important discovery is in resolving the issue.

(C) The court may act either on its own initiative (after giving notice) or pursuant to a motion to limit discovery (see Rule 26(c)).

(3) Trial preparation: Materials (work product)

(A) Disclosure: Normally, work product is not discoverable. A party may obtain discovery gathered by another party only if he can show:

(i) That they are within the scope of 26(b)(1)

and (ii) There is a need, meaning:

1. A *"substantial need"* for the materials to prepare his case

and 2. That he cannot obtain the *"substantial equivalent"* of the materials without *"undue hardship"*

(B) Disclosure is limited to materials themselves. Courts will protect opinions or conclusions (e.g., conclusions, theories of recovery, strategies, etc.).

(C) Previously made statements:

1. If a party "previously made a statement" concerning the action or subject matter, she must turn it over to a requesting party.
2. If the other party denies materials—The party seeking discovery may:
   a. Move for a court order to obtain the other party's materials.
   and b. Apply for expenses incurred in relation to the motion (under Rule 37(a)(5)).

E-Z Definition:
A **"previously made statement"** is:

(i) A written statement signed or adopted by the person making it

(ii) A recorded transcript or recording of an oral statement by the person making the "showing"

(Rule 26(b)(3)(C)(i) and (ii))

(4) Trial preparation; obtaining expert opinions:

(A) Expert who may testify:

1. Depositions of any person identified as an expert may be taken and may be used at trial.
2. If an Expert Disclosure Report is required (by Rule 26(a)(2)(B)), the deposition shall be conducted *after* the report is received.

(B) Experts employed only for trial preparation:

1. A party may not discover known facts, or opinions of another party's experts (via deposition or interrogatory) who are not expected to be used at trial
2. Exceptions:
   (i) As provided in Rule 35(b) (Mental and Physical Examinations: Examiner's Report)
   or (ii) If the requesting party shows *exceptional circumstances* that make it impractical to obtain the expert information himself (i.e., by hiring his own expert).

(C) Payment: The court shall require the party requesting the information to pay the following (unless *manifest injustice* will result):

(i) A reasonable fee to the expert for her time spent in responding to Rule 26(b)(4)(A) or (B) discovery requests.

and (ii) A reasonable portion of the expert's fee to the other party for the expert opinions obtained by him under Rule 26(b)(4)(B) only (not (A)).

(5) Claims of privilege or protection of trial-preparation materials.

(A) **Information withheld.** When a party claims privilege or a trial-preparation objection

(i) the party has to make the claim *expressly*

(ii) the party has to describe the nature of the documents (or communications or things) in a way that will enable other parties to assess whether or not privilege exists (without revealing the information itself).

(B) **Information produced.**

1. Notice: If privileged information or protected work product is produced, the party producing it must send a notice to the opposing party.
2. Return of documents:
   a. After being notified, a party:
      i. must promptly return, sequester, or destroy the specified information (and any copies)
      ii. may not use or disclose the information until the claim is resolved.
      iii. may promptly present the information to the court (under seal) for a ruling on the claim.

b. If it's too late: If the receiving party disclosed the information before being notified, it must take reasonable steps to get it back.
c. Preservation of returned information: All information must be preserved (by a producing party) after return, until the court rules on the claim.
d. The receiving party may promptly present the information to the court (under seal) for a determination of the claim.

(c) Protective orders:

(1) In general.

i. Requirements for requesting a Protective Order:
   a. Motion for protection must be made
   b. Showing of Good Cause
   c. Certification of Good-Faith Effort or attempt to settle the matter without the court

ii. A court may make any order *which justice requires* to protect any party from:
   a. Annoyance
   or b. Embarrassment
   or c. Oppression
   or d. Undue burden or expense

iii. Controls which courts may use to protect parties include *one or more of the following*:
   (A) That disclosure or discovery is not to be had
   (B) Disclosure or discovery may be had only on *specified terms and conditions (i.e., time and place)*
   (C) Discovery may be had by a *certain method*
   (D) Discovery scope may be limited to *certain matters*, prohibiting inquiry into other matters
   (E) Designating in whose presence discovery is conducted
   (F) Sealing depositions and allowing them to be opened by court order only
   (G) Trade secrets or confidentiality not to be revealed, or to be revealed in a specified manner
   (H) Parties file simultaneous specified documents and information in sealed envelopes to be opened with a court order

(2) Ordering discovery. If a motion for a protective order is denied (in whole or partially), the court may, *on just terms*, order that any party (or third party) provide or permit discovery.

(3) Awarding expenses. Rule 37(a)(5) applies.

(d) Sequence and timing of discovery[17]

(1) Timing: Unless the court allows, or the parties agree, a party may not seek discovery from any source until after a conference of the parties (pursuant to Rule 26(f)).

(2) Sequence:

- **Normal sequence**
  - (A) The methods of discovery may be used in any order
  - (B) Discovery by one party does not require another party to delay discovery
- **Changing the sequence:** A party may move for a change of sequence and timing based on:
  - i. Injustice
  - or ii. Inconvenience of parties
  - or iii. Inconvenience of witnesses

(e) Supplementing disclosures and responses

(1) In general: A party who responded to a discovery request is required to supplement it with new information if:

- (A) The party learns that the disclosed information/interrogatories are *incomplete* or *incorrect*, and new information has not been made known to the other parties during discovery (or in subsequent writings)
- or (B) as ordered by the court.

(2) Expert witness:

- a. For a Rule 26(a)(2)(B) expert report, the party must supplement both:
  - i. The expert's report
  - and ii. Information given during the expert's deposition
- b. The time limit for these additions or changes is the time Rule 26(a)(3) pretrial disclosures are due.

(f) Meeting of parties:

(1) Conference timing:

- a. The parties shall confer at least 21 days before scheduling a Rule 16(b) conference or order
- b. A court order may exempt the meeting

(2) Conference content; parties' responsibilities:

- a. Parties shall consider:
  1. The nature and basis of claim
  2. Their defenses

---

[17] By amendment in 2000, Rule 26(d) and (f) limit the authority of Local Rules to allow discovery before a 26(f) conference, and to exempt a case from conference altogether. Also, the amendment requires only a "conference," and not necessarily a face-to-face meeting.

3. Possibilities for a prompt settlement
4. Discussing 26(a)(1) disclosures
5. Disclosure arrangements and the creation of a discovery plan
6. Issues relating to preserving discoverable information

b. All attorneys or parties (if *pro se*) are required to set up the conference and to make a *good faith* effort to reach an agreement.

c. A discovery plan must be submitted within 14 days after the conference.

d. A court may order that the parties/attorneys attend the conference in person.

(3) Discovery plan: Discovery plan shall include:

(A) What permitted changes should be made to 26(a) disclosures and when 26(a)(1) disclosures will be made

and (B) What subjects need discovery (and due dates and whether they should be done in phases)

and (C) any issues relating to disclosure or discovery of electronic information, including the form or forms in which it should be produced[18]

and (D) any issues relating to privilege or work product, including whether to ask the court to include any agreement the parties may have made on how to assert claims of privilege or work product after production[19]

and (E) any new limitations or changes in the limitations on discovery imposed by the FRCP or local rules

and (F) any other orders under Rule 26(c) (Protective Orders) or 16(b) or (c) (Scheduling Orders) that should be entered by the court

(4) Expedited schedule: If necessary, the court may (by local rule):

(A) *The Conference:* Decrease the 21-day limit for the conference so that the Rule 16(b) conference occurs closer to the 26(f) conference

or (B) *The Written Plan:*

1. Decrease the 14-day limit for the written plan

or 2. Excuse the written plan

or 3. Require an oral report on the discovery plan at the Rule 16(b) conference.

---

[18] This subsection (C) was added by the December 2006 amendments.

[19] This subsection (D) was added by the December 2006 amendments.

(g) Signing of disclosures, discovery requests, responses, and objections

(1) Signature required; effect of signature:

i. Every 26(A)(1) or (3) disclosure must be signed by at least one attorney (or by the party if not represented) to be valid (recognized by the court).

ii. The signature should include the signer's name and address and email address.

iii. The signature is a certification that to the *best of his knowledge, information, and belief* (formed after reasonable inquiry):

(A) For disclosure: The disclosure is complete and correct (as of the time it was made).

(B) For discovery requests: Every discovery request, response, or objection is:

(i) Consistent with good faith and existing law (including these rules) or a *non-frivolous* argument to extend, modify, or reverse an existing law

(ii) Has a proper purpose—it is not used for purposes such as harassment, delay, or to increase costs of litigation

(iii) Is not unreasonable or unduly burdensome or expensive when considering:

1. The needs of the case

and 2. The discovery already obtained in the case

and 3. The amount in controversy

and 4. The importance of the issues at stake in the litigation

(2) Failure to sign:

a. An unsigned request, response, or objection will be stricken (unless it is signed promptly after the omission is brought to the party's attention)

b. A party need to respond to an unsigned request.

(3) Sanctions:

a. If rules are violated, appropriate sanctions (such as in Rule 11) will be imposed, either by:

i. The court's own initiative

or ii. Motion by the opposing side

b. Sanctions may include an order to pay the amount of the reasonable expenses incurred because of the violation, including *reasonable attorney's fees.*

Rule 27. Depositions to Perpetuate Testimony

(a) Before an action is filed

(1) Petition—A person desiring to obtain testimony of any matter before a case is filed may file a petition showing:
- (A) That the petitioner expects to be a party to a valid cause of action, but is unable to bring it as of yet
- (B) The subject matter of the expected action and the petitioner's interest in the action
- (C) The facts the petitioner hopes to establish with the proposed testimony
- (D) The reasons for desiring to obtain testimony
- (E) The names and descriptions of expected adverse parties (and their locations)
- f. The names of the people to be examined (to testify)
- g. The subject matter of the testimony expected to be elicited
- h. A request for an order authorizing the petitioner to take depositions as testimony

(2) Notice and service

a. Notice.

1. After the petition is filed, the petitioner shall serve upon any expected adverse parties the following:
   - A copy of the petition
   - A notice stating the time and place of the hearing
2. The notice must be served at least 20 days before the hearing.

b. Service.

1. Rule 4 service applies.
2. The notice may be served either inside or outside the district or state.
3. If service cannot be made with *due diligence* on an expected adverse party, the court may order other service (e.g., service by publication).
4. If a party were not served under Rule 4 and is not otherwise represented, the court *must* appoint an attorney to represent and to cross-examine the deponent on that person's behalf.
5. Rule 17(c) ("Infants or Incompetent Persons") applies if any expected adverse party is a minor or is incompetent.

(3) <u>*Order and examination*</u>—If the court believes that delay of the testimony will cause an injustice, the court will:
   a. Make an order designating or describing people who may testify
   b. Specify the subject matter to be examined
   c. Specify the method of testimony (Deposition or Interrogatories)

(4) <u>*Using the deposition*</u>—A deposition may be used as testimony if:
   a. The action is related to the subject matter of the deposition
   and b. It would be admissible evidence in the court of the state in which the deposition was taken.

(b) Pending appeal

(1) In general: If a case is pending appeal, but there is a chance it will return to the district court, a party may request "leave" to take depositions for use in the event of further proceedings in the district court.

(2) Motion: A <u>motion for leave to take deposition</u> must be filed, including:
   (A) The names and addresses of people to be examined and the substance of testimony expected to be elicited
   and (B) The reasons for requesting advance testimony

(3) Court order:
   a. If the court finds that perpetuating the testimony may prevent a failure or delay of justice, the court may:
      i. permit the depositions to be taken
      and ii. may issue orders (e.g., those authorized by Rules 34 and 35).
   b. The depositions may be taken and used like any other district court case deposition.

(c) Perpetuation by action—"This rule does not limit the power of a court to entertain an action to perpetuate testimony."

Rule 28. Persons Before Whom Depositions May Be Taken

(a) Within the United States

(1) In general: Depositions may be taken before *either:*
   (A) An officer "authorized to administer oaths by U.S. law"
   or (B) A person appointed by the court

(2) E-Z Definition:
"Officer": In Rules 30, 31, and 32, "Officer" includes a person:
a. appointed by the court under this Rule 28
or b. designated by the parties under Rule 29(a).

(b) In foreign countries

(1) In general: Depositions may be taken *either:*
(A) Under any applicable treaty or convention
or (B) Under a letter of request (no need to be "rogatory")
or (C) On notice with an oath administrator authorized by U.S. law or the foreign country's law
or (D) With a person commissioned by the court

(2) Issuing a letter of request or a commission. A letter of request, a commission, or both may be issued:
(A) on appropriate terms after an application and notice of it; and
(B) without a showing that taking the deposition in another manner is impracticable or inconvenient.

(3) Form of a request, notice, or commission.
a. The letter (if used according to a treaty or convention) must be captioned as set forth in the treaty or convention.
b. A letter of request may be addressed "To the Appropriate Authority in [name of country]."
c. A deposition notice or a commission must name (by name or title) before whom the deposition is to be taken.

(4) Letter of request—admitting evidence.
a. The following are not reasons for excluding evidence obtained in response to a letter of request:
- it is not a verbatim transcript
- the testimony was not taken under oath
- any similar departure from the requirements for U.S. depositions.

(c) Disqualification: A deposition may not be taken by any interested party, which includes

1. A fiduciary, attorney, employee, or relative of a party or the attorney
or 2. Someone financially interested in the action

Rule 29. Stipulations About Discovery Procedure

Unless the court otherwise mandates, parties may agree *in writing* to:

(a) Provide for depositions, which may be taken before any person, at any time or any place.

and (b) Modify the FRCP's discovery procedures and limitations (except extending time limits that could affect the discovery cutoff, motions, or trial, which may only be extended with court approval).

Rule 30. Depositions by Oral Examination

(a) When leave required for depositions:

(1) Without leave: A party may normally take depositions of anyone *without* leave of court.

(2) With leave: Leave of court is only required if:

(A) If the parties cannot agree and:

(i) The proposed deposition will result in more than 10 depositions (under Rule 30 or 31) by a party.

or (ii) The Person to be examined has already been deposed.

or (iii) A party requests to take a deposition before a Rule 26(f) discovery meeting, *unless a witness is leaving the country and will not be available later.*

or (B) The person to be deposed is in prison

(b) Notice of examination

(1) Notice in general:

a. *Notice to take deposition:* The deposing party must give reasonable notice in writing to every other party in the action, stating:

1. The **time and place** the deposition is to be held
2. The **name and address** of each person to be examined (if known)
3. If name not known, a **general description** sufficient to identify the person or a particular class to which the deponent belongs (if the name and address are unknown)

(2) Producing documents (*Subpoena duces tecum*): If a subpoena duces tecum is to be served, notice must include the materials sought to be produced.

(3) Method of recording

(A) Method stated in notice:

i. The notice shall state the method of deposition recording.

ii. Depositions may be recorded by sound, video, or stenograph.

iii. The party taking the deposition shall bear the cost of recording.

iv. Any party may request a transcript of a deposition *((b)(2) in pre-December 2007 rule).*

(4) By Remote means

a. Upon written agreement of the parties or court order, a party may use a telephone or other "remote electronic means" (e.g., fax) to take a deposition.

b. Depositions will be considered to have been taken where the deponent is located.

(5) Officer's duties

(A) Before the deposition

1. Depositions shall be conducted before a court-appointed officer (unless the parties agree otherwise)

2. A deposition must begin with:

(i) The officer's name and business address

and (ii) The date, time, and place of the deposition

and (iii) The name of the deponent

and (iv) The administration of deponent's oath

and (v) An identification of all persons present

(B) Conducting the deposition

1. If the deposition is not recorded stenographically, the officer shall repeat items (A)(i), (ii), and (iii) at the beginning of each new tape.

2. The appearance or demeanor of a deponent cannot be distorted via camera or recording techniques (e.g., disguising voice).

(C) After the deposition: At the end of the deposition, the officer shall:

1. Say that the deposition is complete

and 2. Explain who will take custody of the record

and 3. Discuss any pertinent matters

(5) Production of documents

Notice to a party deponent may be accompanied by a Rule 34 request for documents and tangible things (which are to be brought to the deposition).

(6) Depositions of organizations

a. A party may name a corporation, business, or governmental agency as a deponent and reasonably describe the matters to be examined.

b. The organization must:

1. Designate one or more officers, directors, or managers to testify on its behalf

2. Describe what each deponent will testify about

c. A subpoena is used to notify a non-party organization
d. An organization's representative shall testify to *"all matters known or reasonably available to the organization."*

(c) Examination and cross examinations

(1) Examination and cross examination:
a. The Examiner of a witness may proceed as provided for in the FRE Rules 103 and 615 for trial
b. The officer should put the witness under oath and record the testimony.

(2) Objections:
a. All objections regarding the following shall be noted on the record (but the deposition proceeds):
i. To the officer's qualifications
ii. The manner of the recording
iii. The evidence presented
iv. Any other aspect of the examination proceeding
b. An objection must be stated:
i. concisely
and ii. in a nonargumentative and nonsuggestive manner
c. A person may instruct a deponent not to answer only in the following cases:
i. when necessary to preserve a privilege
ii. to enforce a court-ordered limitation
or iii. to present a Rule 30(d)(3) motion to terminate or limit the deposition.

(3) Participating through written questions
a. If written depositions are used, questions are delivered to the deposing officer and read to the deponent.
b. The answers are given to the officer, who records them.

(d) Duration; sanction; option to terminate or limit[20]

(1) Duration:
a. A deposition is limited to <u>1 day</u> of <u>7 hours</u>.
b. The court or parties (by stipulation) may change the time limit.
c. <u>Extra time</u> must be allowed if:
i. Extra time is needed for a *fair examination,* **or**
ii. The deponent (or some other person or circumstance) impedes or delays the examination

(2) Sanction: The court may impose sanctions on deponents that impede or needlessly delay a deposition.

---

[20] In 2000, 30(d) was amended to limit depositions to 1 day of 7 hours, unless otherwise ordered or stipulated. 30(f), below, was amended to delete the provision allowing a deposition to be filed with the court.

(3) <u>Motion to terminate examination</u>:

(A) **Grounds:** At any time during a deposition, a party or deponent may move to terminate the examination or change its scope.

<u>Grounds for motion</u>:

1. The deposition is being conducted in bad faith
2. The deposition is unreasonably embarrassing, annoying, or oppressive

(B) **Order:**

1. The court has discretion to make changes or terminate the deposition.
2. The deposition is then suspended until the court has time to review the motion.

(C) **Award of expenses:** Rule 37(a)(5) applies.

(e) Review by witness

(1) Review; statement of changes: If a party or deponent asks to *review* depositions before their completion, the deponent will have <u>30 days</u> after receiving the transcript to:

(A) Review the transcript

and (B) List the changes in a statement with the reasons for each change, and sign the statement.

(f) Certification and delivery; exhibits; copies of the transcript or recording; filing

(1) Certification and delivery:

a. The officer must certify that the deposition was made under oath and was accurately transcribed

b. The certification must be:

i. <u>In writing</u>,

and ii. <u>Sealed</u> in an envelope

and iii. <u>Marked</u> with the case name and the deponent's name

and iv. <u>Sent to an attorney</u> who must protect it against loss, destruction, or tampering

(2) Documents and tangible things:

(A) Originals and copies

a. Any copies of documents and things produced shall be marked and attached to the deposition.

b. Copies of depositions shall be sent to any requesting parties; anyone may inspect the exhibits as well.

c. If the producing party wants to keep the originals, he may:

(i) offer copies to be marked and attached and to be used as originals (provided all parties had a fair opportunity to compare the copies with the originals)

or (ii) give all parties a fair opportunity to inspect and copy the originals after the exhibits are marked (and then the originals are deemed as if attached to the deposition)

(B) Order regarding the originals: Any party may make a motion asking that the originals be attached to the deposition until final disposition of the case.

(3) Copies of the transcript or recording

a. The officer shall retain stenographic notes or copies of the deposition recording.

b. Any party or deponent is entitled to a copy of the transcript, provided they pay *reasonable charges.*

(4) Notice of filing: The party taking the deposition shall give prompt notice of filing to all other parties.

(g) Failure to attend a deposition or serve a subpoena: Any party may recover reasonable expenses (including attorney's fees) for attending a deposition if:

- They expected the deposition to be taken

and • They attend (in person or by counsel)

and • The noticing party either:

(1) Does not attend and proceed with the deposition.

or (2) Fails to serve a subpoena on a non-party witness, who therefore does not attend.

Rule 31. Depositions by Written Questions

(a) Notice of serving questions

(1) Without leave: A party may normally use *written questions* for its deposition without leave of court

(2) With leave: Leave of court is only required if:

(A) The parties cannot agree and:

(i) the proposed deposition will result in more than 10 depositions (under Rules 30 and 31) by a party.

or (ii) the person to be examined has already been deposed.

or (iii) a party makes a request to take the deposition before the Rule 26(f) discovery meeting.

or (B) The person to be deposed is in prison.

(3) Service; required notice: If a party wants to use *written questions* for its deposition, he must serve them to *every* party, stating:

a. The name and address of person to answer them (if known)

b. If the name is unknown, a description sufficient to describe the person or class of which he is a part.

c. The name and title of the officer taking the deposition.

(4) Questions directed to an organization: The following may be deposed by written questions under Rule 30(b)(6):

a. a public or private corporation

b. a partnership

c. an association

d. a governmental agency

(5) Questions from other parties:

a. Within 14 days of service of questions, a party may serve **cross-questions** to all other parties.

b. Within 7 days of being served cross-questions, a party may serve **redirect questions** to all other parties.

c. Within 7 days of redirect-questions, a party may serve **re-cross questions** upon all other parties.

d. Courts may change the above times for cause shown.

(b) Delivery to the officer; officer's duties: All questions and notices shall be copied and given to the recording officer, who then:

(1) asks the questions and takes the deponent's testimony

and (2) prepares and certifies the deposition

and (3) sends the deposition to the party, attaching a copy of the questions and the notice

(c) Notice of completion or filing.

(1) ***Completion.*** The party who noticed the deposition must notify all other parties when it is completed (so that they may make use of the deposition).

(2) ***Filing.*** The party filing must promptly give notice of the filing to all other parties.

Rule 32. Using Depositions in Court Proceedings

(a) Use of depositions

(1) In general: Depositions (if admissible under the FRE) may be used in court against a party provided:

(A) The party was present at time of the deposition or had reasonable notice of the deposition and (B) The portions being used would be admissible (under the FRE) if the deponent was actually testifying

and (C) Rule 32(a)(2) through (8) allows use of the deposition

(2) Impeachment and other uses: The deposition may be used by any party to:

a. contradict or impeach the testimony of a deponent as a witness

or b. for other purposes allowed by the FRE.

(3) Deposition of party, agent, or designee: An adverse party may use a deposition for any purpose provided that the person deposed was the party's officer, director, managing agent, or Rule 30(b)(6) or 31(a)(4) designee.

(4) Unavailable witness: As personal testimony of a non-party to be used by any party for any purpose, if the court finds that:

(A) The witness is dead

or (B) The witness is too far (more than 100 miles from the place of trial, or outside of the U.S.), unless it appears that the witness' absence was procured by a party

or (C) The witness is sick or imprisoned

or (D) A party offering the deposition is unable to procure attendance of the witness by subpoena

or (E) It is "in the interest of justice" *(upon motion with notice)*

(5) Limitations on use:

(A) Deposition taken on short notice: Depositions cannot be used if:

1. The party it's being used against had less than 11 days notice of the deposition

and 2. The party promptly moved for a Rule 26(c)(1)(B) protective order (not to be deposed or to change the time or place)

and 3. The motion was still pending when the deposition was taken

(B) Unavailable deponent; party could not obtain an attorney: Depositions taken without leave of court (under Rule 30(a)(2)(A)(iii)) cannot be used if:

a. The party it's being used against shows that after getting notice of the deposition it could not get an attorney

and b. The party used *diligent* efforts to get an attorney.

(6) Using part of a deposition: If only part of the deposition is used as evidence, an adverse party may require the remainder to be shown for fairness.

(7) Substituting a party: Substituting a party (under Rule 25) has no effect on the right to use a deposition previously taken.

(8) Deposition taken in earlier action: May be used, whether taken in a state or federal case, provided:

a. All of the following are true:
- the deposition was lawfully taken
- and • the deposition was filed in the prior case (if required)
- The later case involves the same subject matter
- The later case is between the same parties (or their representatives or successors)

or b. The FRE allow it

(b) Objections to admissibility:

1. Objections may be made at any time during a trial or hearing as if objecting to the live testimony of the witness.
2. This rule is subject to Rules 28(b) and 32(d)(3).

(c) Forms of presentation

1. Depositions may be given in transcript or non-transcript form, unless the court orders otherwise.
2. In a jury trial, if any party requests, any deposition offered (other than for impeachment) must be in transcript form if available (the court may order otherwise for *good cause* shown).

(d) Effect of errors in depositions

(1) Notice: All errors shall be deemed waived unless written objection is served promptly after the party gave notice.

(2) The officer's qualification: Disqualification of an Officer—waived unless:

(A) An objection is made before the deposition

(B) An objection is made promptly after learning of the officer's disqualification

(3) Taking of the deposition:

(A) *Objection to competence, relevance, or materiality*—not waived unless the objection would have definitely caused the deposition to be removed.

(B) *Objection to an error or irregularity*—waived if:

(i) it relates to:
- how the deposition was taken
- or • the form of a question or answer
- or • the oath/affirmation
- or • a party's conduct
- or • other matters that might have been corrected at that time.

(ii) not made promptly at the deposition.

(C) *Objection to a written question*—waived unless objected to within 5 days after the date that the last authorized questions were served.

(4) Completion/return of deposition, *transcribed, certified, filed*—waived unless a motion to suppress is made within a *reasonable time* (from when *due diligence* would have discovered it).

Rule 33. Interrogatories to Parties

(a) In general

(1) Number

a. A party may not serve more than 25 separate interrogatories

b. Leave of court is needed if a party wants to serve more than 25 interrogatories

(2) Scope

a. An interrogatory may relate to anything that falls under Rule 26(b).

b. An interrogatory may ask for an opinion (that relates to fact) or the application of law to fact

c. A court may order that a party may wait until certain discovery is complete, or until a pretrial conference or until some other time before answering an interrogatory.

(b) Answers and objections

(1) Responding party: The interrogatory should be answered by:

(A) The party to whom directed

(B) An officer or agent (if the party is a company or agency)

(2) Time to respond:

a. Within 30 Days after they were served.

b. The court may change this time limitation, or parties may agree to new limits (under Rule 29).

(3) Answering each interrogatory:

a. Each question, unless it is objected to, must be answered:

1. Separately
2. Fully
3. In Writing
4. Under Oath

(4) Objections:

a. If questions are objected to, the objecting party shall state all objections and answer those questions that are not objectionable.

b. Grounds for objections must be stated with specificity.

c. Any objection not *timely* stated is waived unless *good cause* is shown.

(5) Signature:

a. Answers must be signed by the person writing them

b. Objections — must be signed by the attorney making them

(c) Use at trial: An interrogatory response may be used to the extent allowed by the FRE.

(d) Option to produce business records: The answering party may offer (instead of a written answer) a business record which is responsive, provided:

- **Responsiveness of record.** The answer may indeed be derived from the business record or an audit of the business record(s)

and
- **Burden of research.** The burden of getting the answer is *substantially* the same for the party serving the interrogatory as for the answering party.
- The responding party does both of the following:
  - **(1) Identifying the record with specificity:** Specifies the relevant record in *sufficient detail* to permit the asking party to find and identify it (as quickly as the answering party would have found it).
  - and **(2) Opportunity to inspect:** Gives the asking party a *reasonable opportunity* to see the records and copy or summarize them.

Rule 34. Producing Documents and Tangible Things, or Entering onto Land, for Inspection and Other Purposes

(a) In general:

(1) **Produce documents (and electronic information) for inspection:**

1. A party may request another party to:
   - (A) Produce any document or electronic information in its *possession, custody, or control.*
   - (B) Permit the requesting party to inspect, test, or sample any tangible thing in its *possession, custody, or control.*
2. The data or item produced must be translated into usable form by the responding party.
3. This rule only applies to things that fall within the scope of Rule 26(b).

E-Z Definition:
"Documents" and "Electronically-stored Information" include:

- writings
- drawings
- graphs
- charts
- photographs
- sound recordings
- images
- other data or data compilations stored in *any medium*

Rule 34(a)(1)(A)

(2) **Entry upon land.**

1. A party may also request entry onto land or other property in the *possession or control* of the responding party for the following purposes:
   - inspection and measuring
   - surveying
   - photographing
   - testing and sampling
2. This rule applies to the property or any item on the property.
3. This rule only applies to things that fall within the scope of Rule 26(b).

(b) Procedure

(1) Contents of the request: The request must:

(A) State each item or category of items (must be stated separately) to be inspected with *"reasonable particularity"*

(B) Describe the manner in which the inspection will be done and set a reasonable time and place for inspection

(C) State the form in which electronic information is to be produced

(2) Responses and objections:

(A) Time to respond: Within 30 Days (subject to change by the court or agreement of the parties—see Rule 29 ("Stipulations")) of the request.

(B) Responding to each item: The responding party must state which items are permitted and which are objected to (and reasons for any objections).

(C) Objections: If a party has a partial objection to a category of things being demanded, the responding party should allow inspection of the unobjectionable portion.

(D) <u>Responding to a request for production of electronic information:</u> The responding party should set forth the proposed manner of production, whether:
    a. The manner demanded for the production of electronic information is objected to;
or b. The demanding party did not specify in what form s/he wants the information (in the objection, the responding party must specify a preferred form)

(E) <u>Producing the documents</u> or electronic information:
    (i) Documents must be produced:
        - as they are kept in the usual course of business or
        - organized and labeled to correspond with the categories in the request.
    (ii) Form for producing electronic information—Absent a specific method demanded, information must be produced:
        - as it is *ordinarily maintained*
        or
        - in a form that is *reasonably usable*
    (iii) Electronic information only needs to be produced in one form.

(c) Non-parties—may be compelled to produce documents under Rule 45.

Rule 35. Physical/Mental Examinations

(a) Order of examination

(1) In general: The requesting party must:
    a. Make a motion for a court order
    b. Show that the physical condition (including blood group) is <u>*in controversy*</u>
    c. Have the examination done by a suitably licensed or certified examiner

(2) Motion and notice; contents of the order
    (A) Must give notice to all parties and show *good cause* for the physical or mental examination
    (B) Must specify the:
        a. Examiner
        b. Time and place of examination
        c. Manner and conditions of examination
        d. Scope of examination

(b) Examiner's report

(1) Request by the party or person examined: A party may request a report of the examination and the party must deliver a copy together with all prior findings

(2) Contents: The examiner's report must:

a. be in writing

b. set out the examiner's findings, including:

- diagnoses
- conclusion
- and the results of any tests

(3) Request by the moving party:

a. The moving party may request and receive similar reports of all other (earlier or later) examinations of the same condition.

b. If the party (who controls the person examined) shows that it could not obtain the reports, they do not have to be produced.

(4) Waiver of privilege: By requesting a report or taking an examiner's testimony, the examined party waives the privilege to get another examiner to testify for her.

(5) Failure to deliver a report: The court may order that a party deliver the examination report (and if it's not provided, the court can exclude the testimony).

(6) Scope:

a. This provision agrees to examinations held by the parties' agreement.

b. This section does not preclude conducting an examination under other rules.

Rule 36. Requests for Admission

(a) Scope and procedure

(1) Scope: A party may serve upon another party a written request for an admission (within the scope of Rule 26(b)(1) and for the pending action only) regarding:

(A) statements of opinion or fact, the applicability of law to fact, and the truth of opinions

(B) the genuineness of any documents described

(2) Form; copy of a document

a. Each matter must be separately stated.

b. A request to admit the genuineness of a document must have a copy of the document attached (unless made available before).

(3) **Time to respond; effect of not responding:** If no answer or objection is received within 30 Days (can be changed by agreement of the parties or by the court) of the request for admission, a party is considered to admit the allegation.

(4) **Answer:**

a. Admissions and denials must be specific to the related questions.

b. A party may not give "lack of knowledge and information" as a reason for not answering a request, unless:

i. The party has made a reasonable inquiry

and ii. There is not enough information to enable the party to admit or deny.

(5) **Objections:** If an objection is made, the reasons shall be stated in detail.

(6) **Motion regarding the sufficiency of an answer or objection:**

a. The requesting party may make a motion regarding the sufficiency of an answer/objection.

b. If court does not like an objection, it can order that an answer be made (and if it is not made, the court presumes an admission).

c. The court may wait until a pretrial conference (or some other time before trial) before making a final decision.

d. Award of Expenses: Rule 37(a)(5) applies.

(b) Effect of admission; withdrawing or amending it

1. Any admissions are *conclusively established*, unless the court grants a motion to withdraw or amend the admission.
2. Admissions are made only in regard to the pending action (i.e., cannot be used in other cases).
3. Amendments or withdrawals may be permitted on a showing that the *"presentation of the merits of the action"* would be promoted and if the opposing party cannot show that he will be prejudiced.

Rule 37. Failure to Make Disclosure or Cooperate in Discovery; Sanctions

(a) Motion for order compelling disclosure or discovery

(1) **In general:** A party may move for an order compelling disclosure or discovery, provided:

a. The motion is made notice to other parties and all affected persons.

b. The motion must include a certification that the moving party conferred in a good faith attempt to get the discovery without court action.

(2) Appropriate court:

a. *Where action pending*—motion required where deponent is a party

b. *Where deposition is pending*—motion required if deponent is not a party

(3) Specific motions:

(A) To compel disclosure: If a party fails to disclose (under 26(a)), a party may make a motion to compel disclosure.

(B) To compel a discovery response:

1. If a deponent refuses to answer, a party may make a motion for an order compelling an answer.
2. This includes:
   - (i) Failure of a deponent to answer a question
   - (ii) Failure of a corporation to make a 30(b)(6) or 31(a)(4) designation
   - (iii) Failure of a party to answer an interrogatory
   - (iv) Failure of a party to permit inspection

(C) Related to a deposition: If a deponent refuses to answer, a party may make a motion for an order compelling an answer.

(4) Evasive or incomplete disclosure, answer, or response: An evasive answer is considered failure to answer for these purposes.

(5) Payment of expenses; protective orders:

(A) If the motion is **granted**, or disclosure is made after the motion is filed:

1. The party/deponent must pay reasonable fees spent to make the motion.
2. The court does not award fees and expenses if:
   - (i) the moving party did not attempt to resolve the issue prior to court intervention
   - or (ii) The nondisclosure was *substantially justified*
   - or (iii) Other circumstances make such an award *unjust*

(B) If the motion is **denied**, and the motion is not *substantially justified*, the party making the motion must pay reasonable fees spent to oppose the motion.

(C) If the motion is denied in part and granted in part:

1. expenses may be reasonably apportioned
2. the court may grant a protective order (under Rule 26(c)).

Note: All sanctions and awards under (A) through (C) above must give an opportunity to be heard.

(b) Failure to comply with a court order

(1) Sanctions In district where deposition is taken—Failure to be sworn or provide an answer is considered contempt in that court.
(2) Sanctions in district where action is pending
(A) *For not obeying a discovery order,* the court may:
(i) Conclude that matters sought to be discovered by a party are to be found in that party's favor
(ii) Refuse to allow the disobedient party to support or oppose designated claims or defenses
(iii) Strike a pleading
(iv) Stay proceedings until the order is obeyed
(v) Dismiss the action (in whole or in part)
(vi) Strike a pleading
(vii) Hold the disobedient person in contempt of court (unless it is in regard to a Rule 35 examination)
(B) *For not producing a person for examination,* the court may apply (b)(2)(i)-(vi), above, *unless* the party shows that it cannot produce the person for examination
(C) *Payment of expenses*—The court may require the opposing party to pay reasonable attorney's fees resulting from his disobedience, *unless* the court finds the disobedience *substantially justified* or an award would otherwise be *unjust.*

(c) Failure to disclose, to amend an earlier response, or to admit[21]

(1) Failure to disclose or amend (i.e., information required under Rule 26(a)):
a. The non-disclosing party is not allowed to use the undisclosed information as evidence at trial or at a hearing.
b. Sanctions may be imposed if:
i. There is no *substantial justification* not to disclose the information
and ii. The failure to disclose was harmful
c. This applies to a failure to disclose, and also to a failure to amend a prior response (pursuant to Rule 26(e)).
d. The court may also impose other sanctions, including:
(A) Payment of reasonable expenses and/or attorneys' fees caused by the failure

[21] In 2000, 37(c) was amended to include failure to disclose and failure to amend a prior response (as required by Rule 26(e)(2)) as sanctionable.

(B) Informing the jury of the failure to disclose

(C) Any action authorized under Rule 37(b)(2)(A)(i)-(vi).

(2) Failure to admit (i.e., under Rule 36): If a party refuses to admit to the authenticity of a document and another party proves its authenticity, the court *must* impose fees spent to prove the document's validity, *unless:*

(A) The request was objectionable under Rule 36(a)

or (B) The admission sought was of no substantial importance

or (C) The party failing to admit had reasonable grounds to believe that he would prevail on that matter

or (D) Other good reason is shown

(d) Party's failure to attend its own deposition, serve answers to interrogatories, or respond to a request for inspection—subjects a party to Rule 37(b) sanctions.

(1) In general

(A) *Motion; grounds for sanctions.* The court may, on motion, order sanctions if:

(i) a party (or a person designated under Rule 30(b)(6) or 31(a)(4)) fails to appear for that person's deposition, after being served with proper notice

or (ii) a party, after being properly served with interrogatories (Rule 33) or a request for inspection (Rule 34), fails to serve its answers, objections, or written response.

(B) *Certification.* The moving party must certify that good faith attempts to resolve the discovery issues were attempted before court intervention.

(2) Unacceptable excuse for failing to act. A Rule 37(d)(1)(A) failure is not excused because the request was objectionable, *unless* the party failing to act has a Rule 26(c) motion for a protective order pending.

(3) Types of sanctions.

a. Sanctions may include anything listed in Rule 37(b)(2)(A)(i)-(vi).

b. Instead of or in addition to these sanctions, the court *must* require the party or attorney (or both) to pay the reasonable expenses (including attorney's fees) caused by the failure, *unless*:

i. the failure was *substantially justified*

or ii. other circumstances make an award of expenses *unjust*.

(e) Subpoena of a person in a foreign country—abrogated

(e) Lost electronic information—A court may not (unless there are *"exceptional circumstances"*) impose Rule 37 sanctions on a party for not providing electronic information which was lost as a result of the "routine, good-faith operation" of the electronic information system.

(f) Failure to participate in framing a discovery plan—If a *good faith* effort is not made to agree on a 26(f) discovery plan, reasonable attorney's fees to bring the plan to court will be imposed (after an opportunity to be heard).

ARTICLE VI
TRIALS

Rule 38. Right to a Jury Trial; Demand

(a) Preserved right—The rights of a jury trial guaranteed by the Seventh Amendment of the Constitution shall be preserved to parties "*inviolate*."

(b) Demand—Any party may demand a jury trial on any issue protected by the Constitution or a federal statute, by:

(1) Serving a written "demand" on other parties

and (2) Filing the demand (pursuant to Rule 5) no later than 10 days from service of the last pleading directed to such issue.

(c) Specification of issues:

1. In the demand, the party may specify which issues it wants to be tried by a jury. Otherwise, trial by jury is assumed to be demanded for all issues.
2. If a party specifies only some issues, then the other party has 10 days (unless the court shortens) to serve a "demand" for other issues she wishes to be tried by a jury.

(d) Waiver

1. Failure to serve and file (pursuant to this rule) constitutes a waiver of the right to a jury.
2. Once a demand is made, it may be withdrawn only if both parties consent.

(e) Admiralty claims—These rules do not apply.

Rule 39. Trial by Jury or Court

(a) When demand is made: When a jury trial is demanded, the trial shall proceed as a jury action *unless:*

(1) The parties both consent on record (either in writing or on oral record in a hearing).

or (2) Upon motion or the court's own initiative, the court finds that a right to a jury trial on all or some of the issues does not exist under the Constitution or any federal statute (e.g., the issue arises out of equity).

(b) When no demand is made:

1. If no jury demand is made, the case shall be tried by the court.
2. If a party neglects to make a demand, the court (upon motion) has *discretion* to allow a jury trial, if it finds that such a demand might have been made.

(c) Advisory jury and trial by consent: For cases not triable as of right by jury:

(1) The court may try an issue with an *advisory jury* (by motion or on its own initiative).
(2) The court may allow a jury if both parties agree. Exception: cases against the U.S. in which a statute provides for trial *without* a jury.

Rule 40. Scheduling Cases for Trial

1. Each court must provide (in its local rules) for scheduling trials.
2. The court *must* give priority to cases that are given priority by a federal statute.

Rule 41. Dismissal of Actions

(a) Voluntary dismissal:

(1) By the plaintiff:
(A) *Without a court order:* A case may be dismissed by the π without a court order by:
(i) filing a notice of dismissal at any time before service of an answer or motion for summary judgment is made (whichever is sooner)
or (ii) filing a stipulation of dismissal signed by all parties who have appeared in the action
(B) *Effect:* Dismissal shall be without prejudice, *unless:*
1. Otherwise stated in the notice
2. The case is filed by a π who has already dismissed the action for the same claim in another court (in which case the notice of dismissal operates as an adjudication upon the merits)

Note: This subsection is subject to Rule 23(e), 23.1(c), 23.2, Rule 66, and any other federal statute.

(2) By court order:
a. Unless dismissed under 41(a)(1), a case shall be dismissed only upon a court order.

b. If a counterclaim has been pleaded by the Defendant prior to service of the π's notice of dismissal then:
   1. The case cannot be dismissed if the counterclaim cannot remain as an independent action.
   2. π's claim can be dismissed if the counterclaim can remain as an independent action.

c. Dismissal of 41(a)(2) cases is without prejudice.

(b) Involuntary dismissal:

1. Defendant may move for a dismissal of any claim if π:
   a. Fails to prosecute
   or b. Fails to comply with the Federal Rules of Civil Procedure
   or c. Fails to comply with any court order
2. Dismissal under 41(b) is with prejudice (and operates as an adjudication on the merits), *unless:*
   a. The dismissal order states otherwise
   or b. The case is dismissed for lack of jurisdiction
   or c. The case is dismissed for improper venue
   or d. The case is dismissed for failure to join a party (under Rule 19)

(c) Dismissal of counterclaims

1. This rule applies to any claims, including:
   a. Counterclaims
   and b. Cross-claims
   and c. Third-party claims
2. If a voluntary dismissal is made by the claimant alone (pursuant to 41(a)(1)(A)(i)), it must be made:
   (1) Before responsive pleadings are served
   (2) Before introduction of evidence (at trial or hearing), if there are no responsive pleadings

(d) Costs of previously dismissed actions—If π previously dismissed a case and is now reinstating it (i.e., bringing a case based on or including the same claim against the same Defendant), the court may:

(1) impose costs for the previously dismissed action
and (2) stay the case until the plaintiff complies

Rule 42. Consolidation; Separate Trials

(a) Consolidation of cases—If cases involve a common question of law or fact, a court may:

(1) Order a joint hearing or trial of any issue in the action
or (2) Order a complete consolidation of the cases
or (3) May make orders to avoid costs or delay

(b) Separate trials—A court may split any claims for any of the following reasons:

1. For convenience
2. To avoid prejudice
3. To expedite and economize

Rule 43. Taking Testimony

(a) Form—In all trials, the testimony of witnesses shall be taken orally in open court (unless otherwise provided in the Federal Rules of Evidence, these rules, or another federal statute).

(b) Scope of examination and cross-examination—Abrogated

(c) Record of excluded evidence—Abrogated

(b) Affirmation in lieu of oath—Whenever an oath is required by these rules, a solemn affirmation may be accepted instead.

(c) Evidence on motions—When a motion is based on facts not appearing on the record:

1. The court may hear the matter on affidavits presented by the parties.

or 2. The court may direct the matter to be heard (wholly or partly) with oral testimony or depositions.

(d) Interpreters

1. The court may appoint an interpreter and fix its compensation.
2. The compensation, at the court's discretion:
   a. Shall be paid out of funds provided by law
   or b. Shall be paid by one or more of the parties (as the court directs)
   or c. May be taxed as a cost of the litigation.

Rule 44. Proving an Official Record

(a) Means of proving

(1) Domestic records—Authentication of any records filed in the U.S. may be made by:
   (A) An official publication
   or (B) A copy signed by an officer (or the officer's deputy)

1. The officer must have *legal custody* of the actual record.
2. The copy must be accompanied by a certificate stating that such officer has custody.
3. The accompanying certificate may be made by:
   - (i) A judge of the court or jurisdiction where the record is filed.
   - or (ii) Any public officer having a "seal of office" and official duties in the jurisdiction where the record is kept.

(2) Foreign records

(A) *In general:* May be authenticated by:

- (i) An official publication
- or (ii) A signed copy of record which is:
  1. Signed by a person authorized to make the attestation
  - and 2. Accompanied by either:
    - i. A certificate of genuineness
    - or ii. A certification under treaty/convention where both the U.S. and the foreign country are parties

(B) *Final certification of genuineness:*

1. A final certification may be made by a secretary of an embassy or other U.S. agent in the foreign country.

(C) *Other means of proof:* After reasonable time is given for all parties to investigate the authenticity of the documents, the court may:

- (i) Admit an attested copy without final certification
- or (ii) Allow the foreign official record to be evidenced by an attested summary, with or without final certification

(b) Lack of record — To prove that a record does not exist, or has not been recorded, a party must:

1. Provide a written statement that no record was found after a *diligent search.*
2. Have the statement authenticated by the appropriate authority, pursuant to Rules 44(a)(1) and 44(a)(2)(C)(ii) (above).

(c) Other proof — Any other method of proving the existence of a record or the lack of a record may be permitted if authorized by law.

Rule 44.1. Determining Foreign Law

1. A party intending to raise a question involving foreign law must give notice of his intention in *either*:

   a. The pleadings

   or b. A *reasonable* written notice

2. In determining foreign law, a court may consider any relevant sources and testimony (admissible under the Federal Rules of Evidence).

3. The court's determination on foreign law shall be treated as a **ruling on a question of law.**

Rule 45. Subpoena

(a) In general

(1) Form and contents

(A) Form; requirements: Every subpoena *must:*

(i) state the name of the court from which it is issued

(ii) state:

1. The title of the action
2. The name of the court in which the action is pending
3. The case's civil action number

(iii) command a person, at a specified time and place, to:

1. Attend and give testimony

or 2. Produce (and permit inspection of) documents, electronic information, or tangible things in the person's *possession, custody, or control*

or 3. Permit inspection of premises

(iv) have in it the text of Rule 45(c) and 45(d)

(B) Command to attend a deposition—Notice of the recording method: A subpoena requiring attendance at a deposition must state how the testimony will be recorded.

(C) Combining or separating a command to produce or to permit inspection; specifying the form for electronic information:

1. A subpoena to produce documents (or electronic information or tangible things) or to permit the inspection of premises:

   a. may be included in a subpoena requiring attendance at a deposition, hearing, or trial

   b. or may be set out in a separate subpoena.

2. A subpoena may specify the form in which electronic information is to be produced.

(D) Command to produce; included obligations: A command in a subpoena to produce documents (or electronic information or tangible things) requires the responding party to permit:
- inspection of the materials
- copying of the materials
- testing of the materials
- sampling of the materials

(2) Issued from which court: A subpoena must issue as follows:

(A) Attendance at a trial or hearing: In the name of the court for the district where the trial or hearing is to be held;

(B) Attendance at a deposition: In the name of the court for the district where the deposition is to be taken (the subpoena should state the method for recording the testimony)

(C) Production and inspection (if separate from a subpoena to attend): in the name of the court for the district where the production or inspection is to be made.

(3) Issued by whom:
- The court clerk (the clerk issues it in blank, and the party serving it completes it prior to service)
- An attorney (as officer of the court) may also issue and sign a subpoena on behalf of
  (A) a court in which the attorney is authorized to practice; or
  (B) a court where a deposition or production is to take place, provided the deposition or production pertains to an action pending where the attorney is authorized to practice.

(b) Serving the subpoena

(1) By whom; tendering fees; serving a copy of certain subpoenas: A subpoena may be served—

a. **Who**—By any person who:
- is not a party and
- is 18 years old or older.

b. **How**—

1. By delivering a copy to the person with the required fees.
2. Fees are tendered only if:
   - attendance is required; and
   - the subpoena is issued on behalf of a party other than the United States (or an officer or

agency of the U.S., in which case no fee is required).

3. Prior notice of any subpoena for production or inspection before trial must be served on each party in accordance with Rule 5(b) (Service of Papers).

(2) **Service in the United States:** Other than as provided in Rule 45(c)(3)(A)(ii), a subpoena may be served:
   (A) at any place in the district of the court by which it is issued, or
   (B) at any place outside the district, but within 100 miles of the place of the production, inspection, copying, deposition, or trial, or
   (C) at any place within the state where a state statute or court rule allows service of a subpoena issued by a state court in the place of the production, inspection, copying, deposition, or trial.
   (D) The court, for good reason, may authorize any other place if a federal statute provides for it.

(3) Service in a foreign country: For witnesses (nationals or residents of the United States) in a foreign country, see 28 USC § 1783

(4) Proof of Service (when necessary) is made by filing a certified statement (containing **the name of the person served** and **the date and manner of service**) with the clerk of the court from which the subpoena issued.

(c) Protecting a person subject to a subpoena

(1) Avoiding undue burden or expense; sanctions: A party responsible for issuing a subpoena must take *reasonable steps* to avoid imposing *undue burden or expense* on the person subject to the subpoena. (The court may enforce this duty with sanctions, such as lost earnings and reasonable attorneys' fees.)

(2) Command to produce materials or permit inspection:
   (A) <u>Appearance not required</u>: A person commanded to produce documents or things or to permit inspection need not appear in person, unless he is also commanded to appear for a:
   1. Deposition
   or 2. Hearing
   or 3. Trial
   (B) <u>Objections (subject to Rule 45(d)(2)):</u>
   1. Within <u>14 days</u> of service of the subpoena (or before the time commanded in the subpoena, if

less than 14 days), the party subject to the subpoena may serve a written objection upon the other party or her attorney.

2. Once an objection is made:
    - (i) The person who originally served the subpoena may make a **motion to compel production,** upon notice to the objecting party.
    - (ii) If the court orders production, non-parties should be protected from significant expenses.

(3) Quashing or modifying a subpoena

(A) *When required:* Upon a *timely* motion, the issuing court shall modify or quash a subpoena for any of the following reasons:

(i) It fails to allow *reasonable time* for compliance.

or (ii) It requires a non-party to travel more than 100 miles from his home or regular place of business for anything other than trial.

or (iii) It requires disclosure of privileged or other protected matter, and no exceptions or waivers apply.

or (iv) It subjects a person to *undue burden.*

(B) *When permitted:* The court may quash or modify a subpoena to protect a person affected by it or subject to it if it:

(i) Requires disclosure of a **trade secret** or other **confidential research**, **development**, or **commercial information**

or (ii) Requires disclosure of an unretained expert's opinion or information not directly relating to the dispute and made by an expert but not at the party's request

or (iii) Requires a non-party to travel more than 100 miles to attend a trial

(C) *Specifying conditions as an alternative:* The court may order appearance or production only upon *specific conditions* if:

(i) A substantial need for the testimony or material is shown or discovery cannot be otherwise met without *undue hardship.*

and (ii) The party assures that the person to whom the subpoena is addressed will be *reasonably compensated.*

(d) Duties in responding to subpoena

(1) <u>Producing documents or electronic information</u>:

(A) Documents must be produced:
- as they are kept in the usual course of business or
- organized and labeled to correspond with the categories in the request.

(B) Form for producing electronic information—Absent a specific method demanded, information must be produced:
- as it is *ordinarily maintained* or
- in a form that is *reasonably usable*

(C) Electronic information needs only to be produced in one form.

(D) <u>Undue burden or cost</u>:
1. A responding party does not have to provide electronic information from sources that are not *reasonably accessible* (because of undue burden or cost).
2. On a motion by the requesting party to compel discovery (or by the responding party to quash the subpoena), the responding party has the burden of showing that the information is not *reasonably accessible.*
3. The court may still order discovery from these sources if the requesting party shows *good cause* (but the court should consider the limitations of Rule 26(b)(2)(C)).
4. The court may specify conditions for the discovery.

(2) <u>Privilege or work product</u>

(A) Information withheld: When information is withheld because of privilege or work-product protection, the responding party must:

(i) make an express claim of privilege

and (ii) describe the nature of the documents, communications, or things not produced (enough so that the requesting party can contest the claim or privilege).

(B) Information produced:
1. <u>Notice</u>: If privileged information or work product is produced in response to a subpoena, the producing party may notify anyone who received the information.
2. <u>Return of information</u>: After being notified, a party must promptly return, sequester, or destroy the

information (and any copies) and may not use or disclose the information until the claim is resolved.

3. Presentation to court under seal: A receiving party may promptly present the information to the court under seal for a determination of the claim.
4. If it's too late: If the information was already disclosed, the receiving party must take reasonable steps to get it back. The person who produced the information must preserve the information until the claim is resolved.

(e) Contempt.

1. If any person fails, without an *adequate excuse,* to obey a subpoena, he may be held in contempt.
2. An *adequate cause* exists when a subpoena requires a non-party to attend or produce at a place not within the limits provided by Rule 45(c)(3)(A)(ii).

Rule 46. Objecting to a Rule or Order

1. Formal exceptions to rulings are necessary only where specified.
2. When required, notice of objection may be made at the time the ruling or order of the court is made or sought, by making known to the court:

   a. The action the party desires the court to take

   and b. The party's objections to the court's actions, and the reasons for them

3. The absence of an objection to a ruling does not prejudice a party if he had no opportunity to object to it at the time it was made.

ARTICLE VII
JURY AND TRIAL RULES

Rule 47. Selecting Jurors

(a) Examining jurors

1. The court may permit parties (or their attorneys) to examine prospective jurors (or the court may itself do so).
2. If the court examines the jurors, it *must* permit the parties *("as it deems proper")* to *either*:
    a. Supplement the examination with further inquiry
    or b. Submit to the prospective jurors additional questions prepared by the parties.

(b) Peremptory challenges — The court *must* allow peremptory challenges of jurors (pursuant to 28 USC § 1870).

(c) Excusing a juror — The court may, for good cause, excuse a juror from service during trial or deliberation.

Rule 48. Number of Jurors; Verdict

a. The court shall have between 6 and 12 jurors.

b. All jurors must participate in the verdict, unless excused pursuant to Rule 47(c).

c. Unless the parties otherwise agree,
    1. The verdict shall be unanimous.
    and 2. No verdict shall be taken from a jury reduced to *fewer than* 6 people.

Rule 49. Special Verdict; General Verdict and Questions

(a) Special verdicts:

(1) In general: The court may require a jury to return only a **special verdict.**
1. The special verdict must be in the form of a special <u>written</u> finding upon each issue of fact.
2. The court may submit to the jury:
    (A) Written questions susceptible of absolute or other brief answers

or (B) Written forms of the several special findings which could properly be made from the evidence or pleadings

or (C) Other methods of submitting issues (as it deems appropriate)

(2) Instructions: The court shall give the jury instructions as necessary to facilitate a jury decision.

(3) Issues not submitted:

a. If the court omits any issue of fact for the jury to decide, the parties must demand submission *before the jury retires.*

b. Those issues omitted and not demanded may be decided by the court.

c. If the court makes no finding, it is considered to have made a finding consistent with its special verdict judgment.

(b) General verdict

(1) In general:

1. The court may submit forms for a **general verdict** accompanied by *written* interrogatories on issues of fact necessary to decide a general verdict.
2. The court shall give appropriate instructions to help the jurors make their decision.

(2) Verdict and answers consistent: When the general verdict and written answers are consistent, appropriate judgment shall be made.

(3) Answers inconsistent with the verdict: When answers are consistent with each other, yet one or more answer is inconsistent with the general verdict, the judge may:

(A) Affirm the jury's verdict and enter judgment in accordance with their answers (and not the general verdict).

or (B) Send the jury back for further considerations

or (C) Order a new trial

(4) Answers are inconsistent with each other and inconsistent with the general verdict: The judge shall:

1. Send the jury back for further considerations

or 2. Order a new trial

Rule 50. Judgment as a Matter of Law in a Jury Trial; Related Motion for a New Trial; Conditional Ruling

(a) Judgment as a matter of law

(1) The court may do any of the following in a case where the parties were heard and the court finds that there is no *legally sufficient*

evidentiary basis for a *reasonable* jury to find for a party on a certain issue:

(A) the court may resolve the issue against the party; and

(B) grant a motion for "judgment as a matter of law" against the party where under controlling law the issue is a prerequisite to the claim.

(2) Motion: A Motion for Judgment as a Matter of Law

a. Must be made *before* the case is submitted to the jury

b. Must specify the judgment sought

c. Must state the applicable law and facts

(b) Renewing motion after trial; alternative motion for new trial

1. Renewal of motion for judgment after trial:
   a. If the original motion is denied, the court is deemed to have submitted the case to the jury.
   b. The court may later decide the legal issues raised by the motion (which would control the jury finding).
   c. The motion may be "renewed" after the verdict by filing and serving a motion within 10 days after judgment is entered (or after the jury is discharged, if the issue was not decided by verdict).
2. Alternative motion for a new trial—The movant may also request a new trial (or join a Rule 59 motion for new trial).
3. Ruling on the renewed motion: The court may:

(1) Allow the original judgment to stand (if a verdict was returned)

or (2) Order a new trial

or (3) Direct entry of judgment as a matter of law

(c) Conditions of granting judgment as a matter of law

(1) If a motion for judgment is granted, the court must also rule on a motion for a new trial (if it was made) as follows:

- The Court must decide whether a new trial should be granted if the judgment is vacated or reversed after the JNOV
- The court *must* describe specific grounds for granting or denying the motion for retrial.

(2) Even if the motion for a new trial is conditionally granted (i.e., if the JNOV is later vacated or reversed), the judgment is still final.

- If the JNOV is later reversed on appeal, the new trial goes forward (unless the appellate court ordered otherwise).
- If the motion for retrial is denied, the denial may be appealed. If the JNOV is later reversed on appeal, the appellate court determines what subsequent proceedings take place.

(d) Time for a losing party's new-trial motion: If judgment as a matter of law has been rendered against a party, that party may serve a motion for a new trial (under Rule 59) no later than 10 days after the judgment was entered.

(e) Denying the motion for judgment as a matter of law; reversal on appeal

1. The successful party may, on appeal, request a new trial, if: the motion was *denied*, and the appellate court finds that the trial court erred in denying the motion for judgment.
2. If the appellate court reverses the trial court's judgment it may also find that:
   a. The appellee is entitled to a new trial
   or b. The trial court shall determine if a new trial should be granted

Rule 51. Instructions to Jury; Objections; Preserving a Claim of Error

(a) Requests.

(1) At or before the close of evidence: A party may file (and should give copies to every other party) written requests for jury instructions. This may be done:
   i. at the close of the evidence
   or ii. at an earlier reasonable time that the court directs

(2) After the close of evidence:
   (A) Requests dealt with in Rule 51(a)(1): A party may file requests on issues that could not *reasonably* have been anticipated earlier, and
   (B) All Requests: The court may allow any untimely request on any issue.

(b) Instructions.

(1) Informing the parties: The court *must* inform the parties of its proposed instructions and proposed action on the requests before instructing the jury and before final jury arguments

(2) Allowing objections on the record:
   - The court *must* allow the parties to object on the record before the instructions are given
   - The court *must* allow the objections to the proposed instructions to be made out of the jury's hearing

(3) When to instruct the jury: The court may instruct the jury at any time after trial begins (but before the jury is discharged).

(c) Objections.

(1) ***How to make:*** Objections to an instruction (or failure to instruct) must be made on the record

(2) ***What:*** Objection must state *distinctly* the objection and the grounds

(3) ***When to make:***

(A) If a party has been informed of an instruction before the jury is instructed and before final jury arguments (as provided by Rule 51(b)(1)): Objections must be made pursuant to Rule 51(b)(2).

(B) If a party has not been informed of an instruction before the time for objection in Rule 51(b)(2): Objections must be made *promptly* after learning about the instruction or request (whether it will be given or refused).

(d) Assigning error; plain error.

(1) **Assigning error.**

(A) Instruction given: A party may assign error if she made a proper objection under Rule 51(c)

(B) Failure to give an instruction: A party may assign error if:

1. She made a request under Rule 51(a), and
2. She also made an objection under Rule 51(c) (unless the court made a definitive ruling on the record rejecting the request, in which case a 51(c) objection is not necessary)

(2) **Plain error.** Only if *substantial rights* are affected, a court may consider a plain error that has not been preserved under Rule 51(d)(1), above.

Rule 52. Findings and Conclusions in a Non-jury Proceeding; Judgment on Partial Findings

(a) Findings and conclusions by the court

(1) In general:

a. Scope: This rule applies to cases tried without a jury or with an advisory jury.

b. The court shall state *separately* its conclusions of law and its findings of fact.

c. Findings of fact may be stated orally (and recorded) or written in an opinion or memorandum.

d. Judgment shall be entered pursuant to Rule 58.

(2) For an interlocutory injunction: In granting or refusing interlocutory injunctions, the court *must* also specifically state findings of facts and law as grounds for its conclusion.

(3) For a motion: Findings of fact and conclusions of law are not needed for motions under Rule 12 or Rule 56.

(4) Effect of a master's findings: Findings of a master shall be considered findings of the court.

(5) Questioning the evidentiary support: A party may later question the evidence supporting the findings, whether or not he:

- requested findings
- objected to them
- moved to amend them, or
- moved for partial findings.

(6) Setting aside the findings:

a. The findings of fact shall be set aside only if they are *clearly erroneous.*

b. *Due regard* must be given to the trial judge's opportunity to determine a witness's credibility.

(b) Amended or additional findings

1. Motion to amend:
   a. A motion for amendment may be made within 10 Days after entry of judgment.
   b. The motion may be made along with a motion for a new trial (pursuant to Rule 59).
2. The court may amend its findings or make additional findings, and change the judgment accordingly.
3. When findings of fact are made by the court, a party may raise a question of sufficiency of the evidence, *without:*
   a. Making a motion to amend
   b. Making a motion for judgment
   c. Raising objections to such findings in the district court

(c) Judgment on partial findings ("Mini-trial" or "Partial Judgment")

1. Scope: This subsection applies to trials heard without a jury.
2. A judge may enter judgment as a matter of law *before* all the evidence is heard if:
   a. A party has been fully heard on certain issues
   and b. The claim or defense is controlled by the issues
   and c. The only way the case could be won is if one particular issue was found in favor of that party
   and d. The court did not find the issue in favor of that party
3. The court may also wait until the close of all the evidence to make its decision.
4. The court shall support its decision as required by Rule 52(a).

Rule 53. Masters

(a) Appointment:

(1) Subject matters: A court may appoint a master only for the following (unless a statute provides otherwise):
  - (A) Where the parties consent: Any duty to which the parties have consented
  - (B) Certain non-jury issues: The Master may try issues or recommend findings of fact if
    - (i) there is some exceptional condition warranting a Master, or
    - (ii) the court needs an accounting or help with a difficult damages computation
  - (C) Where a district or magistrate judge is not available (i.e., cannot deal with the matter *timely* and *effectively*): The Master may deal with
    - i. pre-trial matters, and
    - ii. post-trial matters.

(2) Disqualification:
  - a. A master may not be related to
    - the parties
    - counsel
    - the case
    - the judge

E-Z Definition:
"Related" means anything that would require a judge to be disqualified under 28 U.S.C. §455 *(Rule 53(a)(2))*

  - b. The may parties consent (with the court's approval) to waive any such potential disqualification.

(3) Possible expense or delay: The court *must* also consider:
  - i. the fairness of imposing expenses on the parties
  - ii. unreasonable expense or delay

(b) Order appointing master:

(1) Notice:
  - a. The court *must* give the parties notice.
  - b. The court *must* allow the parties to be heard on the matter.
  - c. A party may suggest candidates.

(2) Contents: The order appointing a master must include:
  1. That the Master should proceed with all reasonable diligence

2. Other Required Contents:
   (A) the master's duties (investigation, enforcement duties, etc.) and any limits on his authority (under Rule 53(c));
   (B) whether or not (and, if so, when) the master may communicate *ex parte* with the court or a party
   (C) what record of the master's activities should be kept
   (D) a schedule of time limits, how the record should be filed, other procedures, and how the master's orders, findings, and recommendations will be reviewed.
   and (E) the master's compensation terms (under Rule 53(h)).

(3) Issuing: Before the court enters the order appointing a master:
   (A) the master must file an affidavit disclosing whether there is any ground for disqualification (under 28 USC § 455)
   and (B) If there are grounds for disqualification: only if the parties have consented (with the court's approval) to waive the disqualification.

(4) Amending: The order may be amended at any time, provided:
   a. the court gives the parties notice, and
   b. the court allows the parties to be heard on the matter.

(c) Master's authority (unless the appointing order directs otherwise):

(1) In general
   (A) A Master may regulate all proceedings.
   (B) A Master may take all appropriate measures to perform her duties *fairly* and *efficiently*.
   (C) A master who is conducting an evidentiary hearing may compel, take, and record evidence as would the court.

(2) Sanctions
   a. A Master may (by order) impose a Rule 37 or Rule 45 sanction
   b. A Master may recommend a contempt sanction against a party.
   c. A Master may recommend sanctions against a non-party.

(d) Master's orders:

1. A master who makes an order must file it and promptly serve a copy on each party.
2. The clerk must enter the order on the docket.

(e) Master's reports:

1. A master must report to the court as required by the order appointing him.

2. The master must file the report and promptly serve a copy of the report on each party (unless the court directs otherwise).

(f) Action on master's order, report, or recommendations:

(1) Action in general

i. The court *must* first afford an opportunity to be heard and may receive evidence

ii. Then, the court may:

- adopt or affirm
- modify
- wholly or partly reject or reverse, or
- resubmit to the master with instructions

(2) Time to object or move

a. Objections or motions to adopt or modify must be made no later than 20 days from the time served.

b. The court may set a different time.

(3) Reviewing factual findings

- The court *must* decide all objections to factual findings or recommendations ***de novo.***
- The parties may stipulate (with the court's consent) that:

(A) the master's findings will be reviewed for clear error (and not decided *de novo*),

or (B) The master's findings will be final (this can be done only where the master was appointed under Rule 53(a)(1)(A) or (C), but not (B)).

(4) Reviewing legal conclusions: The court *must* decide all objections to conclusions of law made or recommended by a master ***de novo.***

(5) Reviewing procedural matters: The standard of review to set aside a master's ruling for procedural matters is *abuse of discretion* (unless the order of appointment sets a different standard)

(g) Compensation:

(1) Fixing compensation.

a. This is done by the court either before or after judgment.

b. The court *must* follow his/her order of appointment

c. The court may set new terms after notice and an opportunity to be heard.

(2) Payment. The compensation (set under Rule 53(h)(1)) must be paid either:

(A) by a party or parties; or

(B) from a fund or subject matter of the action within the court's control.

(3) Allocating payment

a. The court *must* allocate payment of the master's compensation among the parties.

b. The court *must* consider:

 i. the nature of the controversy

 ii. the amount of the controversy

 iii. the means of the parties

 iv. how much each party is responsible for the reference to a master.

c. An interim allocation may be amended to reflect a decision on the merits.

(h) Appointment of magistrate judge:

1. A magistrate judge is normally not subject to this rule.
2. The court may, when referring a matter to a Magistrate Judge, provide that the reference is made under Rule 53.

ARTICLE VIII
JUDGMENT

Rule 54. Judgments; Costs

(a) "Judgment"

1. "Judgment" refers to any *appealable* order or decree.
2. A judgment should not contain any of the following:
   a. A recital of the pleadings
   or b. The report of a master
   or c. The record of prior proceedings

(b) Judgments upon multiple claims or parties

1. The judge may direct an entry of a **final judgment** for some (but not all) of the issues (or parties) involved.
2. Requirements for a directed entry:
   a. The Judge must make an "express determination" that there is no *just* reason to delay judgment on an issue.
   and b. The entry of judgment must be specifically directed to the issue (or party) being adjudicated early.
3. If the above requirements are not met, any order or decision adjudicating less than all of the issues or all of the parties involved shall:
   a. Not terminate the action as to any claims or parties (i.e., the decision is not a final judgment and, therefore, not immediately appealable).
   b. Be subject to revision before final judgment on the entire action is entered.

(c) Demand for judgment; relief to be granted

1. Judgments by default: A default judgment cannot exceed (or differ from) what was requested in the pleadings.
2. Judgment without default: Judgments not reached by default may be different from or exceed that which was demanded in the pleadings.

(d) Costs; attorneys' fees

(1) Costs other than attorneys' fees:
   a. Costs may be allowed to the prevailing party *unless:*
      1. The court otherwise directs
      or 2. The rules or statute otherwise direct

b. Costs imposed against a U.S. Government agency or officer are limited to those that are "permitted by law."
c. Costs may be taxed by the clerk on 1 day's notice.
d. To appeal costs, a motion must be served within 5 days of the clerk's notice.

(2) Attorneys' fees[22]

(A) Claims for attorneys' fees (and related nontaxable expenses) shall be made by motion, unless the substantive law governing the action provides that such fees are to be included as damages (to be proved at trial).

(B) Motion to recover attorneys' fees:

(i) Timing: The motion must be filed no later than 14 days after entry of judgment (unless otherwise provided by statute or court order).

(ii) Contents—The motion must specify:

- The judgment
- The statute, rule, or other grounds entitling the moving party to the award

(iii) Must state the amount sought (or a fair estimate)

(iv) The terms of any agreement with respect to fees to be paid (if directed by the court)

(C) Proceedings (adversary submissions):

1. On request of a party (or class member), the court shall allow for adversary submissions (in accordance with Rule 43(e) or Rule 78).
2. The court may determine issues of liability for fees before receiving submissions on issues of the value of services.
3. The court shall make a finding of facts and state its conclusions of law as provided in Rule 52(a) (findings and conclusions in a non-jury proceeding; judgment on partial findings).

(D) Special procedures by local rule; reference to a master:

1. The court may establish (by local rule) special procedures for resolving fee issues without extensive evidentiary hearings.
2. The court may appoint a Rule 53 special master (without regard to Rule 53(a)(1)) to determine the *value of services.*

---

[22] This subparagraph to Rule 54 was amended in December 2002 and no longer requires that a judgment on a motion for attorneys' fees be in a separate document. Also, the rule no longer requires filing and service within 14 days after entry of judgment, but filing only.

3. The court may refer a motion for attorneys' fees to a magistrate judge (under Rule 72(b)) (as if it were a dispositive pretrial matter).

(E) Exceptions: The provisions of subparagraphs (A) through (D) do not apply to claims for fees and expenses resulting from **sanctions** for violating these rules.

Rule 55. Default; Default Judgment

(a) Entering a default: The Clerk shall enter default judgment when:

1. A party has failed to plead (or otherwise defend itself as provided by the rules)

and 2. Affirmative relief is sought against the defaulting party

and 3. The fact that a party defaulted is proved by an affidavit or otherwise

(b) Entering a default judgment

(1) By the clerk—The clerk may enter default judgment if:

a. π's claim is for a sum certain or computable amount

and b. π files an affidavit with the clerk requesting and attesting to the amount due

and c. The Defendant had defaulted for failure to appear

and d. The defaulting party is not an infant or incompetent

(2) By the court—For all other cases, where the amount due is not certain:

a. The party entitled to a judgment by default shall apply to the court for judgment.

b. If a party against whom a default judgment is rendered has already appeared, the defaulting party shall be served with a written notice of the application for default judgment, *at least* 3 days before the hearing for default judgment.

c. Default judgment cannot be made against infants or incompetents, *unless* they are represented in the action by a guardian or other representative who has appeared.

d. The court may conduct a hearing or order references before entering a default judgment, if it is necessary to:

(A) Conduct an Accounting

or (B) Determine the amount of damages

or (C) Establish the truth of any averment with evidence

or (D) Make an investigation on any other matter

e. The court shall extend the right to a jury trial when any federal statute requires.

(c) Setting aside default—The court may set aside an entry for default judgment if:

1. Good cause is shown

or 2. Cause under Rule 60(b) is shown

(d) Judgment against the United States—No default judgment shall be entered against the U.S. government, agency, or officer, unless the claimant established a <u>claim of right</u> to relief with evidence *satisfactory* to the court.

Rule 56. Summary Judgment

(a) By a claiming party: A party may move for summary judgment (with or without supporting affidavits) *after* either:

1. <u>20 days</u> from commencement of the action

or 2. Service of a motion for summary judgment ("SJ") by the adverse party

(b) By a defending party: May move for summary judgment at *any time* (with or without supporting affidavits).

(c) Serving the motion; proceedings

1. A Motion for SJ must be served to the adverse party at least <u>10 days</u> before the scheduled hearings.
2. The adverse party may serve opposing affidavits *at any time* before the hearing.
3. Summary judgment must be based upon:
    a. Pleadings
    b. Depositions
    c. Interrogatories
    d. Admissions
    e. Affidavits
4. Summary judgment shall be rendered if, based on the above:
    a. There is no *genuine issue of any material fact* shown (discretionary)

    and b. The moving party is entitled to judgment *as a matter of law.*

(d) Case not fully adjudicated on the motion

(1) <u>Establishing facts</u>

a. If only part of the case is adjudicated, the court shall determine which facts remain at issue for trial.

b. The Judge shall file an order establishing the "<u>adjudicated facts</u>" and how they affect the amount in controversy.

(2) Establishing liability
Summary judgment may be granted on **liability** alone, even if there is a genuine issue on the **amount of damages.**

(e) Affidavits; further testimony:

(1) In general
a. Must include personal knowledge of facts (admissible under the Federal Rules of Evidence)
b. Shall show that the affiant is competent to testify
c. The court may permit the affidavit to be supplemented by depositions, interrogatories, or other affidavits.

(2) Opposing party's obligation to response:
a. The adverse party must set forth *specific facts* showing that there is a genuine issue for trial (cannot rely on pleadings).
b. If the adverse party cannot show that there is a genuine issue, SJ shall be entered against her *if appropriate* (given an opportunity for discovery).

(f) When affidavits are unavailable
If a party opposing a motion for SJ can show in its affidavit that it cannot obtain affidavits containing facts *essential* to justify its opposition to SJ, then the court may:

(1) Deny the motion
or (2) Order a continuance to permit affidavits to be obtained (or other depositions or discovery to be had)
or (3) Make any just order

(g) Affidavits submitted in bad faith (to delay the proceeding)

1. A party making an improper affidavit shall pay the other party's reasonable expenses (including attorney fees) associated with the motion for SJ.
2. The offending party or attorney may be guilty of contempt.

Rule 57. Declaratory Judgment

a. The existence of another remedy does not preclude a judgment for declaratory relief in cases where it is appropriate.

b. The procedure for obtaining a declaratory judgment pursuant to 28 USC § 2201 shall be in accordance with these rules.

c. The court may order a speedy hearing of a case for a declaratory judgment, and may advance it on the calendar.

d. A jury trial may be demanded (subject to Rules 38 and 39).

Rule 58. Entering Judgment

(a) Separate document.

- Every judgment (this includes amended judgments) must be on a separate document.
- A separate document is not required for the following orders:
  - (1) Deciding a motion for judgment after trial (Rule 50(b))
  - or (2) Deciding a motion to amend or make additional findings of fact (Rule 52(b))
  - or (3) Deciding a motion for attorney fees (Rule 54)
  - or (4) Deciding a motion for a new trial, or to alter or amend the judgment (Rule 59)
  - or (5) Deciding a motion for relief from a judgment or order (Rule 60)

(b) Entering judgment (Subject to Rule 54(b)):

(1) **Without the court's discretion**: In the following cases the clerk must (unless the Court orders otherwise), without waiting for the court's direction, *promptly* prepare, sign, and enter the judgment:
- (A) when the jury returns a general verdict,
- or (B) when the court awards only costs or a sum certain, or
- or (C) when the court denies all relief

(2) **Court's approval required**: In the following cases the court *must promptly* approve the form of the judgment, and the clerk must then promptly enter it:
- (A) when the jury returns a special verdict or a general verdict accompanied by interrogatories
- or (B) when the court grants other relief not described in Rule 58(a)(2)

(c) Time of entry: Judgment is considered "entered" (for purposes of these rules):

(1) If Rule 58(a)(1) does not require a separate document: when it is entered in the civil docket under Rule 79(a)

(2) If Rule 58(a)(1) requires a separate document: when it is entered in the civil docket under Rule 79(a) and when any of the following occurs:
- (A) when it is set forth on a separate document
- or (B) after 150 days from entry in the civil docket.

(d) Request for entry: A party may request that the judgment be a separate document as required by Rule 58(a)(1).

(e) Cost or fee awards

(1) Taxing of costs or awarding fees may not delay the entry of judgment or extend the time to appeal (except as provided in Rule 58(c)(2)).
(2) When a timely motion for attorney fees is made (under Rule 54(d)(2)), the court may decide that the motion has the same effect (under Federal Rule of Appellate Procedure 4(a)(4)) as a timely Rule 59 motion (New trial; Amending a judgment), so long as a notice of appeal has not yet been filed and become effective.

Rule 59. New Trial; Amending a Judgment

(a) In general

(1) Grounds for new trial: A new trial may be granted on all or some of the issues in the following instances:
  (A) Trial by jury—allowed for any reason courts have (until now) allowed a new trial (See Rule 60(b)).
  (B) Trial Without a Jury—Allowed for any reason the courts have (until now) allowed a rehearing.

(2) Further action after a nonjury trial: Upon motion for new trial, courts may:
  a. Open judgment (if one has been entered)
  or b. Take additional testimony
  or c. Amend a finding of fact
  or d. Amend a finding/conclusions of law
  or e. Make new findings of fact or law
  or f. Direct entry of a new judgment (or affirm the original judgment)

(b) Time to file a motion for a new trial: The motion must be served no later than 10 Days after entry of judgment.

(c) Time to serve affidavits

1. When a motion for a new trial is based on affidavits, the affidavits shall be served with the motion.
2. The opposing party has 10 Days after service of the motion to serve opposing affidavits (may be extended to no more than 20 days (total) if good cause is shown or the parties agree).

(d) New trial on court's initiative

1. The court may order a new trial on its own initiative, for any reason it may have granted a new trial by motion.
2. The court may order a new trial for reasons not specified in the motion *after* giving notice and an opportunity to be heard.

3. The court *must* specify the grounds for its decision.
4. The court *must* order a new trial no later than 10 days after entry of judgment.

(e) Motion to alter or amend a judgment: Must be served no later than 10 Days after entry of judgment

Rule 60. Relief from a Judgment or Order

(a) Clerical mistakes, oversights and omissions in judgments, orders, or other parts of the record:

1. Such errors may be corrected by motion or on the court's initiative
2. Such errors may be corrected any time before an appeal is docketed
3. Once an appeal begins, leave of court is needed for a correction to be made.

(b) Grounds for relief from a final judgment or order: The court may relieve a party or its legal representative from a final judgment, order, or proceeding if:

(1) There was mistake, inadvertence, surprise, or excusable neglect.

or (2) Newly discovered evidence was found, which by *due diligence* could not have been discovered in time to move for a new trial.

or (3) There was fraud, misrepresentation, or other misconduct of an adverse party

or (4) The judgment is void (e.g., jurisdiction is not appropriate).

or (5) *Either:*

a. The judgment was satisfied

or b. The judgment has been released or discharged

or c. A prior judgment, upon which the judgment is based, is reversed

or d. It is no longer equitable that the judgment should have prospective application

or (6) There exists any other reason justifying relief from the operation of the judgment.

(c) Time to make motion

(1) Timing:

a. For reasons (1), (2), and (3), a motion must be made within 1 year from when the judgment or order was entered.

b. For reasons (4), (5), and (6), a motion must be made within a *reasonable time* from when the judgment was entered or taken.

(2) Effect on finality: The motion does not affect the judgment's finality or suspend its operation.

(d) Other powers to grant relief. This rule does not limit a court's power to:

(1) entertain an independent action to relieve a party from a judgment, order, or proceeding;

or (2) grant relief under 28 USC § 1655 to a defendant who was not personally notified of the action

or (3) set aside a judgment for fraud on the court.

(e) Bills and writs abolished. The following are abolished: bills of review, bills in the nature of bills of review, and writs of coram nobis, coram vobis, and audita querela.

Rule 61. Harmless Error

a. The following are not valid grounds for granting a new trial, setting aside a verdict, or otherwise altering a judgment, *unless* refusal to take such action appears to the court *inconsistent with substantial justice:*

1. Error in admission or exclusion of evidence
2. Error or defect in ruling or order in anything done or omitted by the court (or by any of the parties).

b. At every stage of the proceeding, the court *must* disregard any error or defect in the proceeding which does not affect the substantial rights of the parties.

Rule 62. Stay of Proceedings to Enforce a Judgment

(a) Automatic stay

1. Except as otherwise stated below, there shall be an automatic stay of 10 days after the date that any judgment or decision is entered for execution.
2. Unless the court orders otherwise, an interlocutory or final judgment should not be stayed during the period after its entry, until the appeal is taken, for judgments involving:
   a. An injunction
   or b. A receivership
   or c. An order directing an accounting in a case for a patent infringement

(b) Stay on motion for new trial or for judgment

1. The court may stay the execution of any order or judgment proceeding to enforce it
   a. In the court's discretion
   b. For the security of the adverse party
2. The stay may be extended, pending the disposition of:
   (1) A motion for judgment or directed verdict (pursuant to Rule 50)
   or (2) A motion to amend or make additional findings (pursuant to Rule 52(b))
   or (3) A motion for new trial or to alter or amend a judgment (pursuant to Rule 59)
   or (4) A motion for relief from a judgment or order (pursuant to Rule 60)

(c) Injunction pending appeal

i. On appeals from interlocutory or final judgments involving injunctions, the court, *in its discretion,* may suspend, modify, grant, or restore an injunction during the pendency of the appeal, upon such terms as it considers proper for the security of the adverse party's rights.
ii. No such order can be made in a district court created by a federal statute, with 3 judges, *unless:*
   (1) It is made by the court sitting in open court
   or (2) All 3 judges assent to and sign the order

(d) Stay on appeal

1. The appellant may obtain a stay by giving court a Supersedeas Bond.
2. The Stay shall be subject to the exceptions in Rule 62(a).
3. The bond may be given at or after the time of filing the notice of appeal.
4. The Stay is effective when the Supersedeas Bond is approved by the court.

(e) Stay in favor of the U.S.—No bond or security is needed from the U.S.

(f) Stay according to state law: A judgment debtor shall be accorded any stay of execution if the state where the property subject to a court lien is located would ordinarily entitle him to such a stay.

(g) Power of the appellate court not limited: This rule does not limit the power of the appellate court to:

(1) Stay proceedings during pendency of an appeal
or (2) Suspend, modify, restore, or grant an injunction during the pendency of an appeal

or (3) Make any *appropriate* order to preserve the status quo or the effectiveness of the judgment to be subsequently entered

(h) Stay of judgment with multiple claims or parties: When a court has ordered a final judgment pursuant to Rule 54(b), the court may:

1. Stay enforcement of the judgment until the entering of a subsequent judgment

and 2. Prescribe such conditions as are necessary to secure satisfaction of a judgment to the party in whose favor it is entered.

Rule 63. Judge's Inability to Proceed

a. If a judge who has commenced a trial or hearing is unable to continue handling the case, any other judge may proceed with it upon:

1. Certifying familiarity with the record

and 2. Determining that the proceedings may be completed without prejudice to the parties

b. In a hearing or trial without a jury, a party may request the recall of any witness, if:

1. The witness's testimony is material and disputed

and 2. The witness is available to testify again, without undue burden

c. The successor judge may also recall any witness at her own initiative.

Rule 64. Seizing a Person or Property

(a) Remedies under state law—in general:

1. All remedies providing for Seizing a person or property (in order to secure the satisfaction of an ultimate judgment) are available pursuant to the state law in which the district court presides.
2. A federal statute governs to the extent applicable.

(b) Specific kinds of remedies:

1. The remedies available under this section include:
   - Arrest

   and • Attachment

   and • Garnishment

   and • Replevin

   and • Sequestration

   and • Other corresponding or equivalent remedies

2. These remedies are available whether or not:
   a. The remedy is ancillary to a state action
   or b. The remedy must be obtained by an independent action

Rule 65. Injunctions and Restraining Orders

(a) Preliminary injunction

(1) Notice—Notice to the adverse party must be given before a preliminary injunction may be issued.

(2) Consolidating hearing with trial on the merits
   a. Before or after hearings on an application for a preliminary injunction begin, the court may order that the trial itself be advanced and consolidated with the preliminary injunction hearing.
   b. Any evidence admitted during the preliminary injunction hearing will become part of the trial record (and therefore need not be repeated at trial).
   c. The court *must* preserve any party's right to have a jury trial.

(b) Temporary restraining order

(1) Issuing without notice: A Temporary Restraining Order ("TRO") may be granted without notice to the adverse party if:
   (A) It clearly appears from specific facts (in an affidavit or verified complaint), that *irreparable and immediate* injury, loss, or damage will result to the applicant before a hearing can be scheduled.
   and (B) The applicant's attorney certifies to the court in writing:
      a. Efforts made, if any, to give notice
      and b. Reasons why notice should not be required.

(2) Contents; expiration:
   a. Every TRO granted without notice must:
      - Be endorsed with the date and hour of issuance
      - Be filed with the clerk's office
      - Be entered on the record
      - Define the injury
      - State why the injury is irreparable
      - State why the order was granted without notice
   b. Duration of TROs issued without notice:
      1. A TRO may not last longer than 10 days.
      2. A TRO time limit may be extended if:
         a. The adverse party consents to the extension
         or b. Within the initial 10-day period, the court extends the period for another 10 days, *for good cause shown.*

3. Reasons for such an extension must be entered on the record.

(3) Expediting the preliminary injunction hearing:

a. When a TRO is granted without notice, the motion for a preliminary injunction shall be scheduled for a hearing at the *earliest possible time,* and takes precedence over all other matters (except for older matters of the same character).

b. If the party requesting the TRO does not appear at the hearing to proceed with the application for a preliminary injunction, the court shall dissolve the TRO.

(4) Motion to dissolve:

a. The adverse party may appear and move to dissolve or modify the TRO with 2 days' notice to the parties who obtained the TRO.

b. If the adverse party moves to dissolve the TRO, the court shall proceed to decide the motion as *"expeditiously as the ends of justice require."*

(c) Security

1. The applicant for a TRO or preliminary injunction must give security for the payment of any costs or damages incurred by the adverse party, if the TRO or preliminary injunction was wrongfully issued.
2. The court will determine the appropriate amount of security that the applicant must pay.
3. The U.S. Government need not post security to obtain a TRO or preliminary injunction.

(d) Contents and scope of every injunction and restraining order

(1) Any restraining order or grant of injunction shall:

(A) Include the reasons for its issuance

(B) State its terms *specifically*

and (C) Describe the acts to be restrained, in reasonable detail (without reference to the complaint or other outside documents)

(2) The order is binding upon the following persons:

(A) The parties to the action

and (B) The parties' officers, agents, servants, employees, and attorneys

and (C) Those people in active concert or participation with the parties who also receive actual notice of the order.

(e) Other laws not modified: These rules do not modify:

(1) Any U.S. statute relating to TROs or preliminary injunctions in the following cases affecting employers and employees

(2) Cases involving interpleader (pursuant to 28 USC § 2361)

(3) Cases relating to 28 USC § 2284, which relate to cases that must be decided by 3 district judges.

(f) Copyright impoundment—This rule applies to copyright impoundment proceedings.

Rule 65.1. Proceeding Against a Surety

a. Scope of Rule: Rule 65.1 applies whenever these rules require or allow the giving of a security payment, and security is given, in the form of a:

1. Bond
or 2. Stipulation
or 3. Any other undertaking involving one or more sureties

b. Jurisdiction and agent: Each surety involved:

1. Automatically submits itself to the jurisdiction of the court
and 2. Irrevocably appoints the court clerk as the surety's agent upon whom papers may be served

c. The surety's liability may be enforced on motion (i.e., there is no need for an independent action).

d. Motions: Motions and notices affecting the surety may be served to the court clerk.

e. Copies: The clerk must mail copies of the papers to the surety, if the address is known.

Rule 66. Receivers

a. Cases in which receivers have been appointed can only be dismissed by a court order.

b. Cases involving receivers shall be governed by these rules, subject to local rules in the district courts.

Rule 67. Deposit into Court

(a) Depositing money: A party may deposit all or part of the relief sought, if:

1. The relief sought is a judgment of:
    a. A sum of money (or the disposition of a sum of money)
    or b. The disposition of an object capable of delivery
and 2. Notice of the deposit is given to every party
and 3. Leave of court is obtained

(b) Investing and withdrawing funds

1. Money paid into the court shall be deposited (pursuant to 28 USC §§ 2041 and 2042, or any like statute).
2. The fund shall be deposited in an interest-bearing account, or a court-approved investment.

Rule 68. Offer of Judgment

(a) Making an offer; judgment on accepted offer

1. **Definition:** Settlements offered at least 10 days before the trial begins.
2. A Defendant may serve upon an adverse party an offer to settle the case before trial.
3. If the adverse party accepts the offer within 10 days, either party may file the acceptance, and the clerk shall enter judgment.

(b) Unaccepted offer

1. If the offer is not accepted, the offer shall be deemed withdrawn.
2. A party rejecting an offer is not precluded from accepting subsequent offers.
3. Unaccepted offers are not admissible as evidence (except in a hearing for costs).

(c) Offer after liability is determined

1. **Definition:** Settlement made after a party is found liable, yet before the amount of damages has been computed.
2. The party being held liable may make an offer to settle the case before it proceeds further.
3. The offer must be made at least 10 days before the hearing to determine the amount of damages due.
4. All other rules pertaining to pre-trial settlements apply to post-trial settlements.

(d) Paying costs after an unaccepted offer: If the judgment after trial is *equal to or less than* the settlement offer, the offeree has to pay the costs incurred after the offer was made.

Rule 69. Execution

(a) In General

(1) Money judgment; applicable procedure

a. A Writ of Execution is issued to enforce a money judgment
b. The procedure for executing the judgment is to be determined by the state law in which the district court sits (subject to applicable federal statutes).

(2) Obtaining discovery: The party entitled to judgment may obtain discovery from anyone (including the judgment debtor) in order to aid the execution.

(b) Execution against certain public officers

1. Final judgment shall be satisfied as provided in federal statutes.
2. A Writ of Execution will not be issued against the following type of public officers if the court has certified that the officer's actions fall within the relevant statutes:
   a. Collector or other officer of revenue, pursuant to 28 USC § 2006
   b. An officer of Congress, pursuant to 2 USC § 118

Rule 70. Enforcing a Judgment for a Specific Act

(a) Party's failure to act; ordering another to act:

1. Scope—This rule applies if a party fails to comply with a judgment directing it to *either:*
   a. Execute a conveyance of land
   or b. Deliver deeds or other documents
   or c. Perform any other specific act
2. If the court appoints another person to do the act of the disobedient party:
   i. The act that the appointed person does has the same effect as if the disobedient party had done it.
   ii. All costs of the act must be paid by the disobedient party.

(b) Vesting title: If real or personal property is within the court's district, the court may divest the title of any party and vest it in others entitled to it.

(Note: This has the same effect as a direct conveyance.)

(c) Obtaining a writ of attachment or sequestration
Upon application to the clerk, the clerk shall issue a Writ of Attachment or Sequestration against the disobedient person's property in order to compel obedience to the judgment.

(d) Obtaining a writ of execution or assistance: When any order or judgment calls for delivery of possession, the entitled party may obtain a Writ of Execution or Assistance, upon application to the clerk.

(e) Holding in contempt: The court may, *in proper cases,* hold the disobedient party in contempt.

Rule 71. Process in Behalf of and Against Non-Parties

Non-parties are subject to the same rules as parties, when non-parties are:

1. Trying to enforce an order

or 2. Subject to enforcement of an order

ARTICLE IX
SPECIAL PROCEEDINGS

Rule 71A: Condemnation of Property (Eminent Domain)

Rule 71.1. Condemning Property (Eminent Domain)

(a) Applicability of other rules—Except as otherwise provided in these rules, the procedure for condemning property (eminent domain) is governed by the district court rules.

(b) Joinder of properties
π may join more than one piece of property in the same action, whether or not it is of different ownership or sought for the same use.

(c) Complaint

(1) Caption
The complaint shall have a caption (pursuant to Rule 10(a)) except that the π shall name the property as Defendant, with the following details:
a. Kind and quality of the property
and b. Location of the property
and c. At least one of the owners of some part or interest in the property

(2) Contents—<u>The complaint shall contain:</u>
(A) A *short* and *plain* statement of authority for taking the property
and (B) The uses for which the property is being taken
and (C) A description of the property sufficient to identify it
and (D) The interests to be acquired
and (E) A designation of the parties joined as owners or interest holders (of each piece of property)

(3) Parties <u>(Whom the π must join)</u>
1. Once a case begins, the π only has to join people having or claiming an interest in the property whose names are then known.
2. Before hearings begin to determine the compensation for the property, π must join <u>all</u> persons having or claiming an interest in the property.
   a. *Reasonable diligence* must be used to search records for interest holders.

b. In determining the level of *reasonable diligence,* the court considers:
   i. The character and value of the property
   and ii. The interests to be acquired
   and iii. Those whose names have otherwise been learned
c. All other owners may be made Defendants, designated as "unknown owners."

(4) Procedure
   a. Service: Process must be served to all Defendants, even those added after the action begins, pursuant to Rule 71.1(d).
   b. Answer: Defendants may answer pursuant to Rule 71.1(e).
   c. Deposit: The court may order a distribution of a deposit as the facts warrant.

(5) Filing: The π must file a copy of the complaint (and additional copies upon request of the clerk or other parties) with
   a. The Court
   and b. The Clerk (for use of the Defendants)

(d) Process

(1) Delivering notice:
   a. After filing the complaint, the π shall deliver to the clerk joint or several notices directed to the Defendants (named in the complaint)
   b. If additional Defendants are added later, the π must give the clerk additional notices for them as well.
   c. The delivery of the notice to the clerk and its service have the same effect as a Rule 4 service of summons.

(2) Contents of the notice:
   (A) Main contents: Each notice must include:
      (i) That the action is to condemn property
      and (ii) The interest to be taken
      and (iii) The authority for taking it
      and (iv) The uses for which the property is to be taken
      and (v) That the Defendant may serve an answer (or notice of appearance) to π's attorney within 20 days after service (of the notice).
      and (vi) That neglecting to answer constitutes consent to:
         a. The taking of the property
         b. The authority of the court to hear the action
         c. The authority of the court to fix the compensation
      (vii) The title of the action

and (viii) The court in which the action is pending

and (ix) The name of the Defendant to whom it is directed

and (x) A description of Defendant's property (sufficient for its identification)

(B) Conclusion: The notice must end with:

1. The name of the π's attorney and e-mail address

and 2. An address within the district of the court, where the attorney may be served

b. The notice does not have to include a list of any other properties to be taken from the Defendants.

(3) <u>Serving the notice:</u>

(A) *Personal service* (without copies of the complaint)—shall be made to Defendants residing in the U.S., at a known address (in accordance with Rule 4)

(B) *Service by publication*

(i) <u>Publication</u>—may only be used if π's attorney files a certificate stating:

a. That he does not believe Defendant can be personally served

b. That a *diligent inquiry* was conducted within the state in which the complaint was filed, and *either:*

1. Defendant's residence cannot be ascertained

or 2. If ascertained, it is beyond the territorial limits of personal service (as provided in this rule)

(ii) <u>Acceptable notice</u>—π shall publish the notice once a week for at least 3 weeks in one of the following:

a. A local newspaper in which the property is located.

b. If no local publication exists, then in a newspaper having a general circulation where the property is located.

(iii) Prior to the last publication, a copy of the notice shall also be mailed to a Defendant who cannot be personally served under these rules, yet whose address is ascertainable.

(iv) Unknown owners may be served by publication in a like manner by a notice addressed to "unknown owners."

(v) When service complete
  a. Service by publication is complete upon the date of the last publication.
  b. Proof of publication and mailing shall be made by certificate of the π's attorney, with an attached copy of the published notice, with the names and dates of the newspaper marked thereon.

(4) Effect of delivery and service: Delivering and serving the notice have the same effect as serving a summons (under Rule 4).

(5) Proof of service; amending the proof or notice:
  a. Service is governed by Rule 4(l)
  b. The court may allow amendments to the notice or proof

(e) Appearance or answer

(1) Notice of appearance: If the Defendant has no objection or defense to the taking of his property, he shall serve a Notice of Appearance, designating the property he has an interest in, so that he can receive notice of all proceedings affecting it.

(2) Answer: If the Defendant has an objection or defense to the taking of his property:
  a. Defendant shall serve an answer within 20 days of the service of π's original notice
  b. The answer shall:
    (A) Identify the property in which the Defendant claims to have an interest
    and (B) State the nature and the extent of the interest claimed
    and (C) State all of Defendant's defenses and objections

(3) Waiver of other objections and defenses evidence on compensation:
  a. A Defendant waives all defenses and objections not stated in the answer (i.e., no other pleadings or motions asserting any additional defenses or objections are allowed)
  b. At trial, the Defendant may present evidence as to the amount of *just compensation* to be paid for the property, whether or not he has previously appeared or answered.

(f) Amending pleadings

1. π is entitled to make amendments to his complaint if:
  a. It is done before the trial on the issue of compensation begins
  b. It does not result in a dismissal, pursuant to Rule 71.1(i)(1) or (2)

2. π need not serve a copy of the amendment, just a notice (pursuant to Rule 5(b)) to that it was filed, to any affected party who has appeared (and to any affected party who has not appeared (pursuant to 71.1(d)).
3. π must give the clerk at least 1 copy of each amendment, and make an additional copy at the request of the clerk or a Defendant.
4. The Defendant may serve an answer to the amendments within <u>20 days</u> of service (pursuant to Rule 71.1(e)).

(g) Substituting parties

1. If a Defendant dies, becomes incompetent, or transfers his property interest after he has already been joined, the court may order a substitution upon motion and notice of a hearing.
2. If the motion and notice of hearing are to be served upon new parties, service shall be made pursuant to Rule 71.1(d)(3).

(h) Trial

(1) Issues other than compensation; compensation: In an eminent domain case, the court tries all issues (including compensation) unless:

(A) An act of Congress appoints a special tribunal to determine the issue of just compensation, in which case the tribunal determines the issue (and not the court).

(B) If there is not an appointed tribunal, but a party demands a jury trial for the issue of compensation (within the time allowed for answer, or a later time as the court may fix)

(2) Appointing a commission; commission's powers and report

(A) *Reasons for appointing*—The court has discretion to refuse a jury trial and appoint its own 3-person commission to determine just compensation, because of either:

1. The character, location, or quantity of the property to be condemned

or 2. Other reasons in the *interest of justice*

(B) *Alternate commissioners*—If a 3-member commission is appointed:

1. The court may direct that no more than 2 additional persons serve as alternate commissioners to hear the case and replace commissioners who become disqualified, or are otherwise unable to perform their duties (before a decision is filed).
2. Alternates who do not end up replacing regular commissioners will be discharged after the commission renders its final decision.

(C) *Examining the prospective commissioners:*

1. Before appointing commissioners and alternates, the court *must* advise the parties of their identity and qualifications, and *may* permit the parties to examine them.
2. Parties may not be allowed to suggest nominees.
3. Each party has a right to object to an appointment for *good cause.*

(D) *Commission's powers and report*

1. The commission shall have the same power as a master (under Rule 53(c)).
2. The commission's actions are decided by majority.
3. Rule 53(e), (f), and (g) also apply to the commission's actions and reports.

(i) Dismissal of the action

(1) By the plaintiff

a. The π may dismiss a case by right and without a court order, if:

1. No hearings on *just compensation* for the property have begun.
2. π has not acquired title or any lesser interest, nor taken possession of the property.

b. To dismiss the action, π must file a Notice of Dismissal, and include a brief description of the property.

(2) By stipulation

π may dismiss a case (in whole or in part) by stipulation or without a court order if:

1. Both parties stipulate to the dismissal.
2. Judgment has not been entered granting π title or any lesser interest in or possession of the property.

(3) By order of the court

a. The court may dismiss a case:

1. Before the time that compensation has been determined and paid
2. After hearings on *just compensation* begin
3. If π has not acquired title or any lesser interest, or taken possession of the property

b. If π has acquired title, possession, or an interest in the property, the court *must* award just compensation for the property that was taken.

c. The court may at any time drop a Defendant who has been unnecessarily or improperly joined

(4) Effect—Dismissal is *without prejudice*, unless otherwise provided in a:
   a. Notice
   b. Stipulation of dismissal
   c. Order of the court

(j) Deposit and its distribution

(1) Deposit
   a. π must make any deposit of money required as a condition to the exercising of the power of eminent domain.
   b. π may make a deposit when permitted by statute (in such a case it helps speed up the process of ascertaining and distributing just compensation).

(2) Distribution
   1. If the award exceeds the amount distributed to the defendant, the court enters judgment against the plaintiff for the deficiency. If the award is less than the amount distributed, the court enters judgment against the defendant for overpayment.
   2. If the deposit is *less than* the final determination of just compensation, the court shall enter judgment against the Defendant to return the balance (overpayment).

(k) Condemnation under a state's power of eminent domain

1. These rules normally apply to cases involving the exercise of the power of eminent domain under the law of the state.
2. If the state makes its own rules providing for trial of any issue by jury or for trial of the *"just compensation"* issue by the jury, commission, or both.

(l) Costs—Costs are not subject to Rule 54(d).

Rule 72. Magistrates; Pretrial Orders

(a) Nondispositive matters

1. Scope: This section applies when the district judge refers to a pre-trial matter which is not dispositive of a party's claim or defense to a magistrate judge.
2. The magistrate judge shall promptly hear and determine the pre-trial matter (as required by the trial judge) and, when appropriate, enter its disposition as a written order into the record.
3. Objections:
   a. If objections are not served and filed within 10 days after the magistrate's order was served, a party loses its

right to object to any error or disposition made by the magistrate.

b. The district judge (to whom the case is assigned) shall consider any objections made (within a 10 day time period) and *either:*
   1. Affirm the magistrate's order
   or 2. Reject it
   or 3. Modify a portion of it

c. The district judge shall reject or modify the magistrate's order only if he finds that it is *either:*
   1. Clearly erroneous
   or 2. Contrary to law

(b) Dispositive motions and prisoner petitions

(1) Findings and recommendations

a. Scope: This section applies when the district judge assigns a case to a magistrate judge *without the consent of the parties,* and:
   1. The matter is dispositive of a party's claim or defense
   or 2. The matter involves a prisoner petition challenging the conditions of confinement

b. The magistrate judge shall promptly conduct such proceedings as are required.

c. The record:
   1. Required material:
      - A record *must* be made of all evidentiary proceedings before the magistrate.
      - The record *must* include a recommendation for disposition of the matter.
   2. Optional material:
      - A record *may* be made of any other proceedings the Magistrate deems necessary.
      - A record *may* include proposed findings of fact, where appropriate.
   3. The clerk *must* mail copies of the record to the parties.

(2) Objections

a. A party objecting to the recommended disposition of the magistrate shall *promptly* arrange for the transcription of all or part of the record (depending on what the parties agree on or the magistrate and district judge deem necessary).

b. A party may serve and file *specific written* objections to the magistrate's recommendation within 10 days of service of the magistrate's recommendation.
c. A party may respond to another party's objections within 10 days of being served with the objection.

(3) Resolving objections

a. The district judge must make a *de novo* determination on any specific written objections.
b. The district judge shall base her decision on:
   1. The magistrate's record
   2. Additional evidence
c. The district judge may either:
   1. Accept the magistrate's recommendation
   or 2. Reject it
   or 3. Modify it
   or 4. Receive further evidence
   or 5. Recommit the matter to the magistrate with instructions

Rule 73. Magistrate Judges; Trial by Consent; Appeal

(a) Trial by consent

1. A magistrate may conduct the court proceedings when:
   a. Authorized by 28 USC § 636(c)
   and b. All parties consent
2. The proceedings could include a jury or non-jury trial, or any other proceedings in a civil case.
3. A record of the proceedings *must* be made in accordance with 28 U.S.C. § 636(c)(5).

(b) Consent procedure

(1) In general

a. When a magistrate has been given the jurisdiction to hear a civil trial, the clerk must notify the parties of their opportunity to consent to it (per 28 USC § 636(c)).
b. If both parties consent, they shall execute and file either a joint form or separate forms, setting forth their mutual consent to a magistrate proceeding.
c. No judge shall be informed of a party's response, unless all the parties consent.

(2) Reminding the parties about consenting

a. A judge or magistrate may remind the parties of their choice to consent to a magistrate.

b. The parties must then be reminded that they are free not to consent.

(3) Vacating a referral: The district judge may vacate a reference of a civil matter to a magistrate only in the following cases:

a. On the judge's motion, only if *good cause* is shown

or b. Under *extraordinary circumstances* shown by a party

(c) Appealing a judgment—Appeal from a magistrate judge's order shall be made in the appellate court, as it would if the district court had decided it.

Rules 74, 75, and 76

These rules were abrogated in 1997 to conform to the Federal Courts Improvement Act of 1996 that repealed the former provisions of 28 U.S.C. § 636(c)(4) and (5), which enabled parties that had agreed to trial before a magistrate judge to also agree that appeals should be taken to the district court.

ARTICLE X
DISTRICT COURTS AND CLERKS

Rule 77. Conducting Business; Clerk's Authority; Notice of an Order of Judgment

(a) When court is open—The district court shall be deemed *always open* for the purposes of:

1. Filing any pleading or other proper paper

and 2. Issuing and returning *mesne* and final process

and 3. Making and directing all interlocutory motions, orders, and rules

(b) Place for trials and other proceedings

1. All trials upon the merits shall be conducted in open court and in a regular and open court room.
2. All other acts and proceedings may be conducted by a judge in chambers:
   a. There is no need for a clerk or other court official to be present.
   b. The proceedings may be held outside of the district.
3. A hearing must be conducted within the district of the court, *unless:*
   a. All affected parties agree otherwise
   b. The hearing is *ex parte*

(c) Clerk's office hours; clerk's orders

(1) Hours

1. The clerk's office will be open during regular business hours on all days except legal holidays and weekends.

(2) Orders

1. The clerk may grant all motions and applications for:

   (A) Issuing process

   and (B) Entering a default

   and (C) Entering a Rule 55(b)(1) default judgment

   and (D) Other proceedings that do not require allowance or court order

2. Upon good cause shown, the clerk's actions may be:

   a. Suspended

   or b. Altered

   or c. Rescinded

(d) Notice of orders or judgments[23]

(1) Service

a. Immediately upon entry of an order or judgment, the clerk *must:*

i. Serve a Notice of Entry (as prescribed by Rule 5(b)) to each party not in default (for failure to appear)

and ii. Make a note of the service in the docket

b. Any party may, in addition, serve a Notice of Entry (as prescribed by Rule 5(b)).

(2) Time to appeal not affected by lack of notice

a. Lack of notice of the entry does not affect the time for appeal or relieve (or authorize the court to relieve) a party for failing to appeal on time

b. Exception: As allowed by Federal Rule of Appellate Procedure (4)(a).

Rule 78. Hearing Motions; Submission on Briefs

(a) Providing a regular schedule for oral hearings. A court may establish regular times and places for oral hearings on motions.

(b) Providing for submission on briefs. The court may order (or impose a rule) whereby motions are submitted and determined on briefs, without oral hearings.

Rule 79. Records Kept by the Clerk

(a) Civil docket

(1) In general

a. The clerk shall keep a "civil docket" in which each civil action applicable to these rules is entered.

b. Cases shall be assigned consecutive file numbers.

c. The file number of each action shall be noted on the folio of the docket, where the first entry of the action is to be made.

(2) Items to be entered: The clerk shall chronologically enter into the docket all of the following (marked with the file number):

(A) Papers filed with the clerk

and (B) Process issued, proofs of service

and (C) Appearances, Orders, Verdicts, and Judgments

---

[23] The 2001 amendment permits courts to serve notices by electronic means on parties who have so consented.

(3) Contents of entries; jury trial demanded

a. Each entry shall be brief, yet detailed enough to show:
- The nature of each paper filed or writ issued

and
- The substance of each order or judgment and of the return showing execution of process.

b. The clerk shall enter the word "jury" on the folio if a trial by jury is properly ordered or demanded.

(b) Civil judgments and orders

The clerk shall keep a correct copy of every:

1. Final judgment

and 2. Appealable order

and 3. Order affecting title to or lien on property

and 4. Any other order which the court may direct be kept

(c) Indexes; calendars

(1) A suitable index shall be maintained for:

a. The civil docket

b. Every civil judgment and order referred to in Rule 79(b)

(2) A calendar shall be prepared for all cases ready for trial, which shall distinguish "jury actions" from "court actions."

(d) Other books and records of the clerk

The clerk shall keep such other books as may be required from time to time by the Director of the Administrative Office of the United States Courts with the approval of the Judicial Conference of the United States.

Rule 80. Transcript as Evidence

Stenographic report or transcript as evidence: If testimony of a witness is admissible as evidence, it may be proved by the transcript if it is *certified* by the person who reported it.

ARTICLE XI
GENERAL PROVISIONS

Rule 81. Applicability of the Rules in General; Removed Actions

(a) Applicability to particular proceedings

(1) Prize proceedings—These rules do not apply to:
   a. Prize proceedings in admiralty (governed by 10 USC §7651–7681)

(2) Bankruptcy—Proceedings in bankruptcy, to the extent provided by the Federal Rules of Bankruptcy

(3) Citizenship
   a. These rules apply to citizenship proceedings if:
      i. The practice in those proceedings is not specified in federal statutes
      and ii. The practice has previously conformed to the practice in civil actions.
   b. 8 USC §1451 (for service by publication and for answer) apply in proceedings to cancel citizenship certificates.

(4) Special writs
   - *Types of Proceedings:*
      - Habeas corpus
      - Quo warranto
   - *Requirements:*
      (A) The practice in these proceedings is not set forth in:
         a. Federal statutes,
         or b. The Rules Governing Section 2254 Cases, or
         or c. The Rules Governing Section 2255 Proceedings
      (B) The practice in these proceedings has previously conformed to civil action practice.

(5) Proceedings involving a subpoena
   a. These rules apply to a subpoena compelling testimony or production of documents according to a subpoena issued by a United States officer or agency under a federal statute.
   b. Exception: Where otherwise provided by:
      - statute
      - or • district court rules
      - or • court order

(6) Other proceedings:

(A) 7 USC §292 and 7 USC §499g(c)—proceedings to review orders of the Secretary of Agriculture.

(B) Arbitration (9 USC)—applies only to the extent not provided for by other statutes.

(C) 15 USC §522—proceedings to review orders of the Secretary of the Interior.

(D) 15 USC §715d(c)—proceedings to review orders of the Petroleum Control Boards, but *"the conduct of such proceedings in the district courts shall be made to conform to these rules as far as possible."*

(E) The orders of the National Labor Relations Board (29 USC §§159-160).

(F) Proceedings for enforcement or review of compensation orders (under the Longshoreman's and Harbor Worker's Compensation Act, pursuant to 33 USC §§918 and 921)

(G) Boards of arbitration of railway labor disputes—applies only to the extent not provided for by other statutes.

(b) Scire facias and mandamus

1. The writs of scire facias and mandamus are abolished
2. Relief may now be obtained by appropriate action or motion prescribed by these rules

(c) Removed actions

(1) Applicability: These rules apply to civil cases removed to the U.S. district court (from state courts)

(2) Further pleading

a. Re-pleading is not necessary unless the court so orders

b. If a Defendant has not answered before action is removed, he must answer or present an objection within the later of:

(A) 20 days—after receipt of the initial pleadings (e.g., complaint)

(B) 20 days—after service of summons upon the initial pleadings filed

(C) 5 days—after the filing of the petition for removal

(3) Demand for a jury trial

(A) As affected by state law

1. If, before removal, a party made an appropriate demand for a jury according to state law, she need not make another demand (after case is remanded).
2. If state law does not require a demand to be made to obtain a jury trial, then the parties only have to

make a demand in the district court if the court so orders (in its own discretion).

3. Failure to make a demand as directed constitutes a waiver by that party of the right to trial by jury.

(B) Under Rule 38: A party will be entitled to a jury trial if:

a. At the time of removal all necessary pleadings have been served

and b. A demand is made within:

(i) For Petitioner: 10 days after filing the petition for removal

(ii) Other Parties: 10 days after notice that the petition for removal has been served

(d) Law applicable

(1) State law — When the law of a state is referred to, the word **"law"** includes the statutes of that state and the state judicial decisions.

(2) District of Columbia

a. Whenever state law is referred to, and for purposes of this rule, **"state"** includes, if appropriate, the District of Columbia

b. When state law applies, in the District of Columbia:

(A) the law applied in the District governs

(B) the term "federal statute" includes any act of Congress that applies locally to the District

Rule 82. Jurisdiction and Venue Unaffected

a. These rules do not extend or limit the U.S. District Court's jurisdiction or venue.

b. An Admiralty or Maritime claim within the meaning of Rule 9(h) is not treated as a civil action for the purposes of 28 USC § 1391-92.

Rule 83. Rules by the District Courts; Judge's Directives

(a) Local rules:

(1) ***In general***

a. A district court may adopt and amend rules governing its practice.

b. Procedure:

i. The court must act by a majority of its district judges.

ii. The court must give public notice and an opportunity for comment

c. Consistency with federal rules:

i. A local rule must be consistent with (but not duplicate):

- federal statutes

and • rules adopted under 28 USC §§ 2072 and 2075

ii. A local rule must conform to any uniform numbering system prescribed by the Judicial Conference of the United States.

d. Effective date:

i. A local rule takes effect on the date specified by the district court

ii. The rule remains in effect unless

- amended by the court

or • abrogated by the judicial council of the circuit

e. Copies: When adopted, copies of rules and amendments must:

i. be given to the judicial council

and ii. be given to the Administrative Office of the United States Courts

and iii. be made available to the public.

(2) ***Requirement of form:*** A local rule that imposes a requirement of form must not be enforced in a way that causes a party to lose any right because of a nonwillful failure to comply.

(b) Procedure when there is no controlling law:

1. A judge may regulate practice in any manner consistent with federal law, rules adopted under 28 USC §§ 2072 and 2075, and the district's local rules.
2. No sanction may be imposed for noncompliance with:

- federal law

or • federal rules

or • the local rules

Rule 84. Forms

"The forms in the Appendix suffice under these rules and illustrate the simplicity and brevity that these rules contemplate."

Rule 85. Title

"These rules may be cited as the Federal Rules of Civil Procedure."

Rule 86. Effective Dates

(a) In general. These rules and any amendments take effect at the time specified by the Supreme Court (subject to 28 USC § 2074) and govern:

(1) proceedings in a case begun after their effective date; and

(2) proceedings after that date in a case then pending *unless:*

(A) the Supreme Court specifies otherwise; or

(B) the court determines that applying them in a particular action would be *infeasible* or work *an injustice.*

* * *

SELECTED STATUTES

UNITED STATES CODE, TITLE 28 ("28 USC")

§ 1291. Appellate Jurisdiction

The **appellate court** has jurisdiction of appeals from all final decisions of the district courts.

§ 1292. Interlocutory Decisions

(a) The **appellate court** has the power to hear a case before final judgment when:

(1) Injunctions — There is an interlocutory order granting, continuing, modifying, refusing, or dissolving an injunction
(2) Receivers — There is an interlocutory order appointing a receiver (within the meaning of Rule 9)
(3) Admiralty cases

(b) Judge's request to appeal

1. If not included in (a), a district judge may request an interlocutory order appeal by *writing* to the appellate court within 10 days after her order, if she believes there is a controlling question of law where there is substantial ground for difference of opinion, an appeal may *materially advance* the ultimate termination of the case.
2. The appellate court has discretion to accept such a request.

(c) U.S. appellate courts have **exclusive jurisdiction** of:

(1) Any case covered by § 1295
and (2) Patent infringement cases which are final, except for an accounting (Where jurisdiction would otherwise lie in the Court of Appeals for the Federal Circuit)

(d) Specific issues:

i. The appellate court has discretion to take a case if:
  1. The application for appeal is made within 10 days of when an order is entered
  and 2. *Either:*
    a. The Chief Judge of the Court of International Trade issues a 256(b) interlocutory order.

or b. The Chief Judge of the Court of Federal Claims issues a 798(b) interlocutory order.

or c. Any judge of the Court of International Trade/ Court of Federal Claims issues an interlocutory order.

and 3. There is a *substantial ground* for difference of opinion on a controlling question of law.

and 4. An immediate appeal may *materially advance* the termination of the suit.

ii. Applicability

(1) The above rules apply to the Court of International Trade.

(2) The above rules apply to the Court of Federal Claims.

(3) Proceedings are not stayed unless the district court or appellate court so orders.

(4) Motion to transfer

(A) The appellate court has exclusive jurisdiction over all of the district court's ordering, granting, or denying of motions to transfer a case (pursuant to 28 USC § 1631).

(B) Cases must be stayed (put on hold) until 60 days after the court has ruled upon a motion to transfer to the Court of Federal Claims. The time may be extended until after the appeal is decided (if an appeal is taken).

§ 1331. Federal Questions

All civil cases *"arising under"* the U.S. Constitution, U.S. laws, or U.S. treaties have original federal jurisdiction.

§ 1332. Diversity of Citizenship

(a) District courts have original jurisdiction if the matter in controversy is *greater than* $75,000 and is between *either:*

(1) Citizens of different states

or (2) Citizens of a state against citizens of foreign states or countries

or (3) Citizens of different states, with additional parties from different states or countries

or (4) Citizens of one state (or different states) against citizens of a foreign state acting as a π (pursuant to 28 USC § 1603(a))

(b) If the final judgment is $75,000 or less, the court may impose costs on π.

(c) "Citizenship" for the purposes of § 1332/§ 1441

(1) a corporation shall be deemed to be a citizen of any State by which it has been incorporated and of the State where it has its principal place of business, except; and

(2) the legal representative of the estate of a decedent shall be deemed to be a citizen only of the same State as the decedent, and the legal representative of an infant or incompetent shall be deemed to be a citizen only of the same State as the infant or incompetent.

1. Corporate citizenship is considered both:
   a. The corporation's state of incorporation
   and b. The corporation's principal place of business[24]
2. Insurance company's citizenship is:
   a. Its state of incorporation
   and b. Its principal place of business
   and c. The state of the insured person (customer) if the insurance company is not joined as a Defendant.
3. Executors/trustees are citizens of the state of the decedent/beneficiary, with regard to related claims.
4. Aliens are citizens of the state where they are domiciled (per § 1332(a)), if they reside there with the intention of becoming a permanent resident of U.S.

* * *

[24] Exception: In any action against an insurance carrier where the insured is not a named defendant, the insurance company is deemed a citizen of both:

a. the State in which the insured is a citizen, and
b. any State by which the insurer has been incorporated
c. the State where it has its principal place of business

INTERPLEADER STATUTES

§ 1335. Interpleader

("Statutory Interpleader" — minimal diversity allowed)

(a) The district court has original jurisdiction over a civil action of interpleader if:

(1) Subject Matter Jurisdiction exists:
a. The controversy is <u>*greater than or equal to* $500</u>
and b. **Minimal Diversity**: At least 2 parties (not all) need diversity of citizenship (as defined in 28 USC § 1332(a) or (d))
and (2) "Stakeholder" posts a bond (or deposits the property in the court)

(b) Interpleader may take place, although

1. There is no common origin among the titles or claims of the conflicting claimants
or 2. The cases are not identical, but are adverse and independent cases.

§ 1397. Interpleader Venue

A § 1335 interpleader action may be brought in a judicial district where *greater than or equal to* one <u>claimant</u> resides.

§ 1367. Supplemental Jurisdiction

(Over subsequent parties or cases)

(a) "Supplemental jurisdiction" — includes jurisdiction over any claims *related* to the claims in a case which form the *same case or controversy* (including joinder or intervention of claims).

(b) Supplemental-diversity jurisdiction — When courts have Subject Matter Jurisdiction based only on diversity, <u>complete diversity must</u> be continued for all counterclaims against third parties.

(c) Court's discretion — A Court may decline Supplemental Jurisdiction if:

1. The claim raises a novel or complex issue of state law
or 2. The claim is *"substantially"* predominant over the original [federal] claim.

or 3. The court dismissed all claims having Subject Matter Jurisdiction
or 4. Exceptional circumstances compel the federal court to decline jurisdiction.

(d) Statute of limitations—is tolled while

1. The supplemental claim is pending
or 2. For a period of 30 days after its dismissal *unless* state law provides for a longer tolling period.

(e) "State" includes the District of Columbia, Puerto Rico, and any other U.S. territory.

VENUE STATUTES

§ 1391. Venue

(a) **Diversity case:** If a case has federal jurisdiction based solely on diversity, it may be brought:

1. In the district court where any Defendant resides, if all Defendants reside in same state.

or 2. In the district court where *substantial* events or property is located.

or 3. If no other district can hear the case, then it may be heard wherever all Defendants are subject to personal jurisdiction at the commencement of the action (if no such place is available, the parties must bring separate suits).

(b) Jurisdiction not based solely on diversity: Suits involving a **federal question** (as defined in § 1331) may be brought:

1. In the district court where any Defendant resides, if all Defendants reside in same state

or 2. In the district court where *substantial* events or property is located

or 3. If no other district is available, then the suit may be brought wherever any one Defendant may be found.

(c) Corporate venue:

1. Wherever a corporation is subject to personal jurisdiction at commencement of the action (any district where "contacts" would give the corporation personal jurisdiction (under the "minimum contacts test")).
2. If none available, look to the district with the most *"significant"* contacts.
3. If there is no one particular district in the state in which the company has enough contacts for personal jurisdiction, but the state as a whole "qualifies" (under the "minimum contacts test"), the entire state is considered to have personal jurisdiction over the Defendant corporation.

(d) Venue of an alien: An alien may be sued in any district.

(e) Venue for an officer or employee of the U.S.

(1) Where a Defendant resides (if all Defendants reside in the same state).

(2) Where *substantial* events or property exist

(3) If no real property is involved, then where the π resides

(f) Venue for a suit against a foreign state (as defined in § 1603(a)):

(1) Where *substantial* events or property exist
(2) Where the vessel or cargo is situated
(3) Wherever the agency is licensed to do business (or actually does business)
(4) If the action is brought against a foreign state: In the D.C. District Court

(g) Venue for a suit where jurisdiction based on § 1369 (multiparty, multiforum jurisdiction):

1. Any district in which any defendant resides

or 2. Any district in which a *substantial* part of the accident (on which the case is based) took place

§ 1392. Multiple Districts

If Defendants reside or have property located in more than 1 district, π can bring the action in any of those districts.

§ 1404. Change of Venue

(a) i. Change of venue may be made for the following reasons:

1. Convenience of parties

or 2. Convenience of witnesses

or 3. *"In the interest of justice"*

ii. A district may transfer a case to any other district where the case *may have been brought.*

(b) Both parties may consent to change venue (subject to the court's discretion)

(c) A district court may order any civil action to be tried at any place within the division in which it is pending.

(d) Definitions:

E-Z Definition:

1. **"District Court"** includes U.S. District Court for the District Court for the Canal Zone.
2. **"District"** includes the territorial jurisdiction of that court.

§ 1406. Waiver of Venue

(a) If venue is wrong, the district court may:

1. Dismiss the case

or 2. Transfer the case to an appropriate district

(b) Even if a party does not make a timely and sufficient objection to venue, jurisdiction <u>will not</u> be destroyed (See Rule 12 for bringing a motion for improper venue).

(c) **Definitions**:

E-Z Definition:

1. **"District Court"** includes U.S. District Court for the District Court for the Canal Zone.

2. **"District"** includes the territorial jurisdiction of that court.

REMOVAL STATUTES

§ 1441. Cases That Can Be Removed to Federal Court

(a) Removal from state court by Defendant

Whenever federal courts have original jurisdiction, a case may be removed from the state court by the Defendant (but not by the π) to the appropriate federal court in the district of original state forum.

(b) Removable subject matters:

1. Any **federal question** case may be removed without regard to residence of the parties
2. **Diversity cases** may be removed as long as any Defendant is not a citizen of the present forum.

(c) Joinder of cause — When an independent federal question is joined with a non-federal subject matter, the court may choose to either:

1. Split the matters and hear only the federal element of the case

or 2. Hear the entire case

or 3. Remand matters where state law predominates

(d) Foreign state defendant — When a π sues a foreign state, the case may be removed by the foreign state (and tried without a jury; the limitations of § 1446(b) may be enlarged).

(e) Other removable cases — cases under § 1369 (multiparty, multiforum jurisdiction):

(1) § 1369 cases may be removed:

a. Aside from § 1441(b), a defendant may remove a case from state court to federal court if:

(A) the action could have been brought in a United States district court under § 1369

or **(B)** the action could not have been brought to district court originally, but the defendant is a party to a case brought under § 1369 (or which could have been brought under § 1369) and arises from the same accident as the action in State court.

b. Procedure and timing:

i. § 1446 procedures must be followed.

ii. A notice of removal may also be filed before trial of the state court action within 30 days after the defendant first becomes a party to a federal court case under § 1369 and that case arises from the same accident as the state court case.

iii. A notice of removal may also be filed before trial of the state court action at a later time with leave of the federal court.

(2) Damage hearings remanded to state court:

a. If a case is removed under this section and the court required additional hearings on damages, the federal court shall remand the damages hearing to the state court

b. Exception: If the court finds that the action should be kept:

i. for the *convenience of parties and witnesses*

and ii. in the *interest of justice.*

(3) Effective date of remand to state court:

a. Effective Date: 60 days after the district court's liability determination and decision to remand.

b. Appeals. An appeal on the liability decision may be taken during that 60-day period (to the Circuit court), in which case the remand is not effective until the appeal is done (after the remand becomes effective, the liability issue can no longer be appealed or reviewed).

(4) Appealing a remand decision: The federal court's decision to remand a damages hearing to state court cannot be appealed or reviewed.

(5) For purposes of this section and §§ 1407, 1697, and 1785, a case removed under this subsection is considered a § 1369 action.

(6) Nothing here restricts the district court's power to transfer or dismiss a case on the ground of inconvenient forum.

(f) No need to re-file: The federal court to which a case is removed may still hear a case that the state court had no jurisdiction over (the case need not be dismissed and re-filed in federal court).

§ 1445. Non-Removable Cases

The following cases may not be removed:

(a) Railroad cases (pursuant to 45 USC § 51-60)

(b) Common carriers if the amount is *greater than or equal to* $10,000 (pursuant to 45 USC § 11707)

(c) State Workers' Compensation law cases

§ 1446. Procedure for Removal

(a) Filing—Must file pursuant to Rule 11, with a:

(1) Short statement of the grounds for removal
(2) Copy of process and pleadings
(3) Copy of orders served upon the Defendant

(b) Limitations

1. Must file within 30 days after (the shorter of):
    a. Defendant's receipt of π's initial pleadings
    b. Service of the summons, if pleadings are not required to be served
2. If π amends the pleadings (making the case removable) the Defendant may file for removal within 30 days after π's amended pleadings are filed and delivered.

* * *

(d) Promptly after filing, the Defendant shall give written notice to all parties and shall file a copy with the clerk. Once the state court is notified, the state court *automatically* loses control.

(e) If a Defendant has actual custody of process issued by the state court, the district court shall issue its writ of habeas corpus, and the marshal shall take the Defendant into his custody, and deliver a copy of the writ to the clerk of the state court.

§ 1447. Procedure After Removal

(a) A court may do "anything" to bring all parties before it.

(b) District court may:

1. Require the party asking for removal to file all records of the state court proceedings with the district court clerk.

and 2. Cause all records to be brought before it by having the state court issue a Writ of Certiorari.

(c) **Motion to remand** (for any defect in removal procedure)

1. A motion to remand (back to state court) may be made by π.
2. The motion must be within 30 days of the § 1446 filing of notice.
3. If the district court lacks subject matter jurisdiction at any time before judgment, the case can be remanded to state court.
4. Orders remanding a case back to the state may require payment of expenses associated with removal.
5. The state court shall proceed with the case once the district court clerk mails a certified copy of the order of remand.

(d) An order to remand is not appealable (unless removed pursuant to § 1443).

(e) If, after removal, the π joins other Defendants that destroy subject matter jurisdiction (i.e., no more complete diversity), the court may:

1. Deny the joinder

or 2. Remand the case to state court

§1651. Writ of Mandamus

1. A Writ of mandamus will allow immediate appeal, contrary to all laws (i.e., the judge may act beyond normal powers).
2. *The Supreme Court (and all other courts established by Act of Congress) may issue all writs necessary or appropriate in their jurisdiction.*

INDEX